T. Harry Williams, *courtesy of Mrs. Estelle Williams*

LEADERSHIP DURING THE CIVIL WAR

The 1989 Deep Delta Civil War Symposium:

THEMES IN HONOR

OF

T. HARRY WILLIAMS

Edited by
Roman J. Heleniak
and
Lawrence L. Hewitt

WHITE MANE PUBLISHING COMPANY, INC.

This White Mane Publishing Company, Inc. book
was printed by
Beidel Printing House, Inc.
63 West Burd Street
Shippensburg, PA 17257 USA

In respect for the scholarship contained herein, the acid-free paper used in this book meets the guidelines for permanence and durability of the Committee on Production Guidelines for Book Longevity of the Council on Library Resources.

For a complete list of available publications
please write
White Mane Publishing Company, Inc.
P.O. Box 152
Shippensburg, PA 17257 USA

Library of Congress Cataloging-in-Publication Data

Deep Delta Civil War Symposium (3rd : 1989 : Southeastern Louisiana
  University)
    Leadership during the Civil War : the 1989 Deep Delta Civil War
  Symposium : themes in honor of T. Harry Williams / edited by Roman
  J. Heleniak and Lawrence L. Hewitt.
      p.   cm.
    Includes bibliographical references and index.
    ISBN 0-942597-33-8(alk. paper) : $29.95. -- ISBN 0-942597-32-X
  (pbk. : alk. paper) : $19.95
      1. United States--History--Civil War, 1861-1865--Congresses.
  2. Political leadership--United States--History--19th century-
  -Congresses.   I. Williams, T. Harry (Thomas Harry), 1909-   .
  II. Heleniak, Roman.   III. Hewitt, Lawrence L.   IV. Title.
  E468.D4   1989
  973.7--dc20   92-19900
                                                                    CIP

PRINTED IN THE UNITED STATES OF AMERICA

Table of Contents

List of Illustrations

Foreword

Roman J. Heleniak

The theme of this year's Deep Delta Civil War Symposium, "Leadership During the Civil War," gave the participants on the panel a wide range of choices and interpretations. Not surprisingly, Abraham Lincoln, Jefferson Davis, and Robert E. Lee received major attention from the historians at the symposium, although the three speakers who focused on these men generally steered clear from military leadership. Only Grady McWhiney's "Jefferson Davis" touched upon Davis' military background and his reputation as a political/military leader of a nation at war.

Davis' counterpart, Abraham Lincoln, gained the attention of Richard Current, but Current chose to explore Lincoln's alleged bending of the United States Constitution, and only briefly did he touch upon the Great Emancipator's military leadership. As most students of American history know, Lincoln's military background could not compare with that possessed by Jefferson Davis when the Civil War began in 1861. Lincoln's brief army career in the Black Hawk War hardly prepared him to lead a nation in the throes of one of the great wars of the nineteenth century, a war of such magnitude that there are those who argue that Lincoln had to stretch the constitution to win it.

Current demurs from his interpretation, and his "Lincoln, the War and the Constitution" is a persuasive case against the views of Jefferson Davis; other nineteenth-century defenders of the South, and contemporary writers such as Gore Vidal and William Safire, all claim that Lincoln exceeded his constitutional prerogatives. On the contrary, Current maintains that Lincoln had great reverence for the Declaration of Independence and the United States Constitution and that, with the possible exception of the Emancipation Proclamation, the President operated within the confines of United States law.

The problems of Jefferson Davis differed from those of Lincoln. As his endless feud with Governor J. E. Brown of Georgia over states' rights illustrates, Davis had to walk a very fine constitutional line in leading the Confederacy. Ironically, the superbly prepared Davis comes under criticism because of his military judgement, particularly his selection of commanders.

While Lincoln's detractors, for the most part, concede that for a man of limited experience he learned the art of war the hard way—but he learned. Jefferson Davis brought to his presidency a wealth of military training and experience. Yet, historians and Civil War students have not been kind to the

Confederate leader. They blame Davis for a variety of mistakes, ranging from his overall strategy to his choice of commanders. On the latter point, they argue that Davis allowed his personal likes and dislikes to influence his choice of commanders.

McWhiney claims that Davis' faith in his own military acumen was not totally unfounded and that many leading Confederates expressed that same kind of confidence in Davis' military prowess. Furthermore, speculation about what might have been is a moot point. Jefferson Davis served as President of the Confederate States of America for the entire war. The for-want-of-a-shoe-the-horse-was-lost bemoaning has no relevancy in historiography.

McWhiney does concede that Jefferson Davis had an antipathy towards certain rebel generals but that political and military considerations proved far more important in the selection process than his personal whims. And, need it be mentioned: Jefferson Davis chose Robert E. Lee to command the Army of Northern Virginia, perhaps Davis' most important decision.

One selection, undefended by McWhiney, was Davis' choice of Braxton Bragg to command the Western Department rather than General Pierre G. T. Beauregard, a man thoroughly disliked by Davis. For all his pomposity, Beauregard enjoys a greater reputation than Bragg, a man with many detractors—some of them are among the speakers at the symposium.

For most students of the Civil War, northern and southern, especially the latter, Robert E. Lee stands out as the premier leader of the conflict. Only Lee has managed to avoid the arrows of second-guessers and debunkers, unless one includes the "Marble Man school of criticism" of Lee. Emory Thomas examines Lee as a young man, from Lee's boyhood to the age of forty—in some quarters that is still considered young. Thomas does not challenge the high opinion of Lee held by most writers that the Virginian was a great man and an outstanding general.

Thomas is more concerned with the forces and people that shaped the first character of Lee, first as a young boy, secondly as a father of youngsters, and finally as a promising junior officer in the United States Army. Can one point to certain chapters of Lee's early life and say that those things steeled the character of Robert E. Lee? Thomas thinks that it can be done.

Thomas is especially intrigued by Lee's relationship with his father. Light Horse Harry Lee, a hero of the American Revolution, proved to be a failure as a father and as a provider for his family. Thomas believes that son Robert set out to be everything that his father was not. This is an interpretation that brings to mind a cruel, but characteristic, observation made by Lyndon B.

Johnson. The Texan once said that if he knew why a man was ashamed of his father, he owned that man. Robert E. Lee was ashamed of his father, but fortunately for him, his opponents in the Civil War did not know this.

In "Young Man Lee," Thomas wades the treacherous and murky waters of Freudian interpretation, which he acknowledges can be very dangerous for a historian. Despite his qualms, Thomas has written a very convincing essay, one in which he ever so gently applies psychology to historiography.

Those who worship every aspect of Lee's life should be warned, however, about what Thomas has to say about Mary Custis Lee. She was an invisible cross borne by Lee throughout his married life, and Thomas openly questions why the methodical, practical, and orderly Lee ever married her in the first place. Yet, in a convoluted way Mary Custis did contribute to the greatness of Lee's character.

A wide gulf separated the leadership ability of Lee from that of most of the other men discussed at the symposium, and some of the selections—eclectic at best—were questioned by Richard McMurry.

Certainly General Braxton Bragg falls into this category. Bragg served as the unwitting foil of the symposium, as more than one participant made disparaging remarks about him, even though Bragg was not the central focus of their papers.

It remained for Larry Hewitt to brave the fire by defending Bragg's leadership in the ill-fated Kentucky invasion in 1862. With only a trace of trepidation, he prefaced his formal remarks with some comments that suggested that it was time someone said something good about Bragg, even though most of the other speakers and many in the audience might voice objections.

Hewitt concedes that the rebel invasion of Kentucky launched by Bragg in 1862 failed; however, he believes that Bragg should not be blamed. The historian, in fact, tries to manufacture gold out of the base metal of Bragg's retreat by hinting that one could credit Bragg with prolonging the Civil War. His is a novel interpretation and should generate new interest in Bragg.

Ed Bearss selected General Nathan Bedford Forrest, another of the South's western warriors, as the subject of his study. In many ways Forrest, of all the men discussed at the symposium, Lee excepted, may come closer to being a true military "leader." Forrest showed no hesitation in riding in front of his men into battle. For better or worse, Forrest was a man of the western region of the Confederacy. Rough hewn and fierce of disposition, he possessed more than his share of physical courage, and in battle he gave no quarter. He was afraid of no man. Despite his lack of formal military training, Forrest earned the reputation of being a brilliant strategist and tactician.

At no other place did the fighting qualities of Forrest shine any brighter than they did at the Battle of Brice's Cross Roads in northern Mississippi. Bearss' account of Forrest's men, the "critter cavalry," in this engagement provides evidence of the general's leadership. Unfortunately, Forrest's post-war affiliation with the Ku Klux Klan has damaged his image. Yet, men who fought with him and against him hold him in high regard. There is no greater praise than that given by a former foe. General William T. Sherman, a man similar to Forrest in temperament, respected the rebel commander and thought highly of his fighting qualities.

Forrest's victory over Union forces in north Mississippi did not change the outcome of the war, of course, for the South had already lost its bid for independence. The event that many claim meant the beginning of the end of Confederate hopes was the fall of New Orleans in early 1862.

The loss of New Orleans cost the Confederacy its most populous city and its greatest port, and when David Farragut demanded and received the city's capitulation, the Union also gained control of the mouth of the Mississippi River and the more than one hundred miles of the waterway from the Gulf to New Orleans. For all practical purposes the western region of the Confederacy lost contact with the outside world.

General Mansfield Lovell earned the notoriety of "losing" New Orleans since he commanded the southern forces defending the city. Understandably, armchair strategists and military historians have heaped more than a fair share of criticism on the shoulders of the transplanted Yankee. Panelist Arthur Bergeron, however, takes issue with Lovell's detractors. Lovell's northern birth and upbringing makes him an easy target for those seeking a scapegoat for one of the South's greatest disasters.

Bergeron dismisses any questions about Lovell's loyalty to the Confederate cause; the general had many ties to the South, including his wife and her family. Instead, Bergeron argues that Southern complacency about New Orleans' impregnability from an attack from the Gulf is a better explanation for the defeat than either Lovell's loyalty or his incompetency. Simply stated, Confederate leaders did not believe that the Union Navy could enter the mouth of the river and run the gauntlet along the lower reaches of the Mississippi up to New Orleans. No, the Yankee assault would come from the north. When Farragut confounded this thinking and forced his way up the river, the thin forces under Lovell's command stood no chance of defending the city. Without firing a shot, Farragut marched across the levee to receive the flag of surrender.

If there were an architect of defeat, Bergeron pins that dubious distinction on the chest of the Confederate President, Jefferson Davis. The historian argues that Davis did not understand the importance of New Orleans to the Confederate cause and, therefore, did not provide adequate support for the city.

In Davis' defense, the southern leader had too few forces to protect so vast a region; the Confederacy spanned more than half of the lower portion of the continental United States, from the Texas/New Mexico border to the outskirts of Washington, D.C. Davis and other southerners believed—correctly or not is one of the great questions about Confederate strategy—that the South could not afford to lose Virginia.

Other than General Robert E. Lee, the southern commander who gained the greatest fame in this theater of the war was General Thomas "Stonewall" Jackson. The brilliance of Jackson's Valley campaign continues to attract the attention of scholars and students of warfare. While the Virginian's genius as a military commander cannot be denied, there are those who credit much of his success to the detailed and accurate maps of the Shenandoah Valley drawn by his cartographer, Lieutenant Jedediah Hotchkiss.

When the war began, Hotchkiss, a native New Yorker, found himself in Virginia where he operated a private school. Forced by circumstances to choose sides, he opted for the Confederacy because he had stronger ties to Virginia than he had to the state of his birth. After joining the rebel forces, Hotchkiss won an assignment to serve under General Jackson who directed him to draw a map of the Shenandoah Valley from Harper's Ferry to Lexington. So successfully did he complete his task that many historians credit the reliability of his maps as a factor in Jackson's string of victories.

However, by no stretch of the imagination could Hotchkiss, a functionary, be labeled a commander, nor could one use the word "heroic" to describe his character. Yet, historian Archie McDonald finds him a worthy subject of study, because Hotchkiss in many ways typified the common man serving in a major war fought by hundreds of thousands of like-minded men. His letters provide details of what life was like for soldiers in the Civil War and of their concerns. At the time, his letters reveal that his domestic interests were more important to him than the events of the war. He engaged in the sale and purchase of real estate and cattle with a cold eye for a favorable deal, actions which almost belied the fact that the nation's greatest war raged on with mounting intensity.

Hotchkiss' pragmatic approach to his affairs served him and Virginia well once the war ended. He not only resumed his work as an educator, but he branched out and assisted in the development of coal fields in Virginia during the post-war period. These activities assisted his adopted state to recover from the financial and emotional damage of the war.

Much the same role was played by General Stephen D. Lee, the commander selected for discussion by Herman Hattaway, a symposium participant. During the post-war period, Lee served as the first president of what is now Mississippi State University, a land grant institution.

Stephen Lee fits the description—if such a creature exists—of the journeyman general, for this man is not remembered for any dashing victories or his bold strategy. He was a survivor, and he managed to see action in virtually every part of the Confederacy, including Virginia, where Lee's accurate artillery fire may have been the key to the rebel victory at Second Manassas.

Hattaway, Stephen Lee's major biographer, is dismayed that Civil War historians have generally ignored his subject's contribution to this Confederate victory, but he is somewhat forgiving; Hattaway notes that Lee's superiors at Second Manassas, Robert E. Lee and James Longstreet, both offered cool remarks about Stephen Lee's performance.

Owing to the generous parameters of what constituted "leadership," Jack Davis chose to examine the subject from the cabinet level of the Confederate government. Most scholars agree that the brilliance of rebel military commanders in the field greatly overshadowed the leadership provided by the Confederate War Department. Most of the men who headed this department either lacked ability or had to put up with constant interference from Jefferson Davis. The author examines one exception to the list of mediocre secretaries, John C. Breckinridge. Appointed in early 1865, when hopes of a Confederate victory survived in only the stoutest of southern hearts, Breckinridge brought to the office more impressive credentials than any of his predecessors, including four years as vice president of the United States.

Consequently, Breckinridge did not have to tolerate Davis' meddling, and to be fair to the Confederate President, Davis gave his secretary a free hand to run the department. Breckinridge's wide experience in government and his mandate from Davis, in the opinion of the author, combined to make Breckinridge the most effective Confederate Secretary of War.

However, his leadership has not produced an abundance of scholarly interest. The hopelessness of the rebel cause by 1865 has not piqued the interest of professional historians and Civil War devotees. When Breckinridge took the oath of office, all southern roads led to Appomattox. Nevertheless, he functioned as a true Secretary of War, and, if nothing else, his cold-eyed realism may have prevented a piecemeal surrender and/or a protracted guerilla war. If true, several generations of his countrymen owe Breckinridge a debt of gratitude.

Davis' demurrals notwithstanding, scholars have devoted much effort and ink to Confederate cabinet officials, even if one excludes Breckinridge from the long list of books and articles. As Jon Wakelyn points out, however, the state governments in the Confederate States of America have been overlooked, especially the speakers of the state legislatures. Wakelyn has examined their leadership abilities and has concluded that for the most part these men failed the test.

Even though the Confederate Constitution gave significant powers to the speakers of the legislatures, these men had to face problems of such magnitude that they were unable to use those powers. Chronic fiscal troubles and the vicissitudes of war did not allow for effective management of state affairs.

Wakelyn does not allow these factors to be used as the reasons for the paucity of great state leaders. Cassius' comment to Brutus applies here: "the fault, dear Brutus, is not in our stars but in ourselves..." Applying Cliometric techniques to his study, Wakelyn notes that, as a group, the speakers lacked the political experience, the education, and the business expertise to be successful leaders.

Richard McMurray, certainly agreed with Wakelyn's assessment, except he would carry it one step further: By virtue of their positions, these men could never have been "military leaders." McMurray took a contrary—and humorous—view of leadership. According to him, most of the other participants at the symposium confused command, political bossism, and military staff work with leadership. These men might have been important but they were not leaders. The real leaders, those who urged their men to follow them into combat, occupied the lower level ranks of the army: the platoons and squads.

McMurray outlined the travails faced by the lower ranking officers and the non-commissioned officers; they had the difficult task of taking hundreds of thousands of raw recruits and transforming them into soldiers within a short period of time. Very few of these leaders had any military experience, yet they had to teach their men drills, discipline, weaponry, and a host of different bugle calls. The results were decidedly mixed.

Since Virginia had one of the better state militias before the war and that state did serve as a major focal point of the conflict, it is not surprising that the Army of Northern Virginia had the largest cadre of men trained in the military tradition. McMurray claims that it should not have shocked anyone that this army, especially under the command of Robert E. Lee, enjoyed the greatest military success of any Confederate army.

McMurray's closing remarks included a plea for more research on the small unit leaders. Based on the audience's response to his paper and the need for original topics of study, it is almost a certainty that his prayer will be answered, perhaps at a future symposium.

Lincoln, the War, and the Constitution

Richard N. Current

"Lincoln stomped all over the Constitution to preserve the nation," wrote a *Boston Globe* columnist at about the time of President's Day, 1988. This notion of Lincoln the Constitution-stomper seems to pass nowadays as accepted knowledge. Fiction writers have given the idea wide circulation. According to Gore Vidal, Lincoln badly abused the "inherent powers" of the presidency. According to William Safire, he "departed from the forms of civil liberty" and "stretched and at times seemed to ignore the Constitution." According to Edmund Wilson, he was really expressing his own ambition when, as a young man, he warned against dictatorship. It was an ambition he eventually realized; just like Bismarck and Lenin, he "became an uncompromising dictator."[1]

These recent writers are, in essence, repeating what Lincoln's critics said during the Civil War (and are ignoring what he and his supporters said in his defense). They are echoing the contemporary charges of Confederates in the South and Copperheads in the North. Jefferson Davis congratulated Southerners on having severed their connection with a government that "tramples on all the principles of constitutional liberty." (To say that Lincoln "trampled on all the principles" of the Constitution, I suppose, has pretty much the same meaning as to say he "stomped all over" it.) The Richmond journalist and historian E. A. Pollard denounced Lincoln for his "ruthless despotism"—until concluding that Davis' "military tyranny" was even worse. A Harvard law professor, who was also a bitterly partisan Democrat, declared that Lincoln was "not only a monarch" but his was "an absolute, irresponsible, uncontrollable government; a perfect military despotism."[2]

Admirers as well as contemners of Lincoln have looked upon him as an all-powerful President, one who could possibly be called a dictator, if only a "benevolent" one. He "was driven by circumstances to the use of more arbitrary power than perhaps any other President has seized," J. G. Randall wrote soon after the First World War. Randall added, "It would not be easy to state what Lincoln conceived to be the limit of his powers."[3]

So-called "strong" Presidents of the twentieth century have used what they considered to be the Lincoln precedent to justify their own bold use of executive authority. Harry S. Truman is only one example. After his seizure of the steel mills during the Korean War, Truman was asked at a press conference, "Are there any limitations at all over a President's actions during an emergency?" He replied, in effect, that there were none. "Mr. Lincoln," he explained, "exercised the powers of the President to meet the emergencies with which he was faced."[4]

Supposedly. Lincoln flouted the Constitution in the following ways: 1. He asserted a new presidential "war power" and used it to justify measures as unwarranted as the confiscation of private property—property in slaves, that is. 2. He authorized the military arrest and imprisonment of thousands of citizens whose only offense was disagreeing with his conduct of war. 3. He silenced opposition not only by imprisoning dissenters but also by censoring and even closing down unfriendly newspapers.

*   *   *   *   *

Now, it certainly would have been ironic if Lincoln had, in fact, ignored or disregarded the Constitution. No man in public life had been more devoted to that document than he. True, he gave his devotion to the *Union* primarily, to the *Declaration of Independence* secondarily, and to the *Constitution* only after that. Yet in his mind the Union, the Declaration, and the Constitution formed a sacred and inseparable triad. To maintain the Constitution, he had to preserve the Union.

In interpreting the Constitution, Lincoln liked to take into account the original intent of its framers. "I do not mean to say we are bound to follow implicitly in what our fathers did," he explained in 1860. "To do so, would be to disregard all the lights of current experience—to reject all progress—all improvement. What I do say is that, if we would supplant the opinions and policy of our fathers in any case, we should do so upon evidence so conclusive, and arguments so clear, that even their great authority, fairly considered and weighed, cannot stand."[5]

"But," Lincoln added a year later, in his first inaugural, "no organic law can ever be framed with a provision specifically applicable to every question which may occur in practical administration." Inevitably there would arise questions to which the Constitution gave no explicit answers. "From questions of this class," Lincoln said, "spring all our constitutional controversies." And from questions of this class sprang the constitutional controversies of the Lincoln presidency.

*   *   *   *   *

After the firing on Fort Sumter he faced a problem that the framers of the Constitution had not fully anticipated. They had provided for declaring a foreign war but not for dealing with a civil war, though they had taken into account the possibility of a rebellion. Now Lincoln had to cope with a rebellion that quickly broadened into a civil war. Believing as he did that the Union and the Constitution were two components of a national trinity, he could never concede that secession might be a perfectly legal and constitutional undertaking. Certainly the Constitution itself contained no provision for a state's withdrawal from the Union. But it did require the President, as Lincoln said, to see that "the laws of the Union are faithfully executed in all the States."[6]

In opposing the Union's assailants, Lincoln at the outset had to proceed on the basis of such executive authority as he could find without looking to Congress for it, since Congress was not in session. When he first called upon the states for troops, he had a congressional act to go on, the Militia Act of 1795, which he invoked. This authorized him to use the state militia against "combinations too powerful to be suppressed by the ordinary course of judicial proceedings" whenever such combinations were resisting federal laws. By implication, the Militia Act would seem to justify the use of various warlike measures to put down the insurgents, but Lincoln did not refer to it when he took such additional steps as enlarging the army and navy and proclaiming a blockade of Southern ports. He simply said that "no choice was left but to call out the war power of the Government; and so to resist force, employed for its destruction, by force, for its preservation."[7]

After Congress met, on July 4, it retroactively authorized Lincoln's exercise of legislative functions in regard to the army and the navy. So, if he had exceeded his constitutional authority in those respects, Congress did what it could to excuse him. But there remained the question of his "war power" in general and his blockading power in particular. The question of the blockade came before the Supreme Court in the Prize Cases, which it decided in 1863. According to the decision, while Congress alone can declare war, the President by himself can and must deal with an insurrection "in fulfilling his duties as Commander-in-Chief." And "he must determine what degree of force the crisis demands." Thus the Supreme Court vindicated Lincoln to the extent that he had exercised his "war power" in a strictly military and naval sense.[8]

*   *   *   *   *

Already, however, he had carried the "war power" beyond that limit by using it to justify his Emancipation Proclamation. At first, he had found nothing in the Constitution that would have allowed him to proclaim freedom for the slaves. He promptly overruled Major General John C. Frémont when Frémont issued an emancipation proclamation for Missouri. A commanding general, he told Frémont, could temporarily seize property he needed for his operations; this was "within military law, because within military necessity." But the general could not permanently confiscate private property, including property in slaves. "That must be settled according to laws made by law-makers, and not by military proclamations. The proclamation in point in question is simply 'dictatorship,'" Lincoln expostulated. "Can it be pretended that it is any longer the government of the U.S.—any government of Constitution and laws,—wherein a General, or a President, may make permanent rules of property by proclamation?"[9]

Lincoln wrote that letter to Frémont on September 22, 1861. Exactly one year later, one year to the day, on September 22, 1862, Lincoln issued his own preliminary Proclamation of Emancipation.

Obviously, he had changed his mind, but if his mind had changed, so had the situation, and perhaps he was a little less inconsistent than he appeared to be. In late 1861 the border slave states, Kentucky in particular, were still wavering between the Union and the Confederacy, and an antislavery edict might have driven them into secession. Such an edict at that time would therefore have been no "military necessity"; instead, it would have been a military liability. By late 1862 the border states were quite firmly in the Union, and an emancipation proclamation then might be considered so advantageous as to be necessary for the winning of the war.

Shortly before issuing the proclamation, Lincoln responded to a group of Chicago Christians who were petitioning him to do just that. To parry their appeal, and to keep his intentions hidden, he asked them whether such a decree might not be "inoperative, like the Pope's bull against the comet." But he hastened to add, "Understand, I raise no objection against it on legal or constitutional grounds; for, as commander-in-chief of the army and navy, in time of war, I suppose I have a right to take any measure which may best subdue the enemy." Later he replied to a group of Democrats who had held a mass meeting in Springfield, Illinois, to denounce the proclamation: "You say it is unconstitutional—I think differently. I think the constitution invests its commander-in-chief with the law of war in time of war. ...[S]laves are property. Is there—has there ever been—any question that, by the law of war, property both of enemies and [of] friends may be taken when needed?"[10]

This, of course, is precisely what Lincoln had told Frémont no general and no President could constitutionally do. It was, in the words of a hostile pamphleteer, an assertion of "transcendent executive power" and had no basis in the Constitution. But, according to a friendly pamphleteer, the power needed no basis in the Constitution except for the clause making the chief executive the commander-in-chief. Such a commander was the "depository" of "all the war powers, rights, and discretion which belong to the nation," this defender of Lincoln argued. Throughout history, every nation at war had had that kind of officer, and in pursuit of victory he was "authorized and bound to use any and all accessible means not forbidden by the laws of war." "Constitutionality and unconstitutionality cannot, therefore, be predicated of the acts of the *commander-in-chief.*"[11]

That was much farther than Lincoln himself ever went in asserting a presidential "war power." He never suggested that the constitutionality of the acts of the commander-in-chief was irrelevant. On the contrary, he repeatedly insisted that his own acts as commander-in-chief—including his Proclamation of Emancipation—were constitutional. Yet, despite his insistence, he continued to have doubts, which were reminiscent of the objections he had earlier expressed to Frémont. He took it for granted that his proclamation could be subject to judicial review, and when he proposed a loyalty oath for ex-rebels, he asked them to swear to abide by the proclamation only "so long and so far as not modified or declared void by decision of the Supreme Court." When urging the adoption of the Thirteenth Amendment, he said the proclamation "falls short of what the amendment will be." He admitted, "A question might be raised whether the proclamation was legally valid."[12]

From this questioning, this concern for constitutionality, we may infer that Lincoln had been trying to convince himself when he said, "...I *suppose* I have a right to take any measure which may best subdue the enemy," and "I *think* the constitution invests its commander-in-chief with the law of war in time of war." He did not say he *knew* he had the right or was *certain* the Constitution invested him with it. Taken together, taken in context, his words really give little or no support to those pundits and Presidents who in more recent times have quoted him selectively to bolster their claim of unlimited power for the chief executive.

* * * * *

Besides asserting and exercising a "war power," however, Lincoln also did other things that might seem to sustain his reputation (in some quarters) as a high-handed ruler and an oppressor of the people. He had the army seize and hold a great many of the people without allowing them any opportunity for a legal defense. The arrests began only a couple of weeks after the firing on Fort Sumter. On April 27, 1861, Lincoln directed the commanding general of the army to suspend the privilege of the writ of *habeas corpus* "at any point on or in the vicinity of the military line" between Washington and Philadelphia. This meant, in effect, that those arrested in that strip could no longer obtain a court order assuring them of a hearing or a trial.[13]

One of those arrested, a Marylander named John Merryman, nevertheless applied to the federal circuit court for a writ of *habeas corpus*. His fellow Marylander Chief Justice Roger B. Taney, sitting on circuit duty, readily granted the writ, demanding that Merryman's captors have his "body" in court to "make known the day and cause of the capture and detention." The military authorities, not least among them the commander-in-chief, ignored Taney's writ.

In this case, *Ex parte Merryman*, Taney maintained that only Congress could suspend the privilege of the writ and that Lincoln, though under oath to "take care that the laws be faithfully executed," was himself violating the law. Taney contended, further, that the courts in the area were freely functioning, so the army had no real need to deprive civilians of their right to a trial. "There was," he declared, "no danger of any obstruction or resistance to the action of the civil authorities, and therefore no reason whatever for the interposition of the military."[14]

Let us look at what was going on at the time and place of Merryman's arrest to see if Taney was correct in saying there was "no reason whatever" for the military to intervene. Then, after looking at some subsequent military arrests, let us consider the question whether Taney was justified in denying the President any constitutional power to suspend *habeas corpus*.

In those first few days and weeks after the firing on Fort Sumter, the Lincoln government stood in real danger of losing the capital and even the country. The seceders, militarily on the offensive, were rapidly gaining ground. They seemed on the verge of making good the Confederate war secretary's boast that the flag flying over Montgomery, Alabama, would soon be flying also over Washington, D.C.

On April 17 Virginia seceded. The next day the Virginia secessionists captured the federal arsenal at Harper's Ferry and, two days after that, the federal navy yard at Norfolk. It only remained for Maryland to secede, and Washington would be surrounded. Already the rebellious Marylanders had bestirred themselves. On April 19 a pro-Confederate mob fell upon soldiers from Massachusetts as they tried to get through Baltimore on their way to the defense of Washington. Killed were four of the soldiers and a dozen members of the mob; many others were wounded. The Maryland secessionists, now thoroughly enraged, determined to prevent additional Northern troops from reaching Washington. Pro-Confederate militia companies gathered from various parts of the state. They set about burning bridges and cutting telegraph lines along the Philadelphia-Washington route.

These armed and mounted men were doing the work of the Confederacy just as surely as if they had been wearing the uniforms of Confederate cavalry. They sent to Richmond for additional arms. The Virginia governor quickly forwarded two thousand muskets and promised twenty heavy guns. Jefferson Davis encouraged the governor. "Sustain Baltimore, if practicable," Davis telegraphed him. "We reinforce you." As good as his word, Davis ordered thirteen regiments of Confederate troops to concentrate in Virginia and be ready to assist the Virginians in the campaign for Maryland.

Such was the situation that Lincoln confronted when he suspended *habeas corpus*. Such was the activity that John Merryman—Lieutenant Merryman—

had been engaged in when he was arrested. As commander of the Baltimore County Horse Guards, he had been doing his part to disrupt communications between Washington and the North.[15]

It makes no sense to say, as Taney did in Merryman's behalf, "There was no danger of any obstruction or resistance to the action of the civil authorities, and therefore no reason whatever for the interposition of the military." On the contrary, there is no reason whatever to believe that Merryman, if the civil authorities had been inclined to arrest and prosecute him, would have yielded with no "obstruction or resistance" on the part of his militiamen and their allies. There is good reason to believe, however, that had it not been for the "interposition of the military" on Lincoln's part, Maryland might have been lost and the future of the Union put in real jeopardy.

*   *   *   *   *

Maryland remained at risk throughout the summer of 1861. When the state legislature met in July, a majority of its members showed their sympathy with the secessionists by adopting a protest against the military arrests. The legislature then adjourned until September 17. If it should reassemble at that time, the pro-Confederate majority could be expected to take steps toward the secession of the state. So, before September 17, the U.S. troops not only apprehended the mayor and other officials of Baltimore but also rounded up enough of the secessionist legislators to deprive them of a majority in the general assembly. Through a Baltimore newspaper, Lincoln assured the people of Maryland that "no arrest has been made, or will be made, not based on substantial and unmistakable complicity with those in armed rebellion against the Government of the United States."[16]

During the fall and winter of 1861-62 the military arrests continued. They were not confined to the Washington-Philadelphia corridor where Lincoln had suspended *habeas corpus*. Many occurred on the Eastern Shore of Maryland (a part of the state even more rebellious than Baltimore) and in Kentucky, Missouri, and northern Virginia. Very few of the arrests took place anywhere north of the border slave states.

Lincoln did not intend for the army to harass civilians unnecessarily. "Our wish is to make as few arrests as possible compatible with the safety of the Government, and never if they can be avoided for merely words spoken." That was what Secretary of State William H. Seward, in charge of the military arrests, instructed the U.S. attorney in Cincinnati. Brigadier General Robert Anderson, commanding U.S. troops in Kentucky, ordered them "not to make any arrests except where the parties are attempting to join the rebels or are engaged in giving aid or information to them." And Major General John A. Dix advised his subordinate on Maryland's rebellious Eastern Shore that "those who have been deceived and misled, instead of being confirmed in their prejudices and driven hopelessly off by harshness on our part, should if possible be reclaimed by kind treatment."[17]

The number of arrests has been grossly exaggerated, and their nature has been even more distorted. In the confusion and urgency of the moment, the troops undoubtedly took prisoners who had been doing nothing to aid the Confederacy. But the great majority of those taken had been doing one or more of the following things for the rebels: spying, passing information, procuring arms and other supplies, recruiting, destroying bridges and committing other acts of sabotage, bushwhacking, robbing and murdering Union soldiers, inducing them to desert, and serving generally as Confederate agents.

Those who were innocent, or whose offense was trivial, could obtain their freedom by taking an oath of allegiance to the United States or giving a "parole of honor" not to assist the enemy. In February 1862 Lincoln ordered the release of practically all the remaining civilian prisoners who would take the oath or give the parole.[18]

*　　*　　*　　*　　*

The first period of military arrests was now over, and for the rest of the war they were to be far fewer. Nevertheless, on paper at least, Lincoln greatly widened their scope with his proclamation of September 24, 1862. He intended thereby to strengthen the enforcement of the draft, which was about to go into effect. The proclamation applied to all persons anywhere in the United States who were discouraging enlistments, resisting the draft, or "affording aid and comfort to the rebels" in any way. Such persons would be "subject to martial law and liable to trail and punishment by Courts Martial or Military Commissions," and the writ of *habeas corpus* would be suspended in these cases.[19]

When the draft began in Ozaukee County, Wisconsin, a mob of farmers, immigrants from Luxembourg, descended on the county seat, Port Washington, and started a wild riot. They drove off the draft commissioner, destroyed the boxes containing the names to be drawn, and went on a spree of "pillage and plunder." Troops finally occupied the town. About 150 of the rioters were arrested and detained under the recent proclamation. But the Wisconsin Supreme Court, in the Kemp case, declared the proclamation unconstitutional on the same grounds as those on which Chief Justice Taney had based his decision in *Ex parte Merryman*—namely, that only Congress had the power to suspend *habeas corpus*. Lincoln's Secretary of War, Edwin M. Stanton, now in charge of military arrests, paroled the prisoners while waiting for the U.S. Supreme Court to review the Kemp case.[20]

In issuing the *habeas corpus* proclamations, Lincoln was confident that he had acted in a perfectly constitutional manner. For authority, he could point to a specific clause in the Constitution: "The privilege of the writ of *habeas corpus* shall not be suspended unless when, in cases of rebellion or invasion, the public safety may require it." Obviously, this meant that the privilege *could* be suspended in case of a rebellion, and just as obviously there was a rebellion in existence. "Now it is insisted that Congress, not the Executive, is vested with this power," Lincoln noted in replying to Taney without mentioning him or the Merryman case. "But," he went on to argue, "the Constitution itself is silent as to which, or who, is to exercise the power; and as the provision was plainly made for a dangerous emergency, it cannot be believed that the framers of the instrument intended that, in every case, the danger should run its course until Congress could be called together...."[21]

In thus referring to the original intent of the framers, Lincoln seems to have had at least as good an argument as Taney, and probably a much better one. Taney based his conclusion on the fact that the *habeas corpus* clause happens to appear in the section of the Constitution dealing with the legislative branch. At the 1787 constitutional convention, however, the clause had originally been part of the article on the *judiciary*. The phrasing originally had included the words "suspended by the legislature." But the convention amended the judiciary article so as to leave out the reference to the legislature, thus (it would seem) deliberately rejecting any implication that the *habeas corpus* power should be confined to Congress alone. Finally the convention's Committee on Style and Arrangement took the clause from the article on the judiciary and put it where it has been located ever since. Pointing all this out, a pro-Lincoln pamphleteer in 1862 declared it "inconclusive and unsafe" to infer anything from the *"position"* of the clause in the Constitution.[22]

Congress itself resolved this *habeas corpus* question in Lincoln's favor, though somewhat equivocally. On March 3, 1863, the congressional majority managed to agree on a bill with this wording: "During the present rebellion the President of the United States, whenever, in his judgment, the public safety may require it, is authorized to suspend the privilege of the writ of *habeas corpus* in any case throughout the United States or any part thereof." Was Congress now granting him the power, or was Congress recognizing that he had possessed it all along? The wording was purposely ambiguous, the bill being a compromise.[23]

Still, this act of Congress settled the matter as far as the U.S. Supreme Court was concerned. The Kemp case from Wisconsin now became moot, and the Court did not bother to review it. The Ozaukee County anti-draft rioters, already on parole, remained at liberty. Lincoln made no attempt to have them rearrested.

*   *   *   *   *

Nor did he intend for the military to arrest Clement L. Vallandigham, the prominent Ohio Democratic politician who was making provocative antiwar speeches. After a military commission had condemned Vallandigham to prison for the duration, Lincoln commuted the sentence to banishment to the Confederacy. And after Vallandigham returned to Ohio and resumed his speech making, Lincoln simply let him alone. Meanwhile Democrats staged protest meetings here and there. One of them, at Albany, New York, sent Lincoln a copy of its resolutions, which maintained that, though possibly constitutional at scenes of actual insurrection, military arrests of civilians were definitely unconstitutional elsewhere.

"Inasmuch, however, as the constitution itself makes no such distinction," Lincoln replied to the New York Democrats, "I am unable to believe that there is any such constitutional distinction." His understanding in the case of Vallandigham, he explained, was that "his arrest was made because he was laboring, with some effect, to prevent the raising of troops, to encourage desertions from the army, and to leave the rebellion without an adequate military force to suppress it." He added, "I have to say it gave me pain when I learned that Mr. V. had been arrested." And he hoped "the necessity for arbitrary dealing" with such cases would soon "cease altogether."[24]

Though not ceasing altogether, such cases were declining in frequency. During the first year of the war, numerous detentions had seemed urgent, not so much to punish treason as to prevent it. The aim was, in Lincoln's words, "preventive" rather than "vindictive." Seldom did the arrests of Northern civilians lead to military trials and convictions. The Vallandigham case was as exceptional as it was conspicuous, and so was the Milligan case.

In the midst of the 1864 political campaign a military commission convicted Lambdin P. Milligan and other Indianans of conspiring to aid the rebels. At that time the Confederates were plotting to seize a U.S. gunboat on Lake Erie, to raid border towns from bases in Canada, to perpetrate various acts of sabotage throughout the North, and to free captured rebels from midwestern prison camps. Republicans feared a "Northwestern Conspiracy" to detach the Old Northwest from the Union and align it with the South. They suspected that Northern traitors were cooperating through the Sons of Liberty, a secret organization of Peace Democrats, or Copperheads. Milligan was a Copperhead and a member of the Sons of Liberty.

The hysteria infected Republicans as highly placed as Governor Richard Yates of Illinois and Governor Oliver P. Morton of Indiana. Yates talked of "shooting home traitors" like "so many dogs," and Morton insisted that, at the very least, they must be tried for treason. A prompt trial, Morton thought, was "essential to the success of the National cause in the autumn elections." Lincoln, too, was anxious about the elections in Indiana, and he urged General William T. Sherman to let his Hoosier troops go home and vote. But Lincoln was quite immune to the rising hysteria. "He holds the Northern section of the conspiracy as not especially worth regarding," his private secretary John Hay noted, "holding it as a mere political organization," and one with more "puerility" than "malice" in it.[25]

Not Lincoln but Morton prodded the military commander in Indiana into arresting Milligan and his associates. A military commission condemned Milligan and two others to death. Indiana Republicans went to Lincoln and demanded that he see to the prompt execution of the three, but Lincoln refrained from setting a date for the firing squad. At the time of his assassination the men were still alive, and soon afterward Milligan petitioned the Federal Circuit Court for a writ of *habeas corpus*. The case went on to the U.S. Supreme Court.

At issue was the constitutionality of the military trial. Earlier, in the Vallandigham case, the Supreme Court had declined to review the proceedings of the military commission, thus letting them stand. That was in 1864, while the war was still going on. The Court did not give its decision in the Milligan case until 1866, after the war was over. The Court now reversed itself. It directed the release of Milligan on the ground that the military commission had had no jurisdiction over him. "A citizen, not connected with the military service, and resident in a State where the courts are all open, and in the proper exercise of their jurisdiction, cannot, even when the privilege of *habeas corpus* is suspended, be tried, convicted, or sentenced otherwise than by the ordinary courts of law."[26]

The decision in the Milligan case has long been hailed as a glorious vindication of civil liberty, and no doubt it was all of that. Certainly the Supreme Court, in rendering the decision, was declaring unconstitutional one part of Lincoln's September 24, 1862, proclamation—the part having to do with martial law and military trials, but not the part having to do with the suspension of the writ of *habeas corpus*.

It has been said that, by implication, the Supreme Court in the Milligan case also rebuked Lincoln and backed Taney in the Merryman case. "The principle in *Milligan* applied to *Merryman*," Safire has asserted; "Taney's opinion...was upheld, and Lincoln's action [with respect to Maryland in 1861] remains condemned to this day."[27] It remains condemned by ill-informed people, to be sure, but it was not condemned by the Supreme Court. In the Merryman case the issue was *habeas corpus*, and the chief justice contended that the President had no power to suspend it. In the Milligan case the justices did not question the President's power to do so; the issue this time was martial law. Besides, the situations differed in the two cases. In Maryland in 1861, armed men were resisting the authority of the United States, and John Merryman was one of them. In Indiana in 1864, there were only rumors of a possible uprising, and Lambdin P. Milligan was guilty of nothing more than antiwar political activity. The Supreme Court disallowed only one of Lincoln's wartime exercises of presidential power, and that was his authorizing military trials of civilians in localities where, at the moment, armed rebels were not in action and the civil courts could therefore function normally.

*   *   *   *   *

According to Lincoln's critics—those both in his time and in ours—he not only infringed upon free speech by means of military arrests. He also infringed upon freedom of speech and press by censoring the news and shutting down critical newspapers.

In fact, the Lincoln government never imposed a strict or effective censorship. With congressional authorization, the war department took control of all the telegraph lines and undertook to supervise the transmission of war news. But the government made no attempt to control the postal service, and newsmen could send in their reports either by messenger or by mail. The newspapers disregarded an 1862 order of Stanton's forbidding them to publish military information. Throughout the war, they freely printed the accounts they received from their correspondents at the front. Robert E. Lee and other Confederate commanders regularly depended on Northern papers for knowledge about the disposition of Union armies.

The military authorities did suppress quite a few newspapers, though most of them for very brief periods. Nearly all of these were pro-Confederate organs located in the border slave states or in the Union-occupied areas of the South. Two conspicuous exceptions were the *Chicago Times* and the *New York World*, both of them rabid Copperhead sheets. The suppression of the *Chicago Times* was not Lincoln's idea; the order, on June 1, 1863, came from Major General Ambrose E. Burnside, the man who also ordered the arrest of Vallandigham. Lincoln regretted Burnside's action in both instances, and after three days he revoked the order suppressing the newspaper. Lincoln himself, on May 18, 1864, ordered the suspension of the *New York World*, after it had published false news potentially damaging to Northern morale—a fake proclamation calling for 400,000 additional troops and setting a day of fasting and prayer. As soon as Lincoln learned that the publishers themselves had been victims of the hoax, he withdrew the order and the paper resumed publication—again after the lapse of only three days.[28]

Other Democratic newspapers in the North—papers as hostile to Lincoln as the *New York World* and the *Chicago Times* were—went on denouncing him without any government interference whatsoever. The *La Crosse* (Wisconsin) *Democrat*, for example, charged during the presidential campaign of 1864 that he was warring "against the constitution of our country" and was therefore himself a traitor. "And if he is elected to misgovern for another four years, we trust some bold hand will pierce his heart with dagger point for the public good." No President with the slightest dictatorial tendencies would have allowed that kind of press freedom to prevail.[29]

And no man of dictatorial bent would have subjected himself to the uncertainty of reelection in 1864. Here was the perfect opportunity for Lincoln, if he had been so inclined, to make himself dictator of the United States. He could have played upon the mounting hysteria about the Sons of Liberty and the "Northwestern Conspiracy." He could then have postponed the election on the grounds of military necessity. "But the election was a necessity," he firmly believed. "We can not have free government without elections," he explained afterward; "and if the rebellion could force us to forego or postpone a national election, it might fairly claim to have already conquered and ruined us."[30]

*   *   *   *   *

This is the man who, they say, "stomped all over the Constitution" and "trampled on all the principles of constitutional liberty." They do not seem fully to appreciate the dilemma he faced—a dilemma that every democracy sooner or later has to confront. As he put it, "Must a government, of necessity, be too *strong* for the liberties of its own people, or too *weak* to maintain its own existence?"[31] In dealing with this problem, Lincoln may at times have unintentionally stretched the Constitution a bit, but he was always sensitive to its limitations, and he never ignored or disregarded it. Indeed, he read the document much more closely and much more understandingly than most of his recent critics appear to have done.

Endnotes

[1] Alan Lupo in the *Boston Globe*, Feb. 20, 1988, p. 19; Gore Vidal, *Lincoln: A Novel* (New York, 1984), 126, 233, and *passim*; William Safire, *Freedom* (New York, 1987), 987, 1083; Edmund Wilson, *Patriotic Gore: Studies in the Literature of the American Civil War* (New York, 1962), xviii, 106-8.

[2] Michael Davis, *The Image of Lincoln in the South* (Knoxville, 1971), 80-81, quoting Jefferson Davis and E. A. Pollard; Arthur A. Ekirch, Jr., *The Civilian and the Military* (New York, 1956), 95, quoting Joel Parker.

[3] J. G. Randall, *Constitutional Problems under Lincoln* (1926; rev. ed., Urbana, Ill., 1951), 47, 513-14. Ekirch, *The Civilian and the Military*, 90, says that during the Civil War "the United States was placed under what, for all practical purposes, amounted to a military dictatorship." Historians and political scientists, even those admiring Lincoln, have quite generally described him as a "constitutional dictator" or some other kind of dictator. For an able review and refutation of such accounts, see Herman Belz, *Lincoln and the Constitution: The Dictatorship Question Reconsidered* (Fort Wayne, Ind., 1984).

[4] Truman at a press conference, Apr. 24, 1952. William Howard Taft, disagreeing with Theodore Roosevelt, said quite correctly that, while Lincoln had sometimes taken steps "the constitutionality of which was seriously questioned," he had "always pointed out the source of the authority which in his opinion justified his acts." Truman and Taft are quoted in Richard N. Current, *Speaking of Abraham Lincoln: The Man and His Meaning for Our Times* (Urbana and Chicago, 1983), 132-33.

[5] Address at Cooper Institute, Feb. 27, 1860, in Roy P. Basler, ed., *The Collected Works of Abraham Lincoln* (New Brunswick, N.J., 1953-55), III, 522, 534-35.

[6] First Inaugural Address, Mar. 4, 1861, *Collected Works*, IV, 264-65, 267.

[7] Message to Congress in Special Session, July 4, 1861, *Collected Works*, IV, 426; Raoul Berger, *Executive Privilege: A Constitutional Myth* (Cambridge, Mass., 1974), 80-81.

[8] Stanley I. Kutler, ed., *The Supreme Court and the Constitution: Readings in American Constitutional History* (Boston, 1969), 161-64.

[9] To Orville H. Browning, Sept. 22, 1861, *Collected Works*, IV, 531-32.

[10] Reply to Emancipation Memorial, Sept. 13, 1862; letter to James C. Conkling, Aug. 26, 1863, *Collected Works*, V, 419-25; VI, 408.

[11] Benjamin Robbins Curtis, *Executive Power* (1862), and Grosvenor P. Lowery, *The Commander-in-Chief; A Defence upon Legal Grounds of the Proclamation of Emancipation; and an Answer to Ex-Judge Curtis' Pamphlet, Entitled "Executive Power"* (1863) in Frank Freidel, ed., *Union Pamphlets of the Civil War, 1861-1865* (Cambridge, Mass., 1967), 453, 480-82.

[12] Proclamation of Amnesty and Reconstruction, Dec. 8, 1863; Response to a Serenade, Feb. 1, 1865, *Collected Works*, VII, 54; VIII, 254.

[13] To Winfield Scott, Apr. 27, 1861, *Collected Works*, IV, 347.

[14] Ekirch, *The Civilian and the Military,* 94, quoting Taney.

[15] Richard N. Current, *Lincoln and the First Shot* (Philadelphia, 1963), 160-66; Dean Sprague, *Freedom under Lincoln* (Boston, 1965), 9, 14-17.

[16] Sprague, *Freedom under Lincoln,* 184-86, 193-99; *Baltimore American,* Sept. 21, 1861, *Collected Works,* IV, 523.

[17] Seward to Flamen Ball, Sept. 14, 1861; Anderson, General Orders No. 5, Oct. 7, 1861; Dix to Henry H. Lockwood, Oct. 14, 1861, *The War of the Rebellion: A Compilation of the Official Records of the Union and Confederate Armies* (Washington, 1880-1901), ser. II, vol. II, pp. 66, 91-92, 103-4.

[18] Randall, *Constitutional Problems,* 151-56. Examples of arrests and charges may be found throughout *Official Records,* ser. II, vol. II; see pp. 277-79 for a listing of 87 of them. See also *Official Records,* ser. II, vol. I, pp. 563-748.

[19] Proclamation Suspending *Habeas Corpus,* Sept. 24, 1862, *Collected Works,* V, 436-37.

[20] Richard N. Current, *The History of Wisconsin: The Civil War Era, 1848-1873* (Madison, 1976), 316, 318-19.

[21] Message to Congress in Special Session, July 4, 1861, *Collected Works,* IV, 430-31.

[22] Horace Binney, *The Privilege of the Writ of Habeas Corpus under the Constitution* (1862), in Freidel, *Union Pamphlets,* 222-29. See also Randall, *Constitutional Problems,* 126.

[23] Randall, *Constitutional Problems,* 128-31.

[24] To Erastus Corning and Others, June 12, 1863, *Collected Works,* VI, 265, 269.

[25] J. G. Randall and Richard N. Current, *Lincoln the President: Last Full Measure* (New York, 1955), 205-7; Kenneth M. Stampp, *Indiana Politics During the Civil War* (Indianapolis, 1949), 230-32, 246-47.

[26] Frank L. Klement, *The Copperheads in the Middle West* (Chicago, 1960), 256; Kutler, *Supreme Court,* 168.

[27] Safire, *Freedom,* 980. Safire adds, 1084: "The lesson in this most extreme of cases is that it is never a proper time to ignore the Constitution in the name of saving the Constitution. To be tolerant of Lincoln's excesses is to encourage future abuses of power." But to exaggerate Lincoln's "excesses," as Safire and likeminded writers do, would seem to be even more likely to encourage future abuses.

In fairness to Safire, it should be pointed out that he did not invent the notion that the Supreme Court in the Milligan case vindicated Taney in the Merryman case. In *Without Fear or Favor: A Biography of Chief Justice Roger Brooke Taney* (Boston, 1965), p. 455, Walker Lewis wrote: "In *Ex Parte Milligan* a Republican dominated Supreme Court held illegal the establishment of military tribunals to try civilians in states where the civil courts were open. In essence the constitutional issue was the same as in the Merryman case and the decision has been regarded as sustaining Taney's position. For example, Charles Warren's *The Supreme Court in United States History* says, 'Never did a fearless Judge receive a more swift or more complete vindication.' "

That, however, is not the view of the best present-day authorities. Both Harold

Hyman and Kenneth Stampp agree with me on this matter (conversation with Hyman in Reno, Nevada, on March 26, 1988, and with Stampp in Berkeley, California, on March 27, 1988). Hyman had protested to Safire when Safire sent him portions of the *Freedom* manuscript dealing with the issue, but Safire did not change the passages that Hyman objected to.

[28] Randall, *Constitutional Problems,* 481-99.

[29] Current, *History of Wisconsin,* 411, quoting *La Crosse Democrat,* Aug. 25, 1864.

[30] Response to a Serenade, Nov. 10, 1864, *Collected Works,* VIII, 101.

[31] Message to Congress in Special Session, July 4, 1861, *Collected Works,* IV, 426.

Jefferson Davis and Confederate Military Leadership

Grady McWhiney

Jefferson Davis was, in the words of a contemporary, "the heart and brains" of the Confederate government. He spent fifteen or more hours a day at his duties—receiving visitors, writing letters, consulting his advisors, revising or initiating projects to win the war. He not only "managed the War Department, in all its various details," noted a contemporary, but found time to devote to "its minutiae,...and the very disbursement of its appropriations." Davis appointed and removed generals, advised them on strategy and tactics, and often decided when and where they should fight. He was the man most responsible for the way the Confederacy fought the Civil War.

Davis seems to have had no doubts about his ability to direct a war. He had spent a dozen years in the army, including four years as a cadet at the United States Military Academy (1824-28), five years as a second lieutenant in the First Infantry (1828-33), two years as a first lieutenant in the First Dragoons (1833-35), and one year as colonel of the First Mississippi Volunteer Rifles during the Mexican War (1846-47). He had participated in the Black Hawk War (1832) and in two Mexican battles. At Monterey and Buena Vista, where he had been wounded in the foot, Davis had fought courageously. In addition to his years in the army, he had served as President Franklin Pierce's Secretary of War (1853-57), and he had been chairman of the Senate's Military Affairs Committee. All of these activities had given him confidence in his military ability. "By early education, by years of service in the army, by other years spent in administering the U.S. War Dept.," Davis boasted, "I had learned the usages of war."[1]

Davis believed that he was a talented soldier. He had said before the Confederacy was formed that he would rather be commander-in-chief of its army than its president. Of course he knew that under the United States Constitution—and he could have guessed that under the Constitution the Confederates would adopt—the President was the army's commander-in-chief. Davis was not a devious man, but neither was he overly modest. He told his wife during the Civil War, "If I could take one wing [of the army] and Lee the other, I think we could wrest a victory from those people."[2]

Contemporaries also had faith in Davis' military ability. When the Mississippi legislature appropriated $150,000 to purchase arms in 1859, Governor John J. Pettis asked Davis' advice on how to spend the money. In 1861 an enthusiastic newspaperman compared "Gen. Davis" favorably with General George Washington, and Louis T. Wigfall, who later would become one of the President's strongest critics, said, "Davis has the wisdom and sagacity of the statesman...the courage and discretion of the soldier....I know of no man so competent to inaugurate a Government at such a time." Just after Davis became President, William L. Yancey declared, "The man and the hour have met." He praised Davis as a "soldier, distinguished upon the field of battle, wise in council, terrible in the charge." A few months later a clerk in the Confederate War Department noted the almost universal belief that Davis "possessed military genius of a high order."[3]

The new Confederate President appeared to be just what the South needed. If war came, the organizers of the Confederacy reasoned, it would be well to have a politician heading the government who had more military experience than any other presidential prospect. They believed that Davis had the knowledge and experience to direct military operations, that he understood strategy and tactics, and that knowing who was who among American professional soldiers he would appoint the ablest men to high rank.[4]

The widespread belief among Southerners at the war's outset that Davis was the right man to lead them soon changed. "When Jeff goes to the encampments [of soldiers]," Mrs. Davis noted in 1861, "they go on like wild Indians, scream, catch hold of him, call out 'I am from Tennessee, I'm from Kentucky, I'm from Mississippi, God bless your soul.' The other day a volunteer stepped up to the carriage and said 'God bless you, Madam, and keep you well,' with a deep bow. They seize little Jeff and kiss him. It seems as if Jeff's stock has...risen." Yet early in 1862 Howell Cobb told his wife that he "might almost use the term *odious*" in describing the attitude of Confederate congressmen toward Davis. Only patriotism prevented them from rebelling against the President, wrote Cobb. "I—(who have never received a kindness at his hands)—have to interpose between him and his former pets to save him from bitter attacks on the floor of Congress." "Davis is perverse and obstinate," insisted Cobb, "and unless we can beat some liberal and just notions into his head, we shall have much trouble in the future...." A few months later an editor considered Davis "cold, haughty, peevish, narrow-minded, pigheaded, malignant" — "the cause of our undoing. While he lives, there is no hope for us." And in November 1862 a major in the commissary department said that he "used to think Jefferson Davis a *mule*, but a good *mule*. He has come to think him a jackass."[5]

Such criticism of Davis would hardly have surprised Winfield Scott. The old general, with whom Davis had feuded when he was Secretary of War, had said in 1861,

> "I am amazed that any man of judgment should hope for the success of any cause in which Jefferson Davis is a leader. There is a

contamination in his touch....He is not a cheap Judas. I do not think he would have sold the Saviour for thirty shillings; but for the successorship of Pontius Pilate he would have betrayed Christ and the apostles and the whole Christian Church!"[6]

If Scott's words seem unduly biased and exaggerated, it is worth nothing that Davis also received criticism from some close associates. The Confederacy's chief of ordnance, Brigadier General Josiah Gorgas, confided to his diary, "The President seems to respect the opinions of no one; and has, I fear, little appreciation of services rendered, unless the party enjoys his good opinion. He seems to be an indifferent judge of men, and is guided more by prejudice than by sound, discriminating judgment." Senator Clement C. Clay, a strong Davis supporter, admitted that the President "will not ask or receive counsel and indeed seems predisposed to go exactly the way his friends advise him not to go."[7]

On the other hand, a number of prominent men continued to praise the President. In August 1864 the editor of *De Bow's Review* said that Davis was as "brave as Ajax and as wise as Ulysses," and in 1865 Congressman Warren Akin wrote

I had a long conversation with the President yesterday. He has been greatly wronged....The President is not the stern, puffed up man he is represented to be. He was as polite, attentive and communicative to me as I could wish. He listened patiently to all I said and when he differed with me he would give his reasons for it. He was very cordial....And many gentlemen tell me the same thing as to his manner with them. His enemies have done him great injustice. He is a patriot and a good man, I think."[8]

Different people simply saw different qualities in Davis. To those who admired him he appeared able, modest, polite, loyal, agreeable, and self-sacrificing—an accomplished and a dedicated patriot. To his enemies he seemed ruthless, cold, stubborn, petty, and prejudiced—an incompetent executive with poor judgement.[9]

On one point friends and enemies of the President agreed: his health was poor. This sick man—who suffered constantly from insomnia, dyspepsia, and neuralgia—was often incapacitated by such diseases as malaria. "Jeff has been for nearly eight weeks confined to the house," admitted Mrs. Davis in 1858. The next year Davis wrote his friend Franklin Pierce, "I...have been seriously ill, though now free of disease, my strength has not been restored and there is therefore constant apprehension of a relapse." Just before the war a reporter described Davis as having "the face of a corpse, the form of a skeleton." "You are surprised to see him walking," wrote Murat Halstead in 1860. "Look at the haggard, sunken, weary eye—the thin white wrinkled lips clasped close upon the teeth in anguish. That is the mouth of a brave but impatient sufferer. See the ghastly white, hollow, bitterly puckered cheek, the high, sharp cheek bone, the pale brow full of fine wrinkles, the grizzly hair, prematurely gray; and see the thin, bloodless, bony, nervous hands!" Almost everyone who saw Davis during the Civil War commented upon his sickly appearance. He seemed, to the English reporter William H. Russell, to have "a very haggard, care-worn, and pain drawn look." In 1861 a future congressman wrote, "The president looks thin and feeble." That same year a war clerk observed: "The President is sick....I did not know until today that he is blind of an eye." Two years later an English officer remarked that Davis looked "older than I expected. He is only fifty-six, but his face is emaciated and much wrinkled. He is nearly six feet high, but is extremely thin and stoops....I was...told he had lost the sight of his left eye from a recent illness."[10]

Not only was the President sickly; so were many of his military advisers. Their gatherings sometimes resembled a hospital ward more than an assembly of war directors. An observer described Davis' first Secretary of War, Leroy Pope Walker, as a "man...whose health is feeble." A war clerk noted in May 1861, "Mr. Walker...is fast working himself down. He has not yet learned how to avoid unnecessary labor....He stands somewhat on ceremony with his brother officials, and accords and exacts the etiquette natural to a sensitive gentleman who has never been broken on the wheel of office. I predict for him a short career." By June Walker's health had failed; he remained Secretary of War until September 1861, but most of the time he was too ill to come to his office. George W. Randolph, Secretary of War for eight months in 1862, had pulmonary tuberculosis, and James A. Seddon, who had the longest tenure of any Secretary of War, was often incapacitated by neuralgia and other illnesses. Albert T. Bledsoe, the Assistant Secretary of War, advised Davis that Seddon was too feeble to head the War Department. "The labor of the office would kill him in one month," insisted Bledsoe. "Mr. Seddon has no physique to sustain him," observed war clerk John B. Jones, who also stated that Seddon lacked both "energy and knowledge of war." "He is...frail in health," noted Jones. "He will not remain long in office if he attempts to perform all the duties." Six months later Jones remarked, "Secretary Seddon is gaunt and emaciated....He looks like a dead man galvanized into muscular animation. His eyes are sunken, and his features have the hue of a man who has been in his grave a full month." After two more months of hard work Seddon looked to Jones like a "corpse which had been buried two months. The circles round his eyes are absolutely black." Another contemporary remembered Seddon as "an old man broken with the storms of state."[11]

Some of the soldiers Davis named to the War Department looked and acted more dead than alive. Three of the most prominent were Colonel Lucius B.

Northrop, the Confederacy's often criticized commissary general; Adjutant and Inspector General Samuel Cooper; and General Braxton Bragg. Colonel Northrop, whom Mrs. Mary Chesnut called an "eccentric creature" because he wore folded newspapers across his chest instead of underwear, had been on permanent sick leave from the United States Army for twenty-two years before Davis appointed him commissary general. "The reason for his appointment to...the most responsible bureau of the War Department was a mystery," admitted a contemporary. General Cooper, often described as too old and too feeble to take the field, had not been in the field for nearly thirty years. During the war he was often ill and out of his office. "Genl. Cooper still sick & can't be seen," wrote an officer in 1862. General Bragg, whom Davis brought to Richmond in 1864 to help him conduct military operations, was at the time the most discredited general in the Confederacy and one of the sickliest. Bragg had enough illnesses to keep a squad of doctors busy—dyspepsia, rheumatism, chronic boils, a liver ailment, extreme nervousness, and severe migraine headaches. Some of his illness—and perhaps his often erratic and irascible behavior—may have been caused by the medicine he took. Before the war Bragg admitted that he was suffering from his "old Florida complaint of the *liver*....Every summer I have these attacks," he explained to a friend, "and I can now only keep about by almost living on Mercury (Blue Mass & Calomel). No constitution can stand it."[12]

A remarkable number of the South's highest ranking field officers had physical handicaps or health problems. Bragg was sick during much of the time he commanded Confederate forces in the West. General John Bell Hood, who lost a leg at Chickamauga and the use of arm at Gettysburg, had to be strapped into his saddle when he commanded the Army of Tennessee. In 1862 General P. G. T. Beauregard had to retire from army command because of illness. General Joseph E. Johnston, who had been wounded seven times in action against Indians and Mexicans before the Civil War, was again hit twice at Fair Oaks—first by a bullet in the shoulder and a few moments later by a shell fragment that unhorsed him. For nearly six months during the critical summer and fall of 1862 he was incapacitated, and even after he returned to duty he often was, in his own words, "too feeble to command an army." In April 1863, when President Davis ordered him to take command of the South's second most important army, Johnston was "seriously sick." He explained, "I...am not now able to serve in the field." Later, when he was ordered to assume command of forces in Mississippi, Johnston replied, "I shall go immediately, although unfit for field-service."[13]

There is a tendency to think of Robert E .Lee as a superman who was never ill, but he was bedridden for several days in the spring of 1863 with "inflammation of the heart-sac" and a serious throat infection. This condition plus occasional attacks of rheumatism "enfeebled" and forced him "to take more rest."

In August 1863, after the Gettysburg Campaign, Lee asked Davis to relieve him from command of the Army of Northern Virginia:

> I do this with the most earnestness because no one is more aware than myself of my inability for the duties of my position. I cannot even accomplish what I myself desire. How can I fulfill the expectations of others? In addition I sensibly feel the growing failure of my bodily strength. I have not yet recovered from the attack I experienced the past spring. I am becoming more and more incapable of exertion, and am thus prevented from making the personal examinations and giving the personal supervision to the operations in the field which I feel to be necessary. I am so dull that in making use of the eyes of others I am frequently misled. Everything, therefore, points to the advantages to be derived from a new commander, and I the more anxiously urge the matter upon Your Excellency from my belief that a younger and abler man than myself can readily be attained.

Though Davis refused to replace Lee, the general's health continued to decline. In October 1863 an attack of "sciatica," "rheumatism," or "lumbago" made it impossible for Lee to ride for about a week, and during the critical campaign against Grant in May and June 1864 Lee was debilitated for ten days by sickness.[14]

Even Lee's trusted lieutenant, Thomas J. (Stonewall) Jackson, had or imagined he had a wide range of ailments—dyspepsia, liver disturbances, nervousness, eye strain, rheumatism, chilblains, cold feet, malaria, bilious attacks, neuralgia, fevers, chronic inflammation of the throat, nose, and ears, as well as "a slight distortion of the spine." By sitting "straight up,...without touching the back of the chair," Jackson believed that he "could keep his internal organs from being constricted." He also treated himself with buttermilk, freshly cooked cornbread, quantities of fruit—especially lemons—and cold water. "I have been quite unwell," he announced before the war, "and had it not have been for my judicious application of water, I can not say what would have been the consequences." Active campaigning seemed to improve his health.[15]

The poor health of many of Davis' subordinates does not necessarily suggest that the Confederate President had a psychological affinity for sick people, though one might speculate that this was the case. Sickness is after all an aspect of weakness, and there is abundant evidence that Davis liked to surround himself with weak subordinates. "He was not only President and secretary of five departments—which naturally caused some errors," stated a contemporary, "but that spice of the dictator in him made him quite willing to shoulder the responsibilities of all the positions...." He had six different Secretaries of War in four years.[16]

If empathy bound Davis to some of his infirm subordinates, there is no evidence that these men received or retained their high offices solely because the President considered them fellow suffers; indeed, he insisted that his military appointments were based on merit alone. "Due care was taken to prevent the appointment of incompetent or unworthy persons to be officers of the army," Davis stated after the war. And several historians have supported his claim. The President "gave just as few high commissions to politicians as possible," insisted one of his biographers. To a critic, Davis wrote: "It would be easy to justify the appointments which have been made of Brig. Genls. by stating the reasons in each case, but suffice it to say that I have endeavored to avoid bad selections by relying on military rather than political recommendations."[17]

Yet political considerations influenced Davis more than he admitted. Nearly thirty percent of the generals he named in 1861 were political appointees. For example, Humphrey Marshall of Kentucky, despite his military training and experience, was clearly a political general. Less than a year after his graduation from the United States Military Academy, Marshall had resigned from the army. Later he served as a volunteer in the Mexican War where, according to one report, his "regiment did some fine running and no fighting." Elected to Congress seven times as a Whig, Marshall had tried to keep Kentucky neutral in 1861. After he had failed, Davis appointed him a Confederate brigadier general. Marshall spent much of his time writing long letters of complaint to Davis. These finally goaded the President into a reply that revealed why he had appointed Marshall. "When you were offered a position of rank and responsibility in our army," Davis stated, "it was my hope that you would prove beneficial to our cause.... [I believed] in your assured conviction of your ability to recruit an army of Kentuckians, who would rally to your standard." But Marshall proved to be neither an able recruiter nor an able general. In 1863 he resigned his army commission and entered the Confederate Congress.[18] Other political generals included: John C. Breckinridge of Kentucky, who had been a member of Congress, vice-president of the United States, and a candidate for President in 1860; Robert Toombs of Georgia, who resigned as Confederate Secretary of State to enter the army; Louis T. Wigfall of Texas, who had been expelled from the United States Senate; James Chesnut, Jr., a former senator from South Carolina and a member of the Provisional Confederate Congress, who became a member of Davis' military staff; Milledge L. Bonham, a South Carolina congressman; Lawrence O. Branch, a member of the politically prominent North Carolina family; Howell Cobb of Georgia, former speaker of the United States House of Representatives; John B. Floyd, at one time Governor of Virginia and recently President Buchanan's Secretary of War; Leroy Pope Walker of Alabama, who was for a short time Davis' Secretary of War; and two former Virginia Governors, William "Extra Billy" Smith and Henry A. Wise.[19]

Pressure to appoint political generals was strong. Davis had the thankless task of organizing an effective army while at the same time including in it officers of diverse political opinion from all states and regions of the South. In a letter of July 13, 1861, Governor Isham G. Harris of Tennessee thanked the President for appointing three Tennesseans to the rank of brigadier general, "but," the governor noted, "they are all Democrats." He wanted Davis to name some "other generals" from Tennessee, including a few Whigs. "It is a political necessity," Harris explained, "that the Whig element be fully recognized." Davis agreed; in fact, he had appointed two additional generals from Tennessee just a few days before receiving Harris' letter. One of these men was Felix Zollicoffer, an influential Whig, who had supported John Bell for the presidency in 1860 and had been a member of the aborted Washington Peace Conference. In 1862 two Alabama politicians protested that the President had appointed only five generals from their state. They recommended to him four politicians who "seem to us entitled to respectful consideration in competition with other civilians, from other states, which have already their full proportion, or more, of General officers."[20]

A few of Davis' political generals were assets, but many of them proved to be worthless soldiers and sources of embarrassment to the President. John B. Floyd, for example, was removed from command after he shirked his responsibility at Fort Donelson. Felix Zollicoffer rashly and in violation of orders attacked a Federal force at Mill Springs, Kentucky, in January 1862, where he was killed and his forces were defeated. After much criticism of his conduct at the battle of Elkhorn Tavern, Brigadier General Albert Pike, a prominent Arkansas Whig, resigned from the army. Brigadier General William H. Carroll, a Tennessean whose father had been governor of the state six times, was removed from command "for drunkenness, incompetency, and neglect of duty." Brigadier General Roger A. Pryor, a former Virginia congressman, was left without military duties in 1863. Robert Toombs and Louis T. Wigfall soon resigned from the army and spent much of the war criticizing Davis. In the summer of 1863 Wigfall announced, "Davis's mind is becoming unsettled. No sane man would act as he is acting. I fear that his bad health and bad temper are undermining his reason, and that the foundation is already sapped." Henry A. Wise had been appointed brigadier general because he was popular in the western counties of Virginia. After he had helped raise a number of regiments, Davis ignored him. "The war has produced no more emphatic a failure than Wise," remarked a member of the administration. Outraged by this ignominy, Wise denounced the President and his family as "little, low, vulgar people."[21]

Davis liked to tell certain people that none of his appointees were political generals, but he also liked to say to others—especially to demanding politicians—that he had appointed a fair number of representatives from each state and party. Thus two conflicting impressions grew—that the President appointed either too many or almost no politicians to high military positions. A general complained that professional soldiers "have seen themselves overlooked by their government, while their juniors in years of service and I think their inferiors...were put over them in rank...." Civilians, on the other hand, often objected to what one man called the President's "irresponsible *West Pointism.*" Davis tried to defend himself against both charges. "I know that among some of our people," he wrote in 1863, "an impression prevailed that I was unduly partial to those officers who had received an education at the Military Academy and was willing to concede something to that impression though I did not recognize its justice."[22]

Davis knew that, whatever his personal desires, all of his generals could not be West Point graduates. First, there simply were not that many West Pointers available. A common misconception is that in 1861 most of America's experienced soldiers were Southerners who resigned their commissions in the United States Army to join the Confederacy. Actually, Northerners comprised nearly sixty percent of the regular army officers at the outbreak of the Civil War. Of the army's 1,080 officers, only 286 entered the Confederate service; 184 of these were graduates of the United States Military Academy. Over 600 West Point graduates remained in the Federal army. Of the approximately 900 West Point graduates then in civil life, fewer than a fourth joined the Confederate army. Second, too many West Point graduates were young and inexperienced soldiers. Of the 286 men who resigned from the United States Army to enter Confederate service only twenty-four were majors or above in the old army; most of the others were junior officers, some quite recent graduates of West Point. Though the President welcomed those young men, he appointed few of them to high rank early in the war.[23]

The eighty-eight men that Davis appointed generals in 1861 fell into three categories: first, forty regular United States Army officers who resigned their commission in 1861 to join the Confederacy (all but two of them—David E. Twiggs and William W. Loring—were West Point graduates)[24]; second, twenty-three West Pointers who had resigned from the regular army some years prior to 1861; and third, twenty-five men who had neither attended the United States Military Academy nor served in the regular army. All of these men had in common at least one thing—they were civil or military leaders. The forty regulars who became Confederate generals in 1861 had been captains or above in the United States Army at the war's outset.[25]

Military training alone did not insure high rank. Fewer than half of the West Point graduates who offered their services to the Confederacy ever became generals. Between 1861 and 1865 Jefferson Davis appointed 425 men to the rank of brigadier general or higher. Almost two-thirds of these men had had some military experience prior to the Civil War, but much of that experience had consisted of militia service, attendance at military schools, or expeditions against Indians. No fewer than 153 Confederate generals were lawyers or politicians when the Civil War began; fifty-five were businessmen, and forty-two were farmers or planters. Only thirty-four percent of the Confederate generals were graduates of the United States Military Academy, and only twenty-nine percent were professional soldiers when the war began.[26]

Some men, it was charged, received or were denied high rank simply because the President liked or disliked them. William L. Yancey claimed that Davis' appointments "are often conferred as rewards to friends and are refused as punishments inflicted upon enemies." Senator James L. Orr said that the "President's attachment for Genl. Bragg could be likened to nothing else than the blind and gloating love of a mother for a deformed and misshapen offspring."[27]

Despite Davis' disclaimer to a critic—"nor will I consent to be influenced in the exercise of the appointing power which I hold as a trust for the public good, by personal favor or personal resentment"—there is evidence to support the charge that the President did reward his friends. In 1861 he commissioned at least five generals who had little military experience, but were his close friends. Three of these men had been with him at West Point: Thomas F. Drayton, Hugh W. Mercer, and Leonidas Polk. All had left the United States Army while they were still lieutenants. Drayton became a planter and a railroad builder in South Carolina; Mercer became cashier of a bank in Savannah; and Polk became the Episcopal Missionary Bishop of the Southwest. At the time Davis appointed these men Confederate generals, they had been out of military service for twenty-five or more years. Polk, who had spent a grand total of five months as an officer after his graduation from West Point in 1827, was made a major general by Davis on June 25, 1861.[28]

Richard Griffith, while a lieutenant in the First Mississippi Rifles during the Mexican War, had "formed a warm and lasting friendship with his commanding officer, Jefferson Davis." This brief military association must have been enough to convince Davis that Griffith had leadership ability. He was appointed a brigadier general in the Confederate service before he had been in a Civil War battle.[29]

Richard Taylor, son of General Zachary Taylor, was the brother of Davis' first wife. Taylor had no military experience prior to the Civil War except that gained from a childhood spent at various army posts, but Davis quickly promoted him to brigadier general. "This promotion," Taylor recalled, "seriously embarrassed me. Of the four colonels whose regiments constituted the brigade,

I was the junior in commission, and the three others had been present and 'won their spurs' at the recent battle [of First Manassas], so far the only important one of the war. Besides, my known friendship for President Davis...would justify the opinion that my promotion was due to favouritism."[30]

At times Davis also used his appointing power to punish his enemies. He apparently struck the name of Arthur M. Manigault off the list of colonels recommended for promotion to brigadier because a personal letter of Manigault's that was critical of Davis had been published. "I admit having written the letter and must abide the consequences," explained Manigault. "It is a matter of...great surprise to me..., its publication in any newspaper, ...as to the best of my recollection, I placed it in the post office at Knoxville myself."[31]

Contrary to the claims of Davis and certain historians, it is clear that qualities other than military ability and experience influenced the appointment of some generals, but what about the Confederacy's highest ranking officers? Did political considerations, friendship with the President, or other factors effect their selection and promotion?

Only six men—Samuel Cooper, Albert Sidney Johnston, Robert E. Lee, Joseph E. Johnston, Pierre Gustave Toutant Beauregard, and Braxton Bragg— ever became full generals in the regular Confederate army.[32] The Confederacy's senior general both in age and in rank was Samuel Cooper. When the President appointed him the highest ranking general in the Confederacy, Cooper was sixty-four years old. No one could deny that he had years of military experience. At the time he joined the Confederacy, he could boast of forty-eight years of continuous service in the United States Army; since 1838 Cooper had been in Washington, D.C., at a desk job. He became the adjutant and inspector general of the Confederacy, the position he had held in the old army since 1852.[33]

In time of peace, Cooper might have been a satisfactory figurehead for the adjutant general's office. But he was incapable of handling the complex and demanding task of organizing and administering the Confederacy's armies. The chief of the Confederate bureau of war, Robert G. H. Kean, claimed that Cooper was totally incompetent: "It is so manifest that nothing but the irrepressible *West Pointism* of the President, and that other peculiarity of preferring accommodating, civil-spoken persons of small capacity about him, can account for his retention." Kean charged that Cooper had no idea of the condition of any army. "There has never been a time when the A[djutant and] I[nspector] General could give even a tolerably close *guess* of the whole force on the rolls of the army, still less of the *effective* force. He is most of the time *out* of his office. There is no one paper a week which bears evidence of his personal examination. He never decides anything, rarely ever *reports* upon a question, and when he does the report is very thin."[34]

Kean believed that Davis appointed and retained Cooper because the President favored professional soldiers and graduates of the United States Military Academy and liked "civil-spoken persons of small capacity about him." When Davis was President Pierce's Secretary of War, he had worked closely and gotten along well with Cooper. "Having known him most favorably and intimately as Adjutant-General of the United States Army," recalled Davis, "the value of his services in the organization of a new army was considered so great that I invited him to take the position of Adjutant-General of the Confederate Army, which he accepted without a question either as to relative rank or anything else."[35] Like most people, Davis generally favored individuals who agreed with him. If they did not, they usually left his administration.

Perhaps another reason why Davis appointed Cooper adjutant and inspector general was that there was simply nothing else to do with the man. Contemporaries agreed that he was unsuited for field service. What could the President do other than give Cooper the same job that he had held for the past nine years? To have done otherwise would have insulted Cooper—a native of New Jersey who had sacrificed a secure position to join the Confederacy—and created political problems for the Davis administration, for Cooper was married to the sister of Senator James M. Mason of Virginia.[36]

If the appointment of Cooper appears to have been motivated by personal and political considerations, that of the second highest ranking Confederate general—Albert Sidney Johnston—was based upon personal friendship and admiration. Davis and Sidney Johnston had been friends for years. They may have met while students at Transylvania University; they attended West Point together, where Johnston treated Davis like a younger brother; they had served together on the Illinois frontier as young lieutenants in the Black Hawk War; and they had been under fire together at Monterey in the Mexican War.[37]

Johnston was fifty-eight years old when the Civil War began; twenty-seven of those years had been spent in active military service or training. After four years at West Point (1822-26), he served eight years as a lieutenant in the Sixth Infantry. He resigned from the army in 1834, but two years later he enlisted as a private in the Army of the Texas Republic. Johnston quickly rose to the rank of senior brigadier general. He next served two years (1838-40) as Texas' Secretary of War. After Texas became a part of the United States and the Mexican War began, Johnston assumed command of the First Texas Volunteer Infantry with the rank of colonel. A month later, when the unit's enlistment ended, most of the men went home and Johnston was left without a command. But he remained in Mexico and Major General Zachary Taylor appointed him inspector general on the staff of General William O. Butler, commander of a division of volunteers. Johnston helped steady the volunteers when Butler was wounded at Monterey. After Taylor became President, he appointed Johnston a major in the army's paymaster department. Relief from this position, which Johnston disliked, came six years later when he was promoted to the rank of full colonel and given command of the Second United States Cavalry. Political influence, including the support of Jefferson Davis, who was then Secretary of War, helped Johnston get his new command. His next opportunity came in 1857 when he was selected to lead an army to Utah to prevent a Mormon uprising. His successful occupation of Utah won him promotion to brevet brigadier general. When the Civil War began, Johnston was in California commanding the Department of the Pacific. He immediately resigned his commission and started overland with a small party. He arrived in Richmond in September 1861 and called at the Confederate White House only to be told that the President was too ill to see visitors. Davis, who from his sickbed heard sounds on the floor below, supposedly called out, "That is Sidney Johnston's step. Bring him up." Davis got out of bed and "for several days at various intervals," he recalled, "we conversed with the freedom and confidence belonging to the close friendship which had existed between us for many years. Consequent upon a remark made by me, he [Johnston] asked to what duty I would assign him, and, when answered, to serve in the West, he expressed his pleasure at service in that section, but inquired how he was to raise his command, and for the first time learned that he had been nominated and confirmed as a [full] general in the Army of the Confederacy."[38]

Robert E. Lee, a fifty-five-year-old professional soldier and the third highest ranking Confederate general, was also Jefferson Davis' friend. The President and Lee had been students together at West Point. While Secretary of War, Davis had aided Lee's military career; Lee, in turn, had defended Secretary Davis against a newspaper critic. Davis later stated that in 1861 he had "unqualified confidence" in Lee, "both as a man and a patriot." Tactful, courteous, and modest, Lee proved repeatedly throughout the war that he knew how to get along with President Davis. Lee never demanded; he got what he wanted by subtle persuasion. He always referred to Davis as "Your Excellency." The President even believed that Lee cared nothing about rank: "He had been appointed a full general," recalled Davis, "but so wholly had his heart and his mind been consecrated to the public service, that he had not remembered, if he ever knew, of his advancement."[39]

The appointment of Lee was inextricably linked with that of Joseph E. Johnston, the fourth highest ranking Confederate general. Joe Johnston and Robert E. Lee were the same age; they were graduated from West Point in the same class (1829); they were both professional soldiers; they had served together in the Mexican War, where both had received the brevet rank of colonel for gallant conduct under fire. After the Mexican War, on the same date (March 3, 1855), both were promoted to lieutenant colonel and assigned to cavalry regiments—Lee to the Second Cavalry; Johnston to the First Cavalry. On June

28, 1860, Johnston left the cavalry to become the army's quartermaster general with the rank of brigadier general. Lee remained in the cavalry and was not promoted to the rank of full colonel until March 16, 1861.[40]

Thus, when the two men left the United States Army to join the Confederacy, Johnston, a brigadier general, outranked Lee, a colonel. Consequently, when the list of Confederate full generals appeared, Johnston was shocked and angered to discover that his old friend and rival now outranked him. A proud man, Johnston believed that he had been treated unfairly by the President. Johnston recalled that he had not been Davis' choice for quartermaster general in 1860; Davis, then chairman of the Senate's Military Affairs Committee, had favored Sidney Johnston for the position. Now, it must have appeared to Joe Johnston, that Davis was taking his revenge. Honor demanded a protest. In an angry letter to the President, Johnston argued that Confederate law guaranteed "that the relative rank of officers of each grade shall be determined by their former commissions in the U.S. Army." Since he was the highest ranking officer of the old army to join the Confederacy, it was unfair and illegal to appoint others above him. "I now and here declare my claim," he wrote, "that notwithstanding these nominations by the President and their confirmation by Congress, I...rightfully hold the rank of first general in the Armies of the Southern Confederacy." Davis considered the letter insubordinate; his reply was cold and brief: "I have just received and read your letter....Its language is, as you say, unusual; its arguments and statements utterly one-sided, and its insinuations as unfounded as they are unbecoming." From that point on the men never trusted each other. In October 1863 a close observer noted, "the President detests Joe Johnston...and General Joe returns the compliment with compound interest. His hatred of Jeff Davis amounts to a religion. With him it colors all things."[41]

The President came to dislike and to mistrust the fifth highest ranking full general—Pierre Gustave Toutant Beauregard—as much or more than Joe Johnston. Beauregard was one of the bright young professional soldiers who joined the Confederacy. Forty-three years old when the war started, he had been graduated second in his class at West Point in 1838 and assigned to the elite engineering corps. During the Mexican War, while serving on General Winfield Scott's staff, he had received brevet promotions to captain and to major for gallant and meritorious conduct in battle. Beauregard became the Confederacy's first hero after Fort Sumter fell to his forces; he won additional fame at First Manassas. But his high opinion of his own military ability and his jealousy of those generals above him in rank, especially Joe Johnston, caused problems. After the war Beauregard explained why he considered himself better qualified in 1861 for high command than Johnston:

> Having been attached...to the staff of...General Scott, in the Mexican
> War, General Beauregard had taken a leading part in the recon-

naissances and conferences that had led and determined the marches and battles of that campaign; and as to what was really essential in those respects to the command of an army he had a practical military experience beyond any opportunities of General Johnston.

Beauregard, a vain man, could be haughty when he considered his prerogatives impinged. Soon after First Manassas he became engaged in a series of disputes with the administration over supplies, military law, and army command. For a time the President tried to be conciliatory, but gradually he grew impatient. In January 1862, after another argument between Beauregard and Davis, an observer in the War Department noted, "Beauregard has been ordered to the West. I knew the doom was upon him."[42]

Following the death of Sidney Johnston at Shiloh, Beauregard became commander of the western forces, but in June 1862 he left his headquarters in northern Mississippi without the President's permission. Beauregard merely informed the government that his health was bad and that he was going to Alabama to recover. "I desire to be back...to retake the offensive as soon as our forces shall have been sufficiently reorganized," he explained. "I must have a short rest." Davis jumped at this opportunity to appoint Braxton Bragg to the permanent command of the western department. Beauregard would never again command a major army. The President no longer trusted him. Davis later told another general, "Beauregard was tried as Commander of the army of the West and left it without leave, when the troops were demoralized and the country he was sent to protect was threatened with conquest."[43]

The sixth highest ranking general was Braxton Bragg, the man who replaced Beauregard as commander of the western department. Forty-four years old when the war began, Bragg too was a professional soldier but he had left the old army in 1856 to become a Louisiana sugar cane planter. He had served for nineteen years in the Third Artillery after being graduated fifth in his class at West Point in 1837. He had received three brevet promotions during the Mexican War for gallant conduct. At Buena Vista, he became a national hero when his battery stopped the final Mexican charge "with a little more grape."[44]

Bragg, it is often charged, received promotion to full general only because he and President Davis had long been friends. Such was not the case. One reason why Bragg had resigned from the United States Army was because he disliked Davis, who was then Secretary of War. In 1855 Bragg informed his friend William T. Sherman, "To judge from high sounding words in reports and bills before Congress, Mr. Jeff. Davis intends to have an Army after his own heart (not a very good one by the way). We are all to be placed at his mercy, and to be rearranged to suit his pleasure and convenience." Bragg considered Davis "a good deal of the pettifogger and special pleader." Years later Sherman recalled that

"Bragg hated Davis bitterly" for sending him to the frontier, "as Bragg expressed it 'to chase Indians with six-pounders [cannons].' "[45]

Davis certainly never knew that for years Bragg had disliked and distrusted
him. When the Civil War began, Bragg feared that he would be ignored by the
Confederate President. Nor was Bragg reassured when Davis gave him command of forces near Pensacola, Florida, in 1861. Only after receiving extensive
reports from people he trusted did Bragg become convinced that the President
was not his enemy. In the spring of 1862 Congressman James L. Pugh, formerly
a soldier at Pensacola, wrote that he "was delighted to find" in the Confederate
capital

> the highest confidence in my old Genl. Bragg. It gives me pleasure
> to assure you that no General in the army has more of public con-
> fidence and admiration. Your praise is on the lips of every
> man....President Davis said that 'you had shown a most self sacrific-
> ing devotion to that cause, and was about the only General who had
> accomplished all you undertook.

And Bragg's brother, who was a member of Davis' cabinet, noted that the president "spoke [favorably] of Gen'l Bragg—said he had put down drinking and that
his had been the only well disciplined and managed army in the field. That
he set a proper example to his men. In speaking of other Generals, their qualities
&c, he [Davis] ranked him [Bragg] with Sidney Johns[t]on." Bragg owed his promotion to full general not to a close friendship with the President, but to the
reputation Bragg had gained as an organizer and administrator. When Bragg
moved north to reinforce Sidney Johnston before Shiloh, Davis wrote his old
friend, "General Bragg brings you disciplined troops, and you will find in him
the highest administrative capacity."[46]

It is easy enough, using hindsight, to blame Davis for appointing at the war's
outset too many generals who would later prove to be less than outstanding
soldiers, but such a judgement is unfair—a misuse of history. Before censuring
Davis for failing to pick the right men to lead the Confederate armies, historians
should ask themselves what, given the circumstances, Davis could have done
differently. He had to pick some political generals; he understandably picked
some of his friends. What obvious leaders did he overlook? The six men he
promoted to full general were all experienced and distinguished soldiers. They
were reputed to be the elite of the old army. Another man, less well acquainted
with military affairs, might have selected different generals. But Davis simply
could not. His own military experience and knowledge forced him to appoint
the men he did to high rank. He had fought beside some of them, and—as
Secretary of War and as chairman of the Senate's Military Affairs Committee—he
had helped to advance their careers. They were already, before the Civil War, his

men. If, as has been charged, his judgement of military ability left something to be desired; if he relied too heavily upon his youthful impressions of men; if he regarded criticism of his appointees as criticism of himself and stubbornly defended proved incompetents, it was because Davis was imprisoned by his own character and background. And so was the Confederacy.

If the fathers of the Confederacy failed, it was in their selection of Jefferson Davis to lead the "Lost Cause." Once he became President the pattern of leadership was established. The major appointments to high positions, especially to high military positions, were his. He picked, assigned, and replaced. When the Provisional Congress chose the Confederacy's President, it indirectly chose its generals.

Endnotes

1. Thomas C. DeLeon, *Four Years in Rebel Capitals: An Inside View of Life in the Southern Confederacy from Birth to Death* (New York, 1962), 54; Hudson Strode, *Jefferson Davis: American Patriot, 1809-1861* (New York, 1955); Francis B. Heitman, *Historical Register and Dictionary of the United States Army* (2 vols., Washington, 1903), I, 358; Jefferson Davis to C. J. Wright, February 12, 1876 (copy), Jefferson Davis Papers, Library of Congress.

2. E. Merton Coulter, *The Confederate States of America. 1861-1865* (Baton Rouge, 1950), 24; Varina H. Davis, *Jefferson Davis...A Memoir* (2 vols., New York, 1890), II, 392.

3. John J. Pettis to Jefferson Davis, December 20, 1859, John J. Pettis Papers, Chicago Historical Society; Bell I. Wiley, *The Road to Appomattox* (Memphis, 1956), 6-7; *Montgomery Daily Post,* February 18, 1861; John B. Jones, *A Rebel War Clerk's Diary,* ed. by Earl Schenck Miers (New York, 1958), 34.

4. Thomas R. R. Cobb, "Correspondence of Thomas Reade Rootes Cobb, 1860-1862," ed. by A. L. Hull, Southern History Association, *Publications,* XI (1907), 147-85; Mary B. Chesnut, *A Diary from Dixie,* ed. by Ben Ames Williams (Boston, 1949), 5; Wilfred B. Yearns, *The Confederate Congress* (Athens, Ga., 1960), 31.

5. Jefferson Davis, *Jefferson Davis: Private Letters, 1823-1889,* ed. by Hudson Strode (New York, 1966), 124; Horace Montgomery, *Howell Cobb's Confederate Career* (Tuscaloosa, Ala., 1959), 48-49; George W. Bagby's Notebook, March 1862, George William Bagby Papers, Virginia Historical Society, Richmond; Robert G. H. Kean, *Inside the Confederate Government: The Diary of Robert Garlick Hill Kean,* ed. by Edward Younger (New York, 1957), 34.

6. Charles W. Elliott, *Winfield Scott: The Soldier and the Man* (New York, 1937), 712.

7. Josiah Gorgas, *The Civil War Diary of General Josiah Gorgas,* ed. by Frank E. Vandiver (University, Ala., 1947), 58; Clement C. Clay to William L. Yancey [1863?], William L. Yancey Papers, Alabama State Archives, Montgomery.

8. *De Bow's Review,* XXXIV (July-August 1864), 102; Warren Akin, *Letters of Warren Akin, Confederate Congressman,* ed. by Bell I. Wiley (Athens, Ga., 1959), 75.

9. Wiley, *Road to Appomattox,* 1-42, gives an excellent analysis of Davis' personality.

10. Mrs. Jefferson Davis to Mrs. Franklin Pierce [c. April 4] 1858, Franklin Pierce Papers, Library of Congress; Jefferson Davis to Franklin Pierce, September 2, 1859, *ibid.*; Murat Halstead, *Three Against Lincoln: Murat Halstead reports the Caucuses of 1860,* ed. by William B. Hesseltine (Baton Rouge, 1960), 121; William H. Russell, *My Diary North and South* (2 vols., London, 1863), I, 250; Akin, *Letters,* 20; Jones, *Rebel War Clerk's Diary,* 41; Arthur J. L. Fremantle, *The Fremantle Diary,* ed. by Walter Lord (Boston, 1954), 167-68. See also Justus Scheibert, *Seven Months in the Rebel States During the North American War, 1863,* ed. by Wm. Stanley Hoole (Tuscaloosa, Ala., 1958), 128; U.S. War Dept., *The War of the Rebellion: A Compilation of the Official Records of the Union and Confederate Armies* (128 vols., Washington, 1880-1901), Series 1, V, 829 (hereafter cited as *OR,* and unless otherwise indicated all references are to Series 1).

11 Halstead, *Three Against Lincoln,* 23; Fremantle, *Diary,* 170, 174; Albert T. Bledsoe to Jefferson Davis, November 12, 1862, Jefferson Davis Paper, Duke University; Jones, *Rebel War Clerk's Diary,* 17, 121, 202, 242, 433-434, 447; William Brierly Memoir, 1864, William Brierly Papers, Chicago Historical Society.

12 Chesnut, *Diary from Dixie,* 285; DeLeon, *Four Years,* 136; Ezra J. Warner, *Generals in Gray: Lives of the Confederate Commanders* (Baton Rouge, 1959), 225; Heitman, *Historical Register,* I, 751, 326; William W. Mackall to his wife, [October, 1862], William W. Mackall Papers, Southern Historical Collection, University of North Carolina, Chapel Hill; Grady McWhiney, *Braxton Bragg and Confederate Defeat, vol. 1: Field Command* (New York, 1969), 179-180; Braxton Bragg to William T. Sherman, June 3, 1855, William T. Sherman Papers, Library of Congress.

13 Richard M. McMurry, *John Bell Hood and the War for Southern Independence* (Lexington, 1982), 75, 77-80, 83-84; John P. Dyer, *The Gallant Hood* (Indianapolis, 1950), 238; T. Harry Williams, *P. G. T. Beauregard, Napoleon in Gray* (Baton Rouge, 1955), 155-158; Robert M. Hughes, *General Johnston* (New York, 1893), 21, 25, 32, 144; Heitman, *Historical Register,* II, 26; Joseph E. Johnston, *Narrative of Military Operations,* ed. by Frank E. Vandiver (Bloomington, 1959), 164, 186, 173; *OR,* XXIII (pt. 2), 708, 745.

14 Robert E. Lee, *The Wartime Papers of R. E. Lee,* ed. by Clifford Dowdey (Boston, 1961), 589-590; Douglas Southall Freeman, *R. E. Lee: A Biography* (4 vols., New York, 1935), II, 502-504; IV, 522.

15 Frank E. Vandiver, *Mighty Stonewall* (New York, 1957), 7, 9, 17, 46, 48-55, *passim;* Lenoir Chambers, *Stonewall Jackson* (2 vols., New York, 1959), I, 63, 71, 153-157, *passim;* II, 75-76; Thomas J. Jackson to his sister, January 1, 1848, April 27, December 3, 1849, September 3, 1850 (photocopies), Thomas Jonathan Jackson Papers, Library of Congress.

16 DeLeon, *Four Years,* 123; *OR,* Series 4, III, 1184. The secretaries and their tenure: Leroy P. Walker, February 21-September 16, 1861; Judah P. Benjamin, September 17, 1861-March 18, 1862; George W. Randolph, March 18-November 17, 1862; Gustavus W. Smith (assigned temporarily), November 17-21, 1862; James A. Seddon, November 21, 1862-February 6, 1865; John C. Breckinridge, February 6-April 26, 1865.

17 Jefferson Davis, *The Rise and Fall of the Confederate Government* (2 vols., New York, 1958), I, 306, 307; Yearns, *The Confederate Congress,* 108; Haskell Monroe, "Early Confederate Political Patronage," *Alabama Review,* XX (1967), 45-61; Hudson Strode, *Jefferson Davis: Confederate President, 1861-1864* (New York, 1959), 138; Davis to W. M. Brooks, March 13, 1862, in Jefferson Davis, *Jefferson Davis, Constitutionalist: His Letters, Papers and Speeches,* ed. by Dunbar Rowland (10 vols., Jackson, Miss., 1923), V, 218.

18 Warner, *Generals in Gray,* 212-213; Heltman, *Historical Register,* I, 691; Braxton Bragg to John Bragg, June 28, 1852, John Bragg Papers, Southern Historical Collection, University of North Carolina, Chapel Hill; Jefferson Davis to Humphrey Marshall, October 6, 1862, in Davis, *Jefferson Davis, Constitutionalist,* V, 348.

19 Warner, *Generals in Gray,* 34, 306-307, 336-337, 48-49, 28-29, 31, 55, 89-90, 320-321, 284-285, 341-342.

[20] *OR,* Series 4, I, 474-475; Warner, *Generals in Gray,* 349-350; William L. Yancey and Clement C. Clay to Jefferson Davis, April 21, 1862, Yancey Papers.

[21] Warner, *Generals in Gray,* 89-90, 350, 240, 44-45, 248, 341-342; *OR,* X (pt. 2), 370-372; Alvy L. King, *Louis T. Wigfall, Southern Fire-eater* (Baton Rouge, 1970); William Y. Thompson, *Robert Toombs of Georgia* (Baton Rouge, 1966); Louis T. Wigfall to Clement C. Clay, August 13, 1863, Clement C. Clay Papers, Duke University; Kean, *Inside the Confederate Government,* 102; Allan Nevins, *The War for the Union* (4 vols., New York, 1959-1971), III, 397.

[22] Braxton Bragg to Samuel Cooper, July 28, 1861 (copy), Braxton Bragg Papers, William F. Palmer Collection, Western Reserve Historical Society, Cleveland; Kean, *Inside the Confederate Government,* 87; Davis, *Jefferson Davis, Constitutionalist,* VI, 44.

[23] Civil War Centennial Commission, *Facts About the Civil War* (Washington, 1960), 7; Ellsworth Eliot, Jr., *West Point in the Confederacy* (New York, 1941), xii-xxxii, *passim.*

[24] Twiggs, who was seventy-one years old and a veteran of both the War of 1812 and the Mexican War, had been in the regular army for nearly half a century. He died in 1862. Loring, after volunteer service against the Seminole Indians, had been commissioned directly into the regular army in 1846 as captain of mounted rifles. When he resigned to join the Confederacy, he was—at age forty-six—the youngest line colonel in the army.

[25] Warner, *Generals in Gray,* 312, 192, 49, 203-204; Heitman, *Historical Register,* I, 976, 642, 299, 625, 670, 826. Only four officers of field grade who left the old army in 1861 failed to become Confederate brigadier generals or higher in the first year of the war. These exceptions—William W. Mackall, Robert H. Chilton, Richard D. Lee, and Thomas G. Rhett—had been staff officers in 1861 and they continued as staff officers in the Confederate service. Apparently they were victims of Davis' opposition to high rank for staff. While Secretary of War in the 1850s, Davis had proposed the abolition of permanent staff assignments. See Davis, *Jefferson Davis, Constitutionalist,* II, 299-406.

[26] Warner, *Generals in Gray,* xix-xxiii.

[27] Yancey to Davis, May 6, 1863, Yancey Papers; Dr. J. H. Claiborne to his wife, March 29, 1864, Dr. J. H. Claiborne Papers, University of Virginia.

[28] Davis to Yancey, June 20, 1863, Yancey Papers; Warner, *Generals in Gray,* 75-76, 216-217, 242-243; Heitman, *Historical Register,* I, 383, 703, 796.

[29] Warner, *Generals in Gray,* 120.

[30] *Ibid.,* 299-300; Charles L. Dufour, *Nine Men in Gray* (New York, 1963), 3; Richard Taylor, *Destruction and Reconstruction* (London, 1879), 19.

[31] *OR,* XX (pt. 2), 449; Manigault to Braxton Bragg, November 30, 1862, Palmer Collection of Bragg Papers.

[32] Edmund Kirby Smith and John Bell Hood were full generals only in the Provisional Confederate Army, and Hood's appointment was temporary and never confirmed.

[33] Warner, *Generals in Gray,* xxiv-xxv, 62-63; Heitman, *Historical Register,* I, 326. Actually Cooper was only adjutant general of the United States Army.

34 Kean, *Inside the Confederate Government,* 87-88.

35 Davis, *Rise and Fall,* I, 308.

36 Warner, *Generals in Gray,* 62-63.

37 Charles P. Roland, *Albert Sidney Johnston: Soldier of Three Republics* (Austin, 1964), 12, 15, 45-46, 135, 137.

38 Heitman, *Historical Register,* I, 577-578; Roland, *Johnston,* 3-259; Davis, *Rise and Fall,* I, 309.

39 Freeman, *Lee,* I, 55, 327, 360, 369; Lee, *Wartime Papers,* 589-590, 700, *passim;* Davis, *Rise and Fall,* I, 340, 309. General Joseph Hooker reportedly said that Lee was a "a courtier" with an "insinuating manner," who was "never much respected in the [United States] army." John Hay, *Letters of John Hay and Extracts from Diary,* ed. by Mrs. John Hay (2 vols., Washington, 1908), I, 99, 100.

40 Heitman, *Historical Register,* I, 578, 625.

41 *OR,* Series 4, I, 605-608; Gilbert E. Govan and James W. Livingood, *A Different Valor: The Story of General Joseph E. Johnston, C.S.A.* (Indianapolis, 1956), 32, 66-71; Hughes, *General Johnston,* 33-34; Jefferson Davis, *The Papers of Jefferson Davis,* ed. by Haskell M. Monroe, Jr., James T. McIntosh, and Lynda L. Crist (6 vols. to date, Baton Rouge, 1971-), VI, 402, 644-45; Mary B. Chesnut, *A Diary from Dixie,* ed. by Isabella D. Martin and Myrta Lockett Avary (Gloucester, Mass., 1961), 248-49.

42 Williams, *Beauregard,* 1-114; Heitman, *Historical Register,* I, 204; G. T. Beauregard, *A Commentary on the Campaign and Battle of Manassas of July, 1861, Together with a Summary of the Art of War* (New York, 1891), 44, 15-16; Jones, *Rebel War Clerk's Diary,* 65.

43 *OR,* XVI (pt. 2), 599; Williams, *Beauregard,* 139-65; Jefferson Davis to E. Kirby Smith, October 29, 1862, Edmund Kirby Smith Papers, Southern Historical Collection, University of North Carolina, Chapel Hill.

44 McWhiney, *Bragg,* 1-101; Heitman, *Historical Register,* I, 240.

45 Bragg to Sherman, February 5, March 15, 1855, Sherman Papers, Library of Congress; William T. Sherman, *Memoirs* (2 vols., Bloomington, Ind., 1957), I, 162.

46 Pugh to Bragg, March 16, 1862, Palmer Collection of Bragg Papers; Thomas Bragg Diary, January 8, 1862, Southern Historical Collection, University of North Carolina, Chapel Hill; *OR,* VII, 912, 258; McWhiney, *Bragg,* 154, 202-203.

Young Man Lee

Emory M. Thomas

The title "Young Man Lee" is an admittedly weak reference to *Young Man Luther: A Study in Psychoanalysis and History* by Erik H. Erikson. This work, published in 1958, all but established the method of inquiry known as psychohistory and established Erikson as its premier practitioner. Erikson focused upon Martin Luther's life during a period after his childhood, but before his fame and influence. Combining his considerable skills as an ego psychologist with traditional techniques of historical research, Erikson reached some very interesting conclusions about Luther, conclusions which continue to be interesting and controversial more than three decades later.[1]

During my current course of conducting research on the life of Robert E. Lee to the purpose of writing his biography, I make no pretension to Eriksonian insight. I lack his training and skills, and I confess that I remain skeptical about much that pretends to be psychohistory. But no one aspires to biography can ignore *Young Man Luther* and Erikson's genius. Historians, after all, are accustomed to using the methods and conclusions of other disciplines. History is an integrative form of knowledge, and we are in a sense the cow birds of the intellectual aviary. We lay eggs (in both senses of the phrase) in nests prepared by others during our attempts to see the world whole.

I am intrigued by Erikson's attention to Luther's young manhood, and I propose to focus appropriate attention upon Lee during those years before he achieved prominence. Lee lived fifty-five years before he took command of the Army of Northern Virginia and began his journey toward legend. He was nearly forty when he first went off to war and eventually performed his first conspicuous service during Winfield Scott's campaign against Mexico City. Lee's biographers have been less than lavish in their attention to those early years. For the record, Douglas S. Freeman devoted 202 pages of a total 2323 to Lee's life before his service in Mexico. Clifford Dowdey gave Lee's first forty years 77 of his 734 pages, and Margaret Sanborn 153 of 720 pages. Those first forty years interest me, especially the young manhood years. Who was young Robert E. Lee? What did he do? About what did he care? What did he think and feel? And what did his contemporaries think about him?[2]

I have little background and less enthusiasm for long-range psychoanalysis. But when Lee or anyone else offers words or deeds which demand some kind of analysis. I hope I have the capacity to call attention to the obvious. People in the nineteenth-century did not know about Sigmund Freud. Consequently, nineteenth-century Americans and others were less guarded in what they wrote about themselves, and sometimes they revealed more about themselves than they knew. When Julia Dent who became Julia Dent Grant confided in her memoirs that she named one of her bedposts "Ulys," a modern reader of that diary should take note. But the modern reader should be careful. Naming bedposts after beaus was common practice among American girls during the nineteenth century. So Julia Dent may have been simply following a fad and not necessarily acting out some Freudian statement about Ulysses S. Grant. Historians who attempt long-range psychoanalysis must beware of Freudian slips.[3]

> There once was a thinker named Eric
> Who pondered a protestant cleric.
> Obsession with feces
> And ninety-five theses?
> O what a connection hysteric!

Here begin, then, some observations about young man Lee, about Lee as career officer, husband, parent, and human being. Let me first rehearse some fundamental facts about those first forty years.

Born on January 19, 1807, at Stratford Hall in Westmoreland County, Virginia, Robert Edward Lee was the son of Anne Hill Carter Lee, second wife of Henry "Light-Horse Harry" Lee. Lee's father had been a hero of the Revolutionary War, Governor of Virginia, and Member of Congress. But he had fallen into political disfavor and financial ruin. When young Robert was six years old, his father left the family and went to Barbados to escape his creditors and to try to reverse his financial woes. He failed again and died in 1818 without returning home. Robert spent his boyhood (1810-1825) in Alexandria with his mother in circumstances which defined "genteel poverty." He attended schools and cared for his mother who was often in ill health.

At age 18 (1825) Lee entered West Point, and in 1829 he graduated second in a class of forty-six. That same summer his mother died. Commissioned an engineer officer, Lee began his military career on Cockspur Island near Savannah, Georgia, working upon the foundations of what later became Fort Pulaski. In 1831 Lee married Mary Anne Randolph Custis, and the young couple moved to Lee's new duty assignment at Old Point Comfort. Lee worked at Fortress Monroe and supervised the sinking of lots of stone and sand at Rip Raps as the foundation of what was supposed to become Fort Calhoun. In 1834 Lee went to work in Washington as assistant to the Chief of Engineers. Mary lived with her family at Arlington, and when his duties and the weather permitted, Lee commuted from Arlington into the Capital. From 1837 to 1840 Lee spent most of his time in St. Louis attempting to alter the channel of the Mississippi River.

Then he spent four years (1840-1844) in New York at work upon Forts Hamilton and Lafayette. He returned to Washington in 1844 as assistant to the Chief of Engineers and received orders to Mexico in August of 1846.

By this time he was Captain Lee; he became a regular army second lieutenant in 1832; first lieutenant in 1836; and captain in 1838. By August, 1846, Mary and Robert Lee had seven children: Custis was almost fourteen; Mary was eleven; William Henry Fitzhugh ("Rooney") was nine; Annie was seven; Agnes was five; Robert Edward, Jr ("Rob") was two; and Mildred was not yet one.[4]

His photograph (daguerreotype) taken at this time displays a strikingly handsome man. He had black, wavy hair, a black mustache, sharp, brown eyes and a high forehead. Lee stood about five feet, ten-and-a-half inches, taller than average for his time, and he carried an athletic, medium build with a soldier's dignity.[5]

This was Lee's life in outline to the time he went off to his first war. In many ways his life had been pretty unspectacular, and much of his military career had been nothing so much as it had been boring. I believe, however, that Lee's first forty years were important. And I believe that several themes emerged in the life of young man Lee which were crucial to his entire life.

I believe Lee responded in various ways to his father's checkered example. He probably possessed few, if any, memories of "Light Horse" Harry, and any memories of his father young Robert might have had would have been about a disastrous period in the life of the Revolutionary hero. Although Lee spent eighteen months at a duty assignment on Cockspur Island near Savannah, he never visited his father's grave on Cumberland Island, less than a hundred miles down the Georgia coast. Only in 1862 did he go to the grave site, and then he remained only "a few moments." He named none of three sons after his father. Yet Lee read his father's published memoirs as a young man, edited a new edition as an old man, and gave considerable attention to the Lee coat-of-arms.[6]

Young man Lee seemed (understandably) to focus upon negative aspects of his family's example. Because his father had failed, Lee was determined to succeed. "Light Horse" Harry's life was mercurial and often out of control; his son sought order and craved control. And if "Light Horse" Harry's example were not sufficiently clear, "Black Horse" Harry's experience certainly was. Lee's older half-brother Henry had inherited the family estate at Stratford when Robert was four. Henry earned the sobriquet "Black Horse" by committing adultery and pregnancy with his wife's seventeen-year-old sister. Henry also squandered so much money that he "lost the farm" in the most literal way possible in 1828. Here was another vivid object lesson in control and self-discipline for Robert Lee.[7]

> There once was a young man named Lee
> A frustrated sibling was he
> Son of an old hero
> With cash flow sub-zero
> And blight on the family tree.

In fact lots of the men Lee might have logically adopted, if not as surrogate fathers, at least as mentors or models provided only milder versions of the same lesson. His older brother Charles Carter went to Harvard and entered a law practice in New York. But he left New York and embarked upon a series of ventures—mill, farm, iron furnace, spa—none of which yielded much financial success. Next older brother Smith was a naval officer, thus often at sea, and Robert complained that Smith never corresponded.

Lee's first commanding officer at Cockspur Island was Major Samuel Babcock. When Lee returned to Cockspur from leave in November, 1830, he wrote to Carter about his "anxiety to see how much the late gales had left us." He described the damage "and what was worst than all, the wharf which cost us so much time and money is destroyed I fear beyond repair, which is the consequence of having our communications on one side of the island instead of the other, about which there was 'issue joined' between the Maj. and myself." Then Lee observed that Babcock was not there; no one knew where he was; and rumor was "that the madame had separated from him and had carried off her youngest child..." Soon thereafter Babcock resigned from the service.[8]

At Fortress Monroe Lee's immediate superior was Captain Andrew Talcott with whom he became fast friends. But Talcott was often away from the fort, and Lee had to carry on alone. In 1836 Talcott resigned his commission and pursued private interests. In Washington Lee worked for Engineer Chief, Brigadier General Charles Gratiot, and from Gratiot he learned a harsh negative lesson about the uncertainty and vicious potential of public service. In 1838, while Lee was in St. Louis, Gratiot left the army in disgrace, charged with defrauding the government. "I believe the news of his *death* would have been less painful to me," Lee wrote to Talcott. "I hardly think of anything of anything else," he added in apparent distraction.[9]

From these men Lee learned many things. He developed friendships, exercised loyalty, and experienced independence. He also learned that the world can be a hostile place where bad things happen to good people. And I believe Lee came to have confidence in himself, to realize that his elders and superiors often lacked his competence, common sense, and sound judgement.

From the example of his father, half-brother, elder brothers, and military superiors, then, young man Lee learned about caution and about his own competence. Whatever the source, caution and competence seemed to characterize Lee's career as professional soldier and family provider. And together these qualities produced considerable frustration from time to time.

Lee worked with skill and diligence at Cockspur, Ft. Monroe, Rip Raps, Washington, St. Louis, and New York. Nevertheless, promotions were slow in peacetime; the army was intensely political; and the Engineer Corps especially depended upon Congressional whim for the appropriations necessary to finance projects on which Lee worked. And so much of that work was so seemingly unfulfilling. At Rip Raps, for example, Lee spent months dumping stone and sand onto a shoal and measuring how much of the material sank and how much his artificial island grew. At Ft. Hamilton Lee spent much of his time ordering stones, rejecting stones of the wrong size and shape, and supervising the placing of the proper stones around the fort. Surely he tired of the tedium.

In early 1837 Lee wrote from Washington to Talcott and spoke to the combination of his career and himself:

> You ask what are my prospects in the Corps? Bad enough unless it is increased and something done for us, and then perhaps they will be better. As to what I intend doing, it is rather hard to answer. There is one thing certain. I must get away from here....I should have made a desperate effort last spring, but Mary's health was so bad, I could not have left her & she could not have gone with me. I am waiting, looking and hoping for some good opportunity to bid an affectionate farewell to my dear Uncle Sam. And I seem to think that said opportunity is to drop in my lap like a ripe pear, for d____l a stir have I made in the matter. And there again I am helped out by the talent I before mentioned I possessed in so eminent a degree [procrastination].[10]

Lee continued to procrastinate and continued in the service.

He even went to some lengths to decline a change of duties, from construction to instruction, an appointment at West Point with the possibility of visiting European military academies as a bonus. To an inquiry from Washington, Lee protested, "There is an *art* in imparting...Knowledge, and in making a subject agreeable to those that learn, which I have never found that I possessed. And you know the character of cadets well enough to be convinced that it is no easy matter to make the labors of mind & body pleasant to them."[11]

Time and foreign tensions finally induced Lee to overcome caution and inertia and to pursue professional advancement more aggressively. In June, 1845, he responded to a query from Chief of Engineers Joseph G. Totten. In the event of an increase in the size of the army, "I would desire a transfer to the new forces with promotion." And Lee added, "In the event of war with any foreign government I should desire to be brought into active service in the field with as high a rank in the regular army as I could obtain. If that could not be accomplished without leaving the Corps of Engineers, I should then desire a transfer...." Finally, over a year after Lee expressed his wish, he received orders to Mexico where he first won fame.[12]

> There once was a young man named Lee
> A frustrated soldier was he
> Never the bold dragoon
> An engineer jejune
> Condemned to drop rocks in the Sea.

During the first seventeen years Lee served in the United States Army, he earned a steady salary. His obligations increased when he married, and eventually nine people depended upon him for support. Mary and the children lived often at her family's estate Arlington and so spared the young officer some of their living expenses. But Mary did not accept charity from her family, and Lee was concerned about money and debt.

Mindful of his father's experience, Lee was extremely careful with money. On one occasion the army paymaster paid Lee's salary twice for the months of May and June, 1845, and Lee did not notice the error. Eventually the paymaster discovered the over-payment and questioned Lee about the matter. Lee claimed that he had been ill at the time, assured the paymaster he intended no deceit, and repaid the money. The incident, Lee wrote, "caused me more mortification that any other act of my life."[13]

Lee's correspondence with his older brother Charles Carter is especially revealing about his personal finances. This is true in part because Carter often asked his younger brother to invest in his various enterprises. To Carter's plans for a spa in southwestern Virginia, Lee responded,

> If it was [sic] not for the pain I feel at the trouble & vexation of your situation, I should have to laugh at the grandeur of your plans & the hopelessness of raising funds from the three main supporters of the firm, yourself, Smith, & myself. The description you give of the Spring & the prospects of the increased value of the property are very flattering, but how in the world are they to be made available. Nothing can be done without money, & it is the very kind of property that requires a large outlay before any profit can be realized & then it will depend upon fashion & prejudice.

Later in the same letter, Lee proclaimed, "I believe if I had a thousand dollars for every hundred dollars I have, I should not have enough for all the demands upon me for money, not so much on my own acct. as...of those near & dear to me who require aid & whom I am powerless to serve."[14]

Lee also corresponded with his older brother about their sister-in-law, Ann, wife then widow of "Black Horse Harry." Lee's half-brother Henry spent the final years of his life in Paris, and when he died in 1837, he left his wife with few resources. Lee was concerned over the plight of "our poor sister in Paris," and alarmed that to maintain her there he, Carter, and Smith would have to provide $900 per year. He proposed, "In her situation she ought not to be left to care of strangers, and indeed I think it wrong for her to remain so far away from those to whom she can look for protection." Lee concluded, "I think she ought at all events be somewhere in this country where she could live comfortably for much less than she is now doing in Paris, and where she would be near her friends."[15] Lee proposed the shrewd solution of prompting Ann's brother Richard Stuart to obtain a court order to restore her property from her husband's creditors and to use the income from this property to support her while she lived and then to let it pass to Henry Lee's creditors at her death. For the present Lee could do little.[16] "The only help I can offer is this," he wrote in August, 1840, "Mr. Lloyd owes me $180 due last March. He has been expecting to pay me all the spring & I relied on that for Mary's use. He however was disappointed in collecting the money. If he can pay it to you, you can send it to Mrs. Lee. It is all I can do...."[17]

While he was en route to Mexico in August, 1846, Lee made his will. In it he listed his various investments—bank stock, state bonds, stock in a railroad, the James River and Kanawa Canal Company, and a St. Louis Company—with an estimated value of 38,750 nineteenth-century dollars.[18] To Mary he wrote while on board a steamboat between New Orleans and Lavaca (Texas):

> The present income of the stocks, bonds, etc., of which you will find the certificates in the package in the bank, is over $2000 per annum. This judiciously expended I hope will be sufficient for their [the children's] education. As I had confined our expenditures pretty much to my military pay, I had been enabled to accumulate this little sum by the annual investment of my private income. While the children were young I might have added to this sum for a few years. But such as it is you must make the most of it.[19]

Despite Lee's protestations to his older brother that he was ever poor, he managed his financial affairs with prudence and skill. As in the case of his career, Lee was cautious and competent in his private investments. But I suspect he wrote the truth when he lamented his inability to meet the needs "of those near & dear to me who require aid & whom I am powerless to serve."

If Lee's career and personal finances sometimes frustrated him, I suspect his marriage often frustrated him. I can think of no good reason why Robert E. Lee married Mary Custis.[20]

Lee had visited the Custis family often at Arlington. Mary's father George Washington Parke Custis was the adopted son of George Washington, and not a whole lot more. He dabbled at farming, drama, poetry, and painting, and when he died in 1857, he left his affairs in such a tangle that his son-in-law was still trying to sort them out as he himself neared death. Mary was the only Custis offspring to survive infancy and her mother and father lavished attention upon her. During the summer of 1830 when heat and pests rendered work on Cockspur Island impossible, Lee took leave, travelled north, and visited again at Arlington. When he returned to duty that fall, he and Mary were informally engaged. "That is," Lee announced to Carter, "she & her mother have given their consent. But the father has not yet made up his mind, though it is supposed will not object." Custis did consent, and the two married at Arlington on June 30, 1831.[21]

Mary Lee's mother once said of her daughter's record as a housekeeper, "The spirit is willing but the flesh is weak." In fact Mrs. Custis' comment well described many facets of Mary's person.[22]

Consider a letter Mary wrote to her mother about a month after she and Robert had settled at Fortress Monroe and had begun their married life together. Mary began with a discussion of her religious zeal and professed "an anxious desire to do something to show forth my gratitude to that all merciful Saviour [sic] who has done all for me but it is hard to find what I can do." She then complained, "The only actively pious family here have not visited me," and that "the rest of the ladies seem not to be exerting themselves to improve the condition of the people here." Next Mary noted, "There is a Sunday School...but I have not seen it nor do I know how it is conducted." She thanked her mother for sending some books, "though I must confess I have not read the others yet." Mary wrote that she and a friend "commenced the life of Luther, but like you she is so much interrupted between children & servants that we have not progressed far." Turning to other topics she said, "There is a Mrs. Halliburton at the tavern who says she is a relation of mine, but I have not seen her yet." "I do not know how it is," she continued, "but we do not seem to find a great deal of time for reading though I hope as we get settled down we shall accomplish more." As for her husband, "Robert has but little time for going about as his duties require his presence daily & keep him pretty well employed...." After reading these fascinating accounts of inaction, I have to agree with Mrs. Custis' judgement and question if indeed "the spirit is willing."[23]

I also must agree with the comment of Mary Lee's youngest son Rob (Robert E. Lee, Jr.) made in a letter to his sister Mildred in 1866. Rob chided his sister:

...you are taking after your Mama & are writing up pieces [of paper] simply because they are pieces. I don't object to your letters in any form but I just would suggest in a brotherly way that the young 'Lord of Romancoke' [Rob] is not accustomed to receive letters gotten up so recklessly, except from his mother.[24]

Mary Lee wrote a rambling stream-of-consciousness about very little of consequence.

One other comment from Mary's letter to her mother deserves emphasis—"What would I give," she wrote, "for one stroll on the hills at Arlington this bright day." She did love Arlington and her family; Mary Lee loved them so much that she spent much of her married life with her parents at Arlington. As newlyweds the Lees settled at Fortress Monroe in early August 1831 and stayed there until December when they both went to Arlington for Christmas. In January, 1832, Robert returned to his duty, and Mary remained with her parents. She remained at Arlington until the middle of June, while Lee threatened to "row up the Bay" to see her. When Mary did rejoin her husband she brought her mother with her to Fortress Monroe. In September Mary gave birth to her first child (George Washington Custis Lee), and by December Mary and her baby were back at Arlington.[25]

This pattern continued, and soon it seemed just fine to Robert. In July of 1833 Lee wrote to his military superior and friend Talcott, "We are all well & Mrs. Custis & Mary have gone up to Shirley which is as much to say that I am as happy as a clam at high water."[26]

Lee sought order and cleanliness in his life. When he first arrived at St. Louis he wrote of the city and himself:

[We] are but poorly accomodated at what is called the best hotel in the city. The house is very crowded, and a dark *dirty* room is the only one we could procure. The dinner was very good indeed, well cooked and well served, but the table is too large and full, and contains too many guests both for the viands and servants. This part could be borne with, but the room is intolerable, and so soon as I close this letter I shall sally out in quest of another. I may be perhaps *over* scrupulous in this respect, but I can readily bear the *clean dirt* of the *earth*, and drink without a strain the mud of the Missouri, and if necessary could live in it and lie in it, though this *domestic* filth is revolting to my taste.[27]

Mary Lee was not only more tolerant of "domestic filth" than her husband; she seems to have promoted it. Lee once warned some prospective house guest, "Tell the ladies that they are aware that Mrs. L. is somewhat addicted to *laziness & forgetfulness* in her housekeeping. But they may be certain she does her best."

In her defense I must point out that Mary Lee was often ill, and under her circumstances she could not always do her best. Time and space do not permit a catalog or complete chronicle of Mary Lee's infirmities here. Let me simply offer one sample from her husband's correspondence.

> Since the commencement of spring she has gradually improved in health and appearance, until about six weeks since, when she was taken with the mumps, which appeared to throw her all back again, and a few days after the disappearance of which, she became extremely ill affected with fevor, which fell upon the brain, and seemed to overthrow her whole nervous system....Her nervous system is much shattered. She has almost a horror of crowded places, an indisposition to make the least effort, and yet a restless anxiety which renders her unhappy and disatisfied.[28]

She recovered from this illness; but Mary Lee's physical infirmities persisted and grew worse with age. By the time of the Civil War, she was an invalid, crippled cruelly by arthritis.

For Robert Lee who had nursed his mother during much of his boyhood, Mary Lee's chronic illnesses must have seemed a sentence of *deja vu*. And Lee was particularly squeamish about physical incapacity. When his son Rooney accidentally cut off the ends of two of his fingers as a child, for example, Lee wrote of the boy having been "ruined for life."[29] Yet Lee spared no expense or effort to relieve the sufferings of his ailing wife, and his letters to her and others indicate that he suffered with and for her.

I believe Lee genuinely loved his wife. He wrote to her often when he was away from her (which was often). He confided in her and shared his hopes and fears. But I also believe that Lee's love for Mary was grounded in duty, rather than the other way around. Mary's adversity and her (superficially, at least) incompatibility with him Lee perceived as challenges to his control of himself. The first significant woman in his life, his mother, invoked similar challenges. The second significant woman in Lee's life, his wife, undoubtedly provoked him. But experiences and observation taught Lee that mothers and wives could be difficult; that was the way the world was. So he did what he believed he ought to do. Lee did his duty, retained his composure, and maintained control.

> There once was a young man named Lee
> A frustrated husband was he
> Was conjugal justice
> Life with Mary Custis
> Let no one say dowries are free.

THEMES IN HONOR OF T. HARRY WILLIAMS

Young parent Lee seemed quite concerned about the control and discipline of his children. Following the child-rearing fashion of his time, Lee made moral lessons out of experiences traumatic and trivial. He wrote to Rooney when the boy was eight about a farm boy who found his father dead in the snow from an accident. The boy was a hero, because he overcame his horror and hauled his father's body home on a sled. Lee then launched into admonitions to Rooney to be good. Lee counselled Mary to "maintain *strict discipline*, & enforce prompt obedience" and proclaimed, "I am sorry indeed Custis has recd so many marks of demerit. Although they may be for *trifles*, yet still if they are required to be observed, they become of *importance* & cannot be considered beneath his attention." Clearly, Lee seemed to be trying to transmit his concern for discipline and control to his children.[30]

But, and this is an important "but," Lee as parent also displayed less rigid, less orthodox qualities. His son Rob recalled, "The two younger children he petted a great deal, and our greatest treat was to get into his bed in the morning and lie close to him, listening while he talked to us in his bright, entertaining way." Rob also remembered, "He was very fond of having his hands tickled, and, what was still more curious, it pleased and delighted him to take off his slippers and place his feet in our laps in order to have them tickled." To his wife Lee wrote of Rob (two at the time), "I long to kiss that fragrant mouth & feel that little heart fluttering against mine." In another letter he said, "I was dreaming of you all last night & thought daughter [Mary] was in the bed with me, & I was wondering how she should be so small, when lo & behold when I awoke in the morng I found it was little Agnes. But I did not see that precious Mildred." Lee was not as formal or unbending as his morality tales or stern precepts indicated. Quite the contrary, he was intimate with his children.[31]

Let me tell one more story about Lee as father. During his tour of duty at Fort Hamilton, Lee agreed to allow young Rooney to accompany him into New York on some errands. Rooney had complained of pains in his legs that morning, and as the day progressed, the pains grew worse. Lee brought the boy home and put him to bed. Later:

> I gave him a dose of salts & at bed time steamed him in a tub of water as hot as he could bare [sic] it. Next day he was better with still some pain. The hot bath was repeated again at night, but the next night as I began to fear it was something of inflammatory rheumatism, I gave him a tepid bath & repeated it in the morng. He then began...to mend, but did not get out of bed for five days, except when lifted & during the first two or three days, even this was attended with great pain. What made it worse, too, was that poor Mary was suffering with her face & Mary Cole [servant] was occupied

> with the baby. So that he had me for chief nurse & except at night
> I could only make him flying visits. Perhaps however it was as well
> as he seemed to think my touch hurt him less than anyone else.[32]

What this story displays is Lee engaged with his child—an important counterpoint to Rob's categorical pronouncement, "I always knew that it was impossible to disobey my father."[33]

Lee's performance as parent is revealing, I believe. He was away from home a lot, and he missed his children. He sought to impart to them lessons about duty, discipline, and self-control because he valued those qualities so much in himself. But he refused to take his lessons or himself too seriously. He played with his children; he touched them and involved himself in their world. Perhaps he was trying vicariously to find in his children the childhood he had missed while he cared for his mother. Whatever the reason, Lee took his children seriously, often more seriously than he took himself.

The ways Lee responded to parenthood were in many ways analogous to the ways he responded to life in general. Surely Lee was frustrated. He was well-born; but his was a prominent family in debt and decline. He never really knew his father, and his mother's illnesses contorted his youth. He became a professional soldier; but he suffered the strains and setbacks of serving in an adjunct arm of a peacetime army. He married well; but his wife was incredibly unlike him and often infirm. He was competent, prudent, and correct in his professional and private life; but these virtues must have seemed valueless while waiting for "opportunity...to drop in my lap like a ripe pear...." And meanwhile he perceived himself ensnared in his own inertia—"for d____l a stir have I made in the matter."

As a parent Lee displayed a capacity to rise above frustration and duty, to cope and compensate. I believe young man Lee developed what I can only call a comic vision of life. He knew human frailty first hand. Had the church not taught the doctrine of original sin, Lee would have invented it. His experience taught him that humanity was less than reliable. At his best he accepted the flaws of a world imperfect. To the human condition in general and his circumstance in particular, Lee had the choice to cry or to laugh. And much of the time he elected to laugh.

Historian Michael O'Brien once challenged me, "Tell us a Lee joke." Lee did not tell jokes. He possessed a wonderful appreciation of the absurd in human affairs, though. And he made humor from the experience of life. When he was not saying and writing those words he believed he ought to say and write, he expressed a lively outlook about life which he refused to take too seriously. Let me offer some examples.

To his friend Andrew Talcott, Lee wrote from St. Louis about an expedition to Des Moines. "Then it was Captain that I regretted not taking your advice, in coming prepared for a regular campaign. How utterly had the *hotels* seen by the Genl. disappeared, and to what miserable *cabins*, few and far between, had the *fine farm houses* been changed!"[34]

To Mary about the same trip he was more expansive and described the man who allowed him to sleep on the "softest log" on his floor.

> This Mr. Adolphus Allen is the nabob of his section of [the] county & lives in a miserable log house on the bank of the river with two rooms and a loft ...; is married a second time, to a young girl of *14*, the sole mistress and *domestic* of his establishment; he's laid off a *town* on his farm, that has nothing to recommend it, but its appearance on paper, with its *projected* canal into the interior and *contemplated* bridge across the river....; is himself engaged in putting up a...mill, and connected with a *company* in erecting a distillery....he tells me his several farms are all lying idle, while he buys his meat and bread, corresponds with the *company*, members of Congress, of the State legislature, and other influencial men....he...has the title of *Doctor*, whether of law, medicine, or science, I have never learned but infer of all three.[35]

Especially to women did Lee write witty, even risqué, epistles. His attention to young women was constant, and it does not require genius to deduce that Lee was compensating for his marriage to Mary Custis. Again, I know Lee loved his wife, and I believe he was physically faithful to her. But one facet of his expansive, comic vision of the world was his succession of relationships with lively young women. He permitted himself such "affairs of the pen" because they were safe; he was certain to remain under control.

He wrote to Harriet Randolph Hackley Talcott through letter to her husband Andrew Talcott and teased her often about his undying love for her. When she gave birth to her first daughter, Lee posed an arranged marriage for the child to his son Custis who was still less than a year old. In mock seriousness he even claimed to be the father of her child:

> The all accomplished & elegant Master Custis Lee begs to place in her hands his happiness & life, being assured that as for her he was born, so for her will he live! His only misery can be her frown, his only delight, her smile. He hopes that her assent will not be witheld from his most ardent wishes, & that in their blissful union Fortune may be indemnified for her miscarriage of the *Affaire du Coeur* of the *Father & Mother*.[36]

While Lee worked at Cockspur Island, he had paid special attention to Jack Mackay's sister Eliza. About six months after his own marriage, Lee learned that Eliza was to marry and on her wedding day he wrote to her, "But Miss E. how do feel about this time? Say 12 o'clock of the day, as you see the shadows commence to fall towards the East and Know that at *last* the sun will set?" He abandoned the letter temporarily and returned to it a few days later; by then Eliza was married. Lee asked (about the wedding night?), "... And how did you disport yourself My Child? Did you go off well, like a torpedo cracker on Christmas morning...."[37]

Sarah Beaumont (Tasy) was the daughter of Dr. William Beaumont with whom Lee and his family shared a house in St. Louis from June, 1838 until May, 1839. Lee commenced his correspondence with Tasy in January, 1840. In March of 1843 Lee wrote to Tasy from Fort Hamilton, New York, and here is some of what he said:

> I wish you were here in person, for I am all alone... Poor Alex K—I pity him. Comfort him Tasy, for if the fire of his heart is so stimulating to the growth of his whiskers there is danger of his being suffocated. What would be the verdict of a jury in that case? Suicide... I hope the sympathy between him & Miss Louise is not so intimate as to produce the same effect upon her, for I should hate her sweet face to be hid by such hairs unless they were—mine....I cannot take leave of it [a story] without a word of advice. It is translated from Theocritus & is an inscription on a statue of Love
>> 'Mild he may be, and innocent to view,
>> Yet who on earth can answer for him? You
>> Who touch the little god, mind what ye do.'
>> Say not that none has cautioned you
>> 'Although short be his arrow, slender his bow;
>> The King Appolo's never wrought such woe.'[38]

Lee was a clever man, and I suspect his correspondents were equally clever. He was certainly a master of the *double entendre*, and his Theocritus poem employs Freudian metaphors thirteen years before Freud was born. As he wrote to his friend Henry Kayser in 1845, "You are right in my interest in the pretty women, & it is strange that I do not lose it with age. But I perceive no diminution."[39]

Later in his life Lee once said in a reflective moment, "I'm always wanting something." Stephen Vincent Benét seized this sentence and emphasized it in his epic poem *John Brown's Body*:
> "I'm always wanting something."...
Picklock biographers,

What could he want that he had never had?

He only said it once—the marble closed—
There was a man enclosed within that image.
There was a force that tried Proportion's rule
And died without a legend or a cue
To bring it back. The shadow-Lees still live.
But the first-person and the singular Lee?[40]

I submit that young man Lee—Lee before forty and before fame—must have wanted lots of things. Frustrated by his heritage, in his profession, about his marriage and family, Lee might have withdrawn from life, or lashed out at life, or waxed sour on life. He did none of the above.

He responded instead by accepting reality flawed and expanding his vision to see life whole. He developed a vision of life I call comic because it was the opposite of tragic. Lee believed that people could and did overcome adversity; he could believe this because his definition of "overcome" was limited, did not require sweetness and light, and included enduring.

Lee made his peace with the world and reconciled his expectations with reality. Some people might say that he achieved psychic wholeness and became Jung man Lee. I would rather observe that Lee was indeed "always wanting something." But he kept his wants in perspective and made the best of what was.

Robert Lee sought something indeed.
"I'm always wanting," he decreed.
But he tried really hard,
Like the Rolling Stones bard
And found that you get what you need.

Endnotes

1 Erik H. Erikson, *Young Man Luther: A Study in Psychoanalysis and History* (New York, 1958). A strong tribute to Erikson is Robert Coles, *Erik H. Erikson: The Growth of His Work* (Boston, 1970).

2 Douglas S. Freeman, *R.E. Lee: A Biography,* 4 vols. (New York, 1934-35); Clifford Dowdey, *Lee* (Boston, 1965); and Margaret Sanborn, *Robert E. Lee,* 2 vols. (Philadelphia, 1966-67).

3 Julia D. Grant, *Personal Memoirs of Julia Dent Grant,* Edited by John Y. Simon (New York, 1975).

4 This outline of Lee's life depends primarily upon Freeman, *Lee,* which is still the standard biography. Sanborn, *Robert E. Lee,* is the best attempt since Freeman.

5 The daguerreotype is reproduced in Freeman, *Lee,* I, 204 (and elsewhere) from a photograph in the Museum of the Confederacy, Richmond, Virginia.

6 Thomas L. Connelly, *The Marble Man: Robert E. Lee and His Image in American Society* (New York, 1977), 5-6; Freeman, *Lee,* I, 66-67, 159-69, IV, 415-18; A. L. Long, *Memoirs of Robert E. Lee* (The Blue and Grey Press edition, Secaucus, N.J., 1983), 22-23.

7 Freeman, *Lee,* I, 97-98.

8 Lee to Charles Carter Lee, November 16, 1830, Robert E. Lee Papers (1085), Alderman Library, University of Virginia.

9 Lee to Andrew Talcott, February 13, June 9, 22, 1836, January 1, 1839, Lee Papers, Virginia Historical Society.

10 Lee to Andrew Talcott, February 2, 1837, Lee Papers, Virginia Historical Society.

11 Lee to Frederick A. Smith, August 12, 1939, Lee Papers, Virginia Historical Society.

12 Lee to Joseph G. Totten, June 17, 1845, Lee Papers, Virginia Historical Society.

13 Lee to Genl. R. Jones, February 16, 1846, Lee Papers, Virginia Historical Society.

14 Lee to Charles Carter Lee, July 24, 1843, Robert E. Lee Papers, Alderman Library, University of Virginia.

15 Lee to Charles Carter Lee, January 30, 1840, Robert E. Lee Papers, Alderman Library, University of Virginia.

16 Lee to Charles Carter Lee, February 23, 1840, Robert E. Lee Papers, Alderman Library, University of Virginia.

17 Lee to Charles Carter Lee, August 22, 1840, Robert E. Lee Papers, Alderman Library, University of Virginia.

18 Among many copies of Lee's will is one in the Robert E. Lee Papers, Library of Congress.

19 Lee to Mary Custis Lee, August 13, 1846, Lee Papers, Virginia Historical Society.

20 Neither can Connelly. See *Marble Man,* 7, 33-37, 171-72.

21 Freeman, *Lee,* I, 92-93, 104-107; Lee to Charles Carter Lee, September 22, 1830, Robert E. Lee Papers, Alderman Library, University of Virginia.

22 Lee to Andrew Talcott, April 10, 1834, Lee Papers, Virginia Historical Society.

23 M. C. Lee to M. S. Custis, Sunday [1831], Lee Papers, Virginia Historical Society.

24 R. E. Lee, Jr. to Mildred Lee, April 8, 1866, Lee Papers, Virginia Historical Society.

25 Connelly, *Marble Man,* 166-67; Lee to M. C. Lee, June 2, 1832, Lee Papers, Virginia Historical Society.

26 Lee to Andrew Talcott, July 3, 1833, printed in George Green Shackelford, ed., "Lieutenant Lee Reports to Captain Talcott on Fort Calhoun's Construction on the Rip Raps," *Virginia Magazine of History and Biography,* 60 (July, 1952), 469.

27 Lee to M. C. Lee, August 5, 1837, Lee Papers, Virginia Historical Society.

28 Lee to Charles Carter Lee, August 2, 1836, Robert E. Lee Papers, Alderman Library, University of Virginia.

29 Lee to Custis Lee, November 30, 1845, Lee Papers, Virginia Historical Society.

30 Lee to Rooney Lee, March 31, 1846; Lee to M. C. Lee, August 4, 1840 and March 24, 1846, Lee Papers, Virginia Historical Society.

31 Robert E. Lee [Jr.], *Recollections and Letters of General Robert E. Lee* (Garden City, N.Y., 1924), 9; Lee to M. C. Lee, March 24, 1846, August 13, 1846, Lee Papers, Virginia Historical Society.

32 Lee to "Mother" [M. S. Custis], April 13, 184?, Lee Papers, Virginia Historical Society.

33 Lee [Jr.], *Recollections and Letters,* 9.

34 Lee to Andrew Talcott, October 11, 1837, Lee Papers, Virginia Historical Society.

35 Lee to M. C. Lee, September 10, 1837, Lee Papers, Virginia Historical Society.

36 Lee to Andrew Talcott, February 21, 1833, Lee Papers, Virginia Historical Society.

37 Quoted in Freeman, *Lee,* I, 113.

38 Lee to Sarah Beaumont, January 21, 1840, March 11, 1840, Lee Papers, Virginia Historical Society.

39 Lee to Henry Kayser, June 16, 1845, Robert E. Lee Papers, Missouri Historical Society, printed in "Letters of Robert E. Lee to Henry Kayser, 1838-1845," *Glimpses of the Past,* III (January-February, 1936), 38.

40 Stephen Vincent Benét, *John Brown's Body* (New York, 1927), 174.

Braxton Bragg and the Confederate Invasion of Kentucky in 1862

Lawrence L. Hewitt

Historians have tarnished the Christ-like image of Robert E. Lee in recent years while the portrait of a contentious Braxton Bragg, Lee's antithesis in the Confederacy, remains unrevised. Bragg's denigration continues with his most recent besmircher describing him as being a "disgusting" individual.[1] I ask you to rid your mind of such preconceptions and to consider a passage from Shakespeare: "The evil that men do lives after them; The good is oft interred with their bones."[2] And so it is with Bragg and his accomplishments as commander of the Western Department.

On June 17, 1862, an ailing General P. G. T. Beauregard relinquished his command of the Western Department to General Braxton Bragg, and three days later President Jefferson Davis confirmed Bragg as permanent commander of that department.[3] Bragg faced a situation that had rapidly deteriorated since January when the Confederates had held all of Tennessee and a large part of Kentucky and had controlled the Misssissippi River from Columbus, Kentucky, to the delta. During the interim, a succession of Confederate defeats left both states virtually under the control of Union forces. Federal flotillas now steamed unmolested both above and below Vicksburg. The Union right flank extended into Mississippi, the vanguard occupied north Alabama, and the left flank threatened Cumberland Gap. Could Bragg devise some plan to halt this momentum of the Union forces?

Bragg's immediate command consisted of the demoralized Army of the Mississippi, an army whose failure to destroy the enemy at Shiloh and its subsequent withdrawal from Corinth to Tupelo had caused its morale to plummet and its desertions to escalate. Shortages of food, of transportation, and of competent junior officers intensified Bragg's concerns as a commander.[4]

Uncertain of the limits of his command, Bragg requested clarification. He was notified that the Western Department embraced "that part of Louisiana east of the Mississippi, the entire States of Mississippi and Alabama, and that portion of Georgia and Florida west of the Chattahoochee and Apalachicola Rivers."[5] Tennessee was not mentioned. Because of this omission, Bragg believed that his command encompassed the whole of Tennessee, because the Western Department had earlier included that entire state.[6] This, Bragg's erroneous assumption concerning the extent of his command, became the primary determinate in bringing about the invasion of Kentucky.

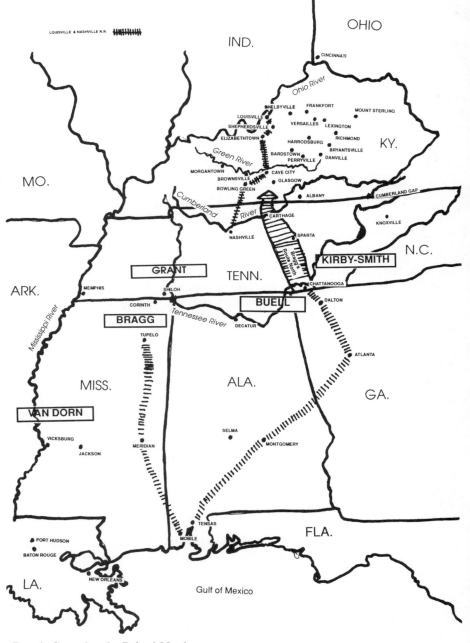

Bragg's Campaign, *by Roland Meariman*

General Braxton Bragg, 1817-1876. *Courtesy of Library of Congress*

The situation that Bragg faced clearly called for a "defensive-offensive" policy, that is, he would assume a defensive posture and only attack should an advantageous opportunity present itself. Union Major General Henry W. Halleck had a combined force of 104,000 troops in and around Corinth. To oppose this horde, Bragg had only 42,000 men. He could augment this field force with 11,000 other Confederates who were scattered from northwestern Mississippi to southeastern Louisiana. Another 4,000 Confederates were already engaged in defending his left flank at Vicksburg, while 7,000 more guarded Mobile.[7]

Bragg considered his right flank to be East Tennessee, where Major General Edmund Kirby Smith had 11,000 men dispersed between Chattanooga and Cumberland Gap. The Federals had 8,000 soldiers in eastern Kentucky threatening Cumberland Gap, 7,000 in northern Alabama threatening Chattanooga, and an additional 7,000 occupying Middle Tennessee.[8] Although the Federals outnumbered the Confederates in East Tennessee, the threats to that area were less ominous than were those to Vicksburg and northern Mississippi.

But Bragg soon learned that fortune had smiled upon him. In early June Union General Halleck had divided his massive force into three armies; one army had the task of securing West Tennessee; another army advanced toward Tupelo, and the remaining army, under Major General Don Carlos Buell, moved eastward through northern Alabama to link up with the forces already poised for an attack upon Chattanooga.[9]

Bragg saw in the breakup of Halleck's forces an opportune moment for the launching of an offensive; however, he felt that, because of their geographically important positions, Vicksburg and East Tennessee would have to be made safe before he could justify any offensive campaign. Once he had secured Vicksburg and Chattanooga and had acquired the necessary transportation for his army, Bragg would strike at Corinth.

Vicksburg required a competent commander. President Davis' first choice had been Bragg, but when Bragg assumed Beauregard's command, Davis chose Major General Earl Van Dorn. Bragg regretted having to detach Van Dorn from Tupelo,[10] but more importantly, Bragg had to furnish him with the troops necessary to defend Vicksburg. Time prohibits a discussion of the ingenuity demonstrated by Bragg in the transfer of these troops to Vicksburg, but his strategy is noteworthy. His yielding of territory of little strategic value in northwestern Mississippi enabled him to reinforce Vicksburg as well as to retain at Tupelo the maximum number of troops for an offensive strike on Corinth.

Since Bragg could now relax his concern for Vicksburg, he focused his attention on East Tennessee. Beauregard, aware that East Tennessee had been established as a separate department in March, had disregarded Kirby Smith's requests for aid. When Adjutant and Inspector General Samuel Cooper had ordered him to reinforce East Tennessee, Beauregard had replied: "It would be fatal to detach any troops from this army at this moment, when I expect daily to meet such superior forces."[11] Mistakenly believing that his own responsibilities included East Tennessee, Bragg reacted differently than had Beauregard.

Before receiving any communication from Kirby Smith, Bragg made the necessary preparations for sending reinforcements to East Tennessee. On June 20, Kirby Smith informed Bragg that he had abandoned Cumberland Gap to avoid being invested and that at least two brigades were necessary to insure the holding of the railroad which constituted the most direct route from Virginia to the western Confederacy.[12]

Bragg, busy readying his forces at Tupelo for an assault on Corinth, withheld the reinforcements and suggested to Cooper on June 22 that East Tennessee should be reinforced from the Atlantic coast. On the following day, Secretary of War George Randolph telegraphed Bragg that reinforcements had already been sent from the Atlantic coast to Chattanooga but that more were needed. Although he urged Bragg to send the additional reinforcements,[13] Bragg took no action, still hoping that troops from elsewhere would be sent to bolster the forces in East Tennessee.

The fact that no further requests to aid East Tennessee were made during the next three days must have eased Bragg's concern for his right flank. When he arose on the morning of the twenty-seventh, he had reason to be assured that two of his three pre-requisites for an offensive had been met—a firm hold on the Mississippi at Vicksburg and a stabilized and seemingly secure front in East Tennessee. Bragg issued a proclamation that day; he announced his formal assumption of permanent command of the Western Department, and he concluded: "A few more days of needful preparation and organization and I shall give your banners to the breeze..."[14] Bragg merely awaited the completion of the final pre-requisite—that of molding the Army of the Mississippi into a potent, offensive force—before launching an attack upon Corinth.

Later in the day a telegram from Kirby Smith shattered Bragg's illusion of East Tennessee's security: "Buell is reported crossing the river at Decatur and daily sending a regiment by rail toward Chattanooga. I have no force to repel such an attack."[15] Bragg acted promptly; he dispatched Major General John P. McCown's 3,000-man division from Tupelo to Chattanooga that same day. Bragg's movement against Corinth would have to be postponed, pending further developments at Chattanooga.[16] Bragg's commitment to securing East Tennessee before attacking Corinth allowed Kirby Smith to dictate Bragg's offensive strategy.

While Bragg waited, he continued to improve his command at Tupelo. His transfer of McCown to East Tennessee cleared the way for Major General Sterling Price to assume command of the Army of the West. This promotion convinced Price, a Missourian, to remain east of the Mississippi, and he raised the spirits of his men by promising to lead them back to their native state by way of Kentucky.[17]

Bragg, in an effort to increase the efficiency of the Army of the Mississippi, promoted Major General Leonidas Polk to second-in-command of the Western Department. Polk's elevation allowed Bragg to resign from immediate command of the Army of the Mississippi and to appoint Major General William J. Hardee as his successor. Bragg felt that Polk made a better bishop than he did a general. In Bragg's opinion, Hardee would provide better training for the troops in Polk's corps. By virtue of his pre-war service, Hardee qualified as the best man available to train the Army of the Mississippi.[18] Bragg's methods, despite some discontent and criticism from the ranks, undoubtedly enhanced the condition of his forces.

Bragg also attempted other improvements within the Western Department. With Corinth garrisoned by Union forces, any strategic movement of troops by Bragg depended upon adequate rail connections through the central Confederacy. Consequently, he repeatedly urged the completion of the railroad from Meridian, Mississippi, to Selma, Alabama.[19]

While Bragg strove to increase the likelihood of his success, events were developing rapidly in East Tennessee, or so it seemed to Kirby Smith. During the first week of July, both Kirby Smith and Bragg received inaccurate reports that Union forces in northern Alabama were moving toward Nashville and even beyond.[20] Both generals chose to believe that the enemy was withdrawing, because that is what they wished to believe. In Bragg's mind, the enemy's retrograde movement would provide him with an opportunity to attack Corinth. For Kirby Smith, the withdrawal of the enemy would relieve the pressure on Chattanooga which, in turn, would enable him to operate against Cumberland Gap.

Kirby Smith did not perceive Buell's true designs until July 10, when he telegraphed Bragg that Buell continued to move on Chattanooga with nearly 30,000 men. Kirby Smith's inability to cope with this situation caused him to magnify the problem in a letter to President Davis on July 14: "I see by the Northern papers that three divisions of Grant's army are to operate against East Tennessee in connection with Buell's corps. This brings an overwhelming force, that cannot be resisted except by Bragg's cooperation."[21] However, Kirby Smith wanted more than just Bragg's cooperation—he wanted Bragg to assume command at Chattanooga personally.

Kirby Smith's letter indicates his unwillingness to assume responsibility for Chattanooga, because he did not ask for reinforcements from Bragg; instead, he wanted Bragg to move his army into Middle Tennessee. The letter also provides an insight into Kirby Smith's future plans: "...the disorders in that State [Kentucky] are extremely propitious for his [John Hunt Morgan's] operations." Kirby Smith reasoned that, because Kentucky had warmly welcomed raiding Confederate cavalry, it would do the same for his entire command.[22] Thus, by July 14, Kirby Smith had determined to invade Kentucky and Bragg would find himself and his army *dragged* along.

Kirby Smith began transferring troops from Chattanooga toward Cumberland Gap on July 17, knowing full well that the threat to that city had not diminished.[23] He was shrewd enough to know that, in order to justify an advance into Kentucky, he would first have to make Chattanooga secure *or*, at least, to shift the responsibility to someone else—namely, Bragg.

On July 18, the Department of East Tennessee was extended to include "that part of the State of Georgia which is north of the railroad leading from Augusta via Atlanta to West Point, and so much of North Carolina as is west of the Blue Ridge Mountains in that State."[24] In as much as this order removed that portion of Georgia which had been a part of the Western Department, Bragg must have been informed of this action. It is not known when he learned of this departmental adjustment, but on the following day he received a telegram from Kirby Smith urging him to move into Middle Tennessee and promising him his cooperation.[25]

This message caused Bragg to reconsider the scope of his command. Apparently, his responsibilities did not include the defense of East Tennessee, after all. On the other hand, the messages from Kirby Smith were becoming more urgent, and if Chattanooga was his responsibility, Bragg would have to act promptly. He wrote to Kirby Smith on July 20:[26]

> I am left in doubt, from what I can learn, whether yours is a separate command, or still, as formerly a part of General [Albert Sidney] Johnston's old department and hence embraced within my command. Can you enlighten me by copies of any orders or instructions you may have? My only desire is to know the precise limits of my responsibilities, not to interfere in the least with your operations and command, as you must know best when and how to act, and have my fullest confidence.

Bragg's uncertainty, as evidenced by the above, offers a rationale for his actions up to this point, and finally, it justifies his most crucial decision, the decision to transfer the Army of the Mississippi to Chattanooga.

Bragg had always considered East Tennessee to be of more importance than northern Mississippi and Alabama. Even before he could establish the limits of his responsibilities, the threat to East Tennessee compelled Bragg to act. Leaving Price and the Army of the West to operate in northern Mississippi and northwestern Alabama, Bragg ordered the Army of the Mississippi to Chattanooga. By moving the infantry stationed at Mobile in advance, reinforcements reached Chattanooga by July 27. Despite some evidence to the contrary, Bragg still had no intention of invading Kentucky.[27] Many have disagreed with this view in the past, because to accept it is to acknowledge that Bragg had the ability to recognize the threats throughout the western theater and enough intelligence to determine the strategic value of each endangered region.

Still, Bragg does not deserve all the credit for moving to Chattanooga, because his failure to learn conclusively that his department did not include Chattanooga greatly influenced his decisions.[28] Had he been informed of the limits of his department prior to July 27 or 28, he undoubtedly would have attacked Corinth, believing that a successful attack there would force the recall of Buell's army.

The odds in northern Mississippi had greatly changed since June 17, when Bragg had succeeded Beauregard. The breaking up of the Union forces at Corinth, begun in early June, continued throughout July. Bragg could now throw his concentrated force against relatively isolated detachments of the enemy forces.[29] By July 27, however, Bragg was committed to transferring his army to Chattanooga.

Bragg met with Kirby Smith in Chattanooga on July 30. Two days later, in a letter to Cooper, Bragg outlined a plan of action that encompassed the entire western theater. Realizing that his own army would not be able to move for at least ten days, he reinforced Kirby Smith with two brigades for a movement against Cumberland Gap. Should this effort prove to be successful, Bragg would be able to withdraw a greater number of troops from the Knoxville region for his own advance against Buell in Middle Tennessee. Bragg realized that Buell would take advantage of any delay to consolidate his position in Middle Tennessee and probably to draw reinforcements from Corinth. Should such a situation develop, Price and Van Dorn could then unite their forces and launch an attack against West Tennessee.[30]

While Bragg awaited the arrival of his wagon train, which was moving overland, Kirby Smith continued to shift his own troops, as well as those on loan from Bragg, to Knoxville in preparation for his advance against Cumberland Gap. On August 9 he notified Bragg that he had a report that the Federals had a month's supply of provisions, adding that, if the information proved to be correct, it would take more time to reduce Cumberland Gap than Bragg had indicated he was willing to take. Further, Kirby Smith requested that he be allowed to move on Lexington, Kentucky, thereby isolating Cumberland Gap.[31]

By this time, Bragg had also begun to think beyond Middle Tennessee. On the tenth of August, he authorized Kirby Smith to move into Kentucky, but urged him to cooperate with a Confederate column moving westward from Virginia, and warned him not to stray too far into Kentucky before Bragg had engaged Buell.[32]

Bragg's reply to Kirby Smith marks a turning point in his planning. He had realized that Buell had had ample time to concentrate his forces in the defenses around Nashville, making an attack too costly even for the combined force of both his and Kirby Smith's armies. He also knew that Buell would be strongly reinforced from West Tennessee, which would enable Price and Van Dorn to drive the Federals from that region. All of these factors prompted Bragg to formulate a new plan of operations—he would attempt, by *maneuvering* and not by fighting, to regain control of the territory in the western theater that had been lost by the Confederacy. In accordance with this new strategy, Bragg authorized Kirby Smith to enter Kentucky prior to the defeat of Buell and the reduction of Cumberland Gap. Likewise, when Bragg learned that Kirby Smith had determined to advance on Lexington, he fully concurred.[33]

Between August 10, when Bragg agreed to let Kirby Smith move into Kentucky, and August 24, when Bragg endorsed Kirby Smith's advance on Lexington, their correspondence and Kirby Smith's actions clearly illuminate the command relationship between the two men; Kirby Smith followed Bragg's instructions to the letter. The leading authorities on this subject content that Bragg and Kirby Smith operated independently of each other, and that Kirby Smith, because he was a department commander, did not have to obey the orders of Bragg, at least, not while the troops of the two commanders were separated. The major weakness of Bragg's offensive, according to these historians, was that he had no control over Kirby Smith's movements and only nominal control over those of Van Dorn and Price; moreover, as each army advanced from its base, communication between Bragg and the army commanders became increasingly more difficult. What has not been pointed out is that, in view of their prior relationship, Bragg had no reason to suspect that Kirby Smith would fail to follow orders after he reached Kentucky.[34]

While Kirby Smith moved on Cumberland Gap and into Kentucky, Bragg hastily prepared his own army for an offensive campaign. In an effort to increase the efficiency of the command, he urged President Davis to relieve several high-ranking generals and to replace them by promoting junior officers, men whom Bragg considered to be more competent. Davis declined, realizing that such action would bring about a barrage of criticism. Moreover, such promotions were not his to make, according to the Confederate Constitution. Criticism voiced against Bragg's proposal resulted in a rift in the army's command system that would ultimately lead to his removal at the end of 1863.[35]

Bragg also continued to press for a concerted movement by Price and Van Dorn against West Tennessee. Such action would either prevent the transfer of Union troops from the Corinth area to reinforce Buell or result in an easy route into Middle or Western Tennessee after the withdrawal of those troops. Unfortunately, Bragg failed to inform the War Department of his instructions to Price and Van Dorn.[36]

On August 28, Bragg moved out of Chattanooga—initiating a campaign that most scholars believe should have resulted in a significant Confederate victory. Historians have long speculated about Bragg's motives when he left Chattanooga. The most prominent among them intimate that Bragg wanted to maneuver Buell out of Middle Tennessee without fighting him. Moreover, they describe Bragg as being indecisive throughout the campaign.[37]

Was Bragg indecisive? Although Kirby Smith was pushing him to move into Kentucky, he also advocated that Bragg first defeat Buell. Davis recommended the same primary action to Bragg—Buell should be defeated first. Tennessee Governor Isham Harris also pressured Bragg to defeat Buell and to retake Nashville before any advance be made into Kentucky.[38] Did Bragg ignore their mutual recommendation because he was indecisive? Hardly. Bragg made his own decisions and remained committed to them until circumstances dictated otherwise. Bragg kept his own council and arrived at the final decision to invade Kentucky; likewise, he alone made the decision to bypass Nashville. He planned to conduct a campaign of maneuver and to engage in combat only when it was to his advantage to do so.

Bragg assumed immediate command of the army at Chattanooga and divided into two corps, one commanded by Polk and the other by Hardee. Crossing the Tennessee River at Chattanooga, the Confederates took up the march toward Middle Tennessee on August 28. By September 3, the advance units had reached Sparta.[39]

Prior to his arrival at Sparta, Bragg had probably intended to move directly toward Lexington via Albany. However, upon his arrival at Sparta on September 4, he was informed that forage was scarce along his projected line of march, that Kirby Smith was in no immediate danger from Federal forces, and that Buell was still at Nashville. These three factors encouraged Bragg to attempt to cut Buell's communications with Louisville.[40]

Bragg captured Munfordville on September 17, thus effectively blocking Buell's direct line of retreat to Louisville. Although Buell had advanced to Bowling Green, Bragg chose not to attack him because of Buell's superior troop strength. Bragg was also unable to lure Buell into launching an assault. A shortage of supplies finally compelled Bragg to move northeastward to Bardstown. If Kirby Smith's forces had been concentrated at nearby Shelbyville, as Bragg expected them to be, the two Confederate armies would then have been in position for a simultaneous advance on Louisville. But, contrary to Bragg's instructions, Kirby Smith had dallied in eastern Kentucky, and Bragg was compelled to allow Buell to reach Louisville without a fight.

Bragg has been severely criticized for not attacking Buell before he reached Louisville, but without support from Kirby Smith, Bragg could only have attacked Buell with 28,000 men at any given time. Buell's force must have numbered more than 39,000 men during the period in which Bragg might have risked battle. Prior to Bragg's withdrawal to Bardstown, Union ranks had swollen to 52,000 troops. Furthermore, Bragg was no Robert E. Lee, and none of his subordinates ever came close to emulating "Stonewall" Jackson. A smashing victory could not have been achieved by such an inferior force, and a defeat, with Confederate units scattered throughout eastern Kentucky, might well have been disastrous to the Confederate cause. The wiser choice was for Bragg to postpone battle until he could unite with Kirby Smith and the Confederate column from Virginia. In an effort to achieve such a concentration of forces, Bragg left Polk in command at Bardstown on September 28 and went to Lexington to confer with the dilatory Kirby Smith.[41]

Bragg was already aware that the invasion had fallen apart. Kirby Smith's faulty deployment prohibited Bragg from uniting more than fifty percent of the Confederates in Kentucky against Buell. The Virginia column had failed to prevent the escape of the Union garrison at Cumberland Gap. Van Dorn and Price had failed to prevent Buell's reinforcement from the Corinth area. Operations at Baton Rouge and Port Hudson had delayed the arrival of reinforcements from Van Dorn. And finally, Kentuckians failed to rally to the Confederate standard.[42]

On October 2, while at Lexington, Bragg learned that Kirby Smith's detachment between Louisville and Frankfort had been driven back by the enemy. Believing that Buell was moving on Frankfort, Bragg planned a Napoleonic concentration of his forces on the battlefield. Kirby Smith would attack Buell's vanguard and Polk would advance directly from the south against the Union right flank. The two Confederate forces would then unite somewhere in the vicinity of Frankfort. Fortunately, Polk discovered that Buell was moving on Bardstown instead of Frankfort, and he acted accordingly. Bragg responded by planning an even larger concentration at Harrodsburg, to the southeast; Polk and Kirby Smith would be joined by other Confederate forces scattered about eastern Kentucky, by the reinforcements from Van Dorn that had finally reached Knoxville, and by a few more fresh recruits. Bragg wired Polk on October 4: "Keep the men in heart by assuring them it is not a retreat, but a concentration for a fight. We can and must defeat them."[43]

About noon on October 7, Bragg learned that Buell was advancing by several routes and that Polk was being pressed near Perryville. Bragg promptly decided to destroy Buell in detail, beginning with the Union column near Perryville. Conflicting orders issued by subordinates and Kirby Smith's failure to ascertain that the Union advance on Frankfort was merely a diversion resulted in Bragg's fighting the Battle of Perryville with only three divisions. Bragg, too, never realized that Buell was concentrating his forces near Perryville.[44] And Buell had mustered quite a force.

On September 29 the last of Buell's forces from Tennessee marched into Louisville where his Army of the Ohio was being reorganized to include reinforcements from West Tennessee and those newly mustered into service. Marching along four routes, Buell led this horde of 87,000 men against Bragg on October 1.[45]

From the outset there was continual skirmishing as the vanguard of Buell's army overtook Polk's rear guard. The pursuit of Polk to Perryville proceeded at a slower pace than did the race for Louisville. The weather was unusually dry and the shortage of water became an acute problem. Although many of the Union soldiers must have dropped out, a forced march the previous evening allowed Buell to concentrate virtually his entire command just west of Perryville by the morning of October 8.[46]

A number of bizarre factors enabled Bragg's vastly outnumbered force to win a tactical victory that day. However, before darkness ended the fighting, Bragg realized that he confronted the preponderance of Buell's army; consequently, he wisely considered discretion to be the better part of valor and made the decision to withdraw. Still hoping that he could achieve a concentration, Bragg issued orders immediately, and early on the ninth of October, the victorious but battered Confederate army moved northeastward toward Harrodsburg. The town was a death trap, because it placed Buell on an almost clear route to Bragg's base of supplies at Bryantsville and his subsequent line of retreat. For Bragg to have done otherwise would have enabled Buell to cut off Kirby Smith. The threat to his rear induced Bragg to abandon all hope of a concentration; he ordered Polk to begin moving south, even before Kirby Smith had reached Harrodsburg.[47]

Buell's slowness to advance, following the battle of Perryville, allowed Bragg to regroup the majority of the dispersed Confederate forces in Kentucky at

Bryantsville. Upon his arrival, Bragg found that very little food had been transferred from Lexington to Bryantsville. The lack of comestibles in the area necessitated a further move. Should Bragg move against Buell, or should he retreat into East Tennessee?[48] Van Dorn's rumored defeat at Corinth, the absence of support from Tennessee, the failure of reinforcements to arrive from Van Dorn, and especially the indifference of the Kentuckians—all indicated that a withdrawal was Bragg's only viable option. Although all of his chief subordinates concurred, it was Bragg who would be held responsible, because the final decision was his alone. When asked about the best test of greatness in a general, the Duke of Wellington responded: "To know when to retreat and to dare to do it."[49] It was fortunate for the Confederacy that Bragg had the courage to order the retreat.

Bragg's army left Bryantsville for Cumberland Gap on October 13, even before all of Kirby Smith's command had reached the former place. At no time during the campaign was the entire available Confederate force united on one field. The only Confederate multi-army offensive had been a failure.[50] Or had it? Just what had Bragg accomplished since succeeding Beauregard barely three months earlier?

The Confederates had invaded Federal territory, whether Kentucky was a border state or not. During the course of the campaign, they had recaptured the strong defensive position at Cumberland Gap; they had virtually annihilated the Federal force sent to Richmond, Kentucky, to stop the movement before it was well underway, and they had captured a garrison of over 4,000 men at Munfordville. In addition, Bragg had won a tactical victory at Perryville against odds of almost four-to-one. Following this engagement, the Confederates were allowed to make an almost unharassed retreat, undoubtedly giving the impression to many Northerners, Southerners, and Europeans alike that the Confederates could come and go almost as they pleased, regardless of the odds.

Bragg had so maneuvered his forces that northern Alabama, Middle Tennessee below Nashville, and East Tennessee were cleared of Federal troops. Bragg's strategy had forced Major General Ulysses S. Grant to detach a considerable force from West Tennessee to aid Buell, and in so doing, Grant was held in check until late in the year by the small force that Bragg had left behind in Mississippi under Van Dorn and Price; a portion of Van Dorn's command had also established a second bastion on the Mississippi River at Port Hudson, thereby giving the Confederates control of a substantial stretch of that waterway as well as the Red River. Moreover, the Federal threat to Chattanooga, an important base for offensive operations for either side, was abated for an entire year. Can it be denied that Bragg's invasion of Kentucky prolonged the war?

Bragg's campaigning by maneuver should have become the primary Confederate strategy in the Western theater. Even if the invasions were to fail, the maneuvers would upset Federal plans and would delay their penetration of the Confederate interior. More importantly, Bragg had demonstrated what a single individual could accomplish when charged with the defense of the entire Western Theater. Between June and October of 1862, Bragg had displayed greater ability at grand strategy than did any other Confederate commander during the entire war; he had accepted responsibility for key positions hundreds of miles from his headquarters and had successfully held them for the Confederacy. The departmentalization of the Western Theater, a process which had begun even before Bragg withdrew from Kentucky, coupled with the assignment of the ineffective Joseph E. Johnston to coordinate activities in the region made a repetition of Bragg's strategy of 1862 a virtual impossibility for the future.

With the advantage of hindsight, it is certain that the rift within the high command of the Army of the Mississippi required major adjustment. It was unfortunate for the Confederacy that Davis selected Joseph E. Johnston instead of Bragg to command the Department of the West, for Bragg had already demonstrated his willingness to assume responsibility, a characteristic sadly lacking in Johnston. Bragg's elevation would have removed him from his disgruntled subordinates in the Army of the Mississippi and provided Davis with the opportunity to select a more congenial but probably less competent commander for that army.

However, Bragg was destined for lesser things. Shortly after his withdrawal from Kentucky, a resident of Middle Tennessee wrote in her diary: "When the History of this war is impartially written, it is my deliberate opinion, that to *Bragg* will be awarded the praise of *having done more with his men and means, than any other Gen. of the War, with equal resources.*"[51] Will the "disgusting" Bragg ever receive an impartial treatment? Possibly, but not before every Southerner has been convinced that Robert E. Lee was only *human*, a mere *mortal* who failed Wellington's test of greatness and senselessly risked the destruction of his army at Sharpsburg.

Endnotes

1 Richard M. McMurry, *Two Great Rebel Armies: An Essay in Confederate Military History* (Chapel Hill & London: The University of North Carolina Press, 1989), p.8.

2 William Shakespeare, *The Tragedy of Julius Caesar* (New York: Washington Square Press, Inc., 1966), p. 56.

3 U.S. War Department, *The War of the Rebellion: A Compilation of the Official Records of the Union and Confederate Armies* (Washington, D.C.: Government Printing Office, 1880-1901), Ser. I, Vol. XVII, Pt. 2, pp. 606, 614, hereinafter cited as *O.R.*, all references are to Series I unless otherwise stated.

4 *O.R.*, XVII, Pt. 2, pp. 627-28.

5 *Ibid.*, 619, 627. In addition to Samuel Cooper, copies were sent President Davis, Secretary of War George Randolph, and General Robert E. Lee.

6 Grady McWhiney, *Braxton Bragg and Confederate Defeat*, Vol. I, *Field Command* (New York and London: Columbia University Press, 1969), 43; U.S. War Department, *The Official Atlas of the Civil War* (New York and London: Thomas Yoseloff, 1958), CLXIII, CLXIV.

7 *O.R.*, X, Pt. 2, p. 235; *ibid.*, XVII, Pt. 2, pp. 635. 661; *ibid.*, XV, 770. Unless otherwise stated, figures represent effective strength.

8 *O.R.*, X, Pt. 2, pp. 235, 573.

9 *Ibid.*, XVII, Pt. 2, p. 3.

10 *Ibid.*, 599, 613, 627-28.

11 *Ibid.*, 630, 644-46, 681; *ibid.*, X, Pt. 2, pp. 307-8; *ibid.*, XVI, Pt. 2, pp. 679-81, 683-85.

12 *O.R.*, XVII, Pt. 2, p. 618; *ibid.*, XVI, Pt. 2, p. 695.

13 *O.R.*, XVI, Pt. 2, pp. 701-702.

14 *Ibid.*, XVII, Pt. 2, pp. 622-26; *ibid.*, XVI, Pt. 2, pp. 704-9.

15 *O.R.*, XVI, Pt. 2, p. 709.

16 *Ibid.*, 710, *ibid.*, XVII, Pt. 2, pp. 651-52.

17 *O.R.*, XVII, Pt. 2, pp. 114, 616, 636, 645-646. Davis had approved the return of Price's three Missouri brigades to the Trans-Mississippi, but such a move was virtually impossible and, following Price's speech on July 17, his soldiers agreed not to make the attempt.

18 *Ibid.*, 636; Marcus J. Wright, *General Officers of the Confederate Army, Officers of the Executive Departments of the Confederate States, Members of the Confederate Congress by States* (New York: Neale Publishing Company, 1911), pp. 21-23; Ezra J. Warner, *Generals in Gray: Lives of the Confederate Commanders* (Baton Rouge: Louisiana State University Press, 1959), pp. 124, 242. Hardee had served as commandant of cadets at West Point and wrote the standard textbook, *Rifle and Light Infantry Tactics* (1853-55).

19 *O.R.*, XVII, Pt. 2, pp. 612, 624; Robert C. Black III, *The Railroads of the Confederacy* (Chapel Hill: The University of North Carolina Press, 1952), pp. 156-57; McWhiney, *Braxton Bragg*, I, 262.

20 *O.R.*, XVI, Pt. 2, pp. 719-23; William P. Palmer Collection, Western Reserve Historical Society, Reel 2, Film 2367, Bragg's return endorsement to Kirby Smith's July 4, 1862, telegram.

21 *O.R.*, XVI, Pt. 2, pp. 725-27.

22 *Ibid.*, 726-27.

23 *Ibid.*, 728.

24 *Ibid.*, 729.

25 Palmer Collection, Western Reserve, Reel 2, Film 2367, Kirby Smith to Bragg, July 19, 1862.

26 *O.R.*, XVII, Pt. 2, pp. 651-52.

27 *Ibid.*, XVI, Pt. 2, pp. 731, 738-39; *ibid.*, XVII, Pt. 2, pp. 638, 651-52. Although many historians contend that Bragg intended to invade Kentucky before his departure from Mississippi, ample evidence exists to disprove this hypotheses, including Bragg's letter to Kirby Smith on July 20 and the movements of Withers' division between June 27 and July 21.

28 *O.R.*, XVII, Pt. 2, p. 627; *ibid.*, XVI, Pt. 2, pp. 734-35, 745-46.

29 *O.R.*, XVII, Pt. 2, pp. 90, 99-102, 114, 143-44, 638, 648. By July 21, Bragg could field a force nearly equal to the 55,000 effective Federal troops that remained in the vicinity. Of these, 13,000 were stationed at Memphis, which had no direct rail connections to Corinth and was farther away from that city than Tupelo; 8,000 men were stationed at Jackson, Tennessee, which was in direct rail communications with both Memphis and Corinth; 5,000 troops were encamped about ten miles due north of Corinth on Clear Creek; 5,000 were located in extreme northwestern Alabama; 14,000 were located in Corinth; and 9,000 were located in an arc around that city to the south at a distance of from ten to fifteen miles.

30 *Ibid.*, 655-56, 662; *ibid.*, XVI, Pt. 2, p. 741.

31 *O.R.*, XVI, Pt. 2, pp. 742-45, 748.

32 *Ibid.*, 748-49, 995.

33 *Ibid.*, 766-67, 775.

34 McWhiney, *Braxton Bragg*, I, 273, 281-82; Thomas L. Connelly, *Army of the Heartland: The Army of Tennessee, 1861-1862* (Baton Rouge: Louisiana State University Press, 1967), pp. 204, 206-209; Stanley F. Horn, "Perryville," in *Civil War Times Illustrated: A nonpartisan magazine of American History*, IV, 10 (February, 1966), p. 6; *O.R.*, XVI, Pt. 2, pp. 734-35, 748, 751, 755.

35 *O.R.*, XVII, Pt. 2, pp. 627-28, 647, 654, 658, 667-68, 671-72; Thomas L. Connelly and Archer Jones, *The Politics of Command: Factions and Ideas in Confederate Strategy* (Baton Rouge: Louisiana State University Press, 1973), p. 50. Although the correspondence cited were written prior to Bragg's arrival at Chattanooga, he continued to push for the replacement of high ranking officers.

36 *O.R.*, XVII, Pt. 2, pp. 666, 675-76, 685, 688, 690, 705-706; McWhiney, *Braxton Bragg*, I, 238-39.

37 McWhiney, *Braxton Bragg*, I, 272-92, 294, 297-98; Connelly, *Army of the Heartland,* 206-9, 217, 221-22, 225, 227-28, 230-32, 234-36, 241, 244-46, 262. Connelly wrote: "The wisdom of this decision was debatable, for it remained to be seen which would secure Kentucky: an early defeat of Buell or an immediate concentration of Confederate strength in the Bluegrass." McWhiney titled the chapter dealing with July 29—September 22, 1862, "By Marching, Not By Fighting."

38 *O.R.*, XVI, Pt. 2, pp. 739-40. 766-67; Dunbar Rowland, *Jefferson Davis, Constitutionalist: His Letters, Papers and Speeches* (Jackson: Mississippi Department of Archives and History, 1923), Vol. V, 313; McWhiney, *Braxton Bragg*, I, 283; Connelly, *Army of the Heartland,* 221.

39 Palmer Collection, Western Reserve, Reel 2, Film 2367: Organization formed at Chattanooga during mid-August, 1862; *O.R.*, XVI, Pt. 2, pp. 759, 772, 782, 784; *ibid.*, XVII, Pt. 2, pp. 618-19; *ibid.*, XVI, Pt. 1, p. 1089; Connelly, *Army of the Heartland,* 224-26.

40 Connelly, *Army of the Heartland,* 224-26.

41 McWhiney, *Braxton Bragg*, I, 286-292, 289n34; Stanley F. Horn, *The Army of Tennessee: A Military History* (1941: rpr. Norman: University of Oklahoma Press, 1953), pp. 170-72; Joseph Howard Parks, *General Edmund Kirby Smith, C.S.A.* (Baton Rouge: Louisiana State University Press, 1954), p. 229; Joseph Howard Parks, *General Leonidas Polk, C.S.A., The Fighting Bishop* (Baton Rouge: Louisiana State University Press, 1962), pp. 259-62; Thomas Robson Hay, "Braxton Bragg and the Southern Confederacy," in *Georgia Historical Quarterly,* IX (1925), p. 270; Joseph Wheeler, "Bragg's Invasion of Kentucky," in Robert Underwood Johnson and Clarence Clough Buel, ed., *Battles and Leaders of the Civil War: being for the most part contributions by Union and Confederate Officers,* Vol. III, *Retreat from Gettysburg* (rpr. New York and London: Thomas Yoseloff, 1956), pp. 8, 10; Connelly, *Army of the Heartland,* 233-36; T. Harry Williams, "The Military Leadership of North and South," in David Donald, ed., *Why the North Won the Civil War* (New York: Collier Books, 1960), p. 42; *O.R.*, XVI, Pt. 2, pp. 246-47, 461, 493, 511-14, 516, 784, 988; *ibid.*, XVII, Pt. 2, pp. 144, 174; *ibid.*, XVI, Pt. 1, pp. 6-726, 1090-91. Because Bragg failed to give battle, T. Harry Williams labeled him "the general of the lost opportunity." The "Abstract from Field Return of the Army of the Mississippi, August 27, 1862" indicates 27,816 men present for duty and includes 1,700 men of Preston Smith's brigade which had previously been transferred to Kirby Smith's command. As Buell's combined force numbered 64,000 men, and 25,000 were detached in Middle Tennessee, he must have marched into Kentucky with 39,000 troops and received an additional 8,000 men when Thomas' division arrived on September 20.

42 *O.R.*, XVI, Pt. 2, p. 876; Connelly, *Army of the Heartland,* 236-39, 241-42; McWhiney, *Braxton Bragg*, I, 295-300.

43 *O.R.*, XVI, Pt. 2, pp. 896-98, 903-905.

44 *Ibid.*, Pt. 1, pp. 1091-92; Don Carlos Buell, "East Tennessee and the Campaign of Perryville," in Robert Underwood Johnson and Clarence Buell, ed., *Battles and Leaders of the Civil War: being for the most part contributions by Union and Confederate Officers,* Vol. III, *Retreat from Gettysburg* (Rep. ed. New York and London: Thomas Yoseloff, 1956), p. 47. Hardee was the immediate commander of the Confederates being pressured near Perryville.

[45] *O.R.*, XVI, Pt. 2, p. 558; Frederick H, Dyer, *A Compendium of the War of the Rebellion,* Vol. I, *Number and Organization of the Armies of the United States* (New York and London: Thomas Yoseloff, 1959), pp 432-437; Charles K. Messmer, "City in Conflict: A History of Louisville, Kentucky, 1860-1865 (Unpublished master's thesis, University of Kentucky, 1953), pp. 183-84. The figure of 87,000 effective troops was arrived at after a careful examination of the returns and organization tables appearing in the *Official Records.* It was not based upon the estimates given by the various officers after the battle, especially those estimates given to the "Buell" commission. Also, the figures do not take into account any stragglers.

[46] Messmer, "City in Conflict," 184-86.

[47] *O.R.*, XVI, Pt. 1, p. 1121; Connelly, *Army of the Heartland,* 267-68.

[48] McWhiney, *Braxton Bragg,* I, 321.

[49] Burton Stevenson, ed., *The Home Book of Quotations: Classical and Modern* (10th ed. New York: Dodd, Mead & Company, 1967), p. 1867; McWhiney, *Braxton Bragg,* I, 321; Connelly, *Army of the Heartland,* 270-76.

[50] Connelly, *Army of the Heartland,* 279-80.

[51] Sarah Ridley Trimble, ed., "Behind the Lines in Middle Tennessee, 1863-1865: The Journal of Bettie Ridley Blackmore," *Tennessee Historical Quarterly,* XII (1953), p. 54, cited in McWhiney, *Braxton Bragg,* I, 383.

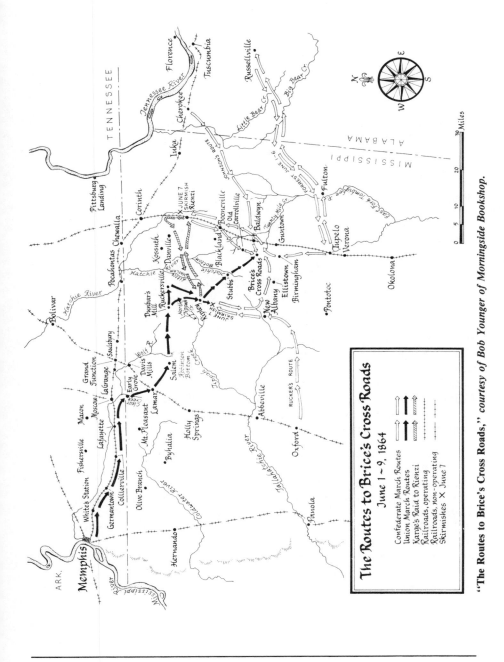

The Routes to Brice's Cross Roads

June 1 ~ 9, 1864

Confederate March Routes
Union March Routes
Karge's Raid to Rienzi
Railroads, operating
Railroads, non-operating
Skirmishes X June 7

"**The Routes to Brice's Cross Roads**," *courtesy of Bob Younger of Morningside Bookshop.*

73

Bedford Forrest and His "Critter" Cavalry at Brice's Cross Roads

Edwin C. Bearss

The spring and summer of 1864 found the attention of the people of the North and of the South focused on the fighting in Virginia and Georgia. In these states, mighty armies fought battles that were to decide whether the United States was to be one nation or two. Interwoven with and having important repercussions on the fighting in Georgia were military operations in northeast Mississippi designed to prevent a Confederate cavalry corps under Nathan Bedford Forrest from striking into Middle Tennessee and destroying the single-track railroads over which Major General William T. Sherman's armies drew their supplies. The Battle of Brice's Cross Roads was fought to protect these railroads.

By the spring of 1864 almost three years of bloodshed and heartbreak had passed since the firing on Fort Sumter signaled the beginning of the Civil War. In the West, an army led by Major General Ulysses S. Grant, supported by the U.S. Navy, had won a series of victories and had forced the surrender of Vicksburg in July of 1863. The fall of Port Hudson a few days later gave Union forces control of the Mississippi River and divided the Confederacy. At Missionary Ridge in the fourth week of November, 1863, armies under Grant had driven the Confederates from the approaches to Chattanooga and recovered the initiative that had belonged to the South in that region since the Battle of Chickamauga in September. In the east, General Robert E. Lee's Army of Northern Virginia, despite its costly defeat at Gettysburg, remained a powerful fighting machine and guarded the approaches to Richmond.

Because of Grant's successes in the west, President Abraham Lincoln brought him east and in early March of 1864, promoted him to lieutenant general, and gave him command of all United States armies. Vowing to defeat the Confederacy, Grant proposed to employ the North's superior resources to grind it down in a war of attrition. Costs would be high, but the North could replace its losses while the South could not. In his planning, there was one factor that Grant could not overlook; if the major Confederate armies were still in the field in November, the electorate might send the Lincoln administration down to defeat at the polls. It was crucial that Northern armies either defeat the South or score sweeping successes by November. A stalemate would be as bad a blow as a defeat.

Grant proposed to concentrate his efforts on the destruction of the two major Confederate armies and thus end the long, drawn-out war. He would personally oversee the movements of the forces whose goal was the defeat of Lee's Army of Northern Virginia, by maintaining his headquarters with the Army of the Potomac. In the west, Sherman, who had succeeded Grant as commander of the Military Division of the Mississippi, was to destroy General Joseph E. Johnston's Army of Tennessee.

On May 7, 1864, coordinating his movements with Grant's, Sherman put his armies in motion through the maze of timber-clad rocky ridges of northwestern Georgia, skillfully employing his superior numbers to outflank successive Confederate positions and compelling Johnston to fall back again and again. But, by May 25, the Federal advance had been checked, for the time being, in front of New Hope Church. Although he had thrust deeply into Confederate territory, Sherman had failed to defeat Johnston, as the Southern leader yielded ground to gain time. As Sherman's troops battled their way forward, their supply lines lengthened and became increasingly vulnerable to Confederate cavalry raids.

There was only one cavalry leader, in the North or the South, whom Sherman respected and that was forty-two-year-old Nathan Bedford Forrest. A self-made man with only six months of schooling, Forrest had entered Confederate service as a private, and by repeated demonstrations of personal bravery, leadership, and audacity, he had risen to the rank of major general.

Holding no respect for soldiers who fought by the book, Forrest attributed his many successes to the simple fact that he "got there first with the most men." Standing six-feet-two inches tall and being of powerful build, he was always ready to engage the foe personally or to thrash any of his own men guilty of malingering. Wounded four times, no other American general has killed as many enemy soldiers with his own hands or has had as many horses—twenty-nine—shot from under him. His words of command as he led a charge were "Forward, men, and mix with 'em!"

Forrest led a cavalry corps based in northeast Mississippi. His corps was effective, because he used it as mounted infantry. The men rode horses and mules to the scene of action, but Forrest habitually made them fight on foot. Unlike most cavalry units, his men worked hard and could wreck a railroad as efficiently as Sherman's infantry. As Sherman's supply line lengthened, the Federal commander feared that "that devil Forrest" would get into Middle Tennessee and break the railroads behind him.

When Forrest was in West Tennessee and western Kentucky in March and April, Sherman telegraphed the commander in Memphis, Major General Cadwalader C. Washburn, not to disturb the Confederate cavalryman, because Forrest could do as much harm by "cavorting over the country" as he could there in West Tennessee. Grant, however, saw that Forrest was recruiting his com-

Major General Nathan Bedford Forrest
Library of Congress

Brigadier General Hylan B. Lyon
Library of Congress

Brigadier General Samuel D. Sturgis
Library of Congress

Colonel Joseph Kargé
Library of Congress

Brigadier General Benjamin H. Grierson
National Archives

Colonel William L. McMillen
Ohio MOLLUS

Colonel George E. Waring
Library of Congress

mand while harassing and destroying isolated Union garrisons, and he directed Sherman to send enough troops to Memphis to chase Forrest back into Mississippi.

Sherman's first task was to find an officer equal to the challenge. Brigadier General Samuel D. Sturgis, an 1846 graduate of U.S. Military Academy and an "old army" man, was chosen. A veteran of Wilson's Creek, where he won promotion for "gallant and meritorious conduct," Sturgis had also served in the Army of the Potomac. In the winter of 1863-64, he had been commended for his cavalry leadership in East Tennessee. He had a chance to test Forrest in the first week of May while the Federals were chasing the Confederates out of West Tennessee. His columns, however, moved too slowly and the Southerners outdistanced them. Reporting to his superiors on May 7, Sturgis wrote: "It was with the greatest reluctance that I resolved to abandon the chase. Although we could not catch the scoundrel we are at least rid of him."

As Sherman's armies pressed deeper into Georgia, Johnston knew that the only way to stop their advance was to destroy the Federal supply line—the railroads from Nashville and Chattanooga. Accordingly, he appealed to Major General Stephen D. Lee for help in breaking these rail lines.

Lee, a graduate of the U.S. Military Academy, commanded the Department of Alabama, Mississippi and East Louisiana. Destined at thirty to become the Confederacy's youngest lieutenant general, his dark hair, beard, and eyes gave him a cavalier look. He had been present when the first shot was fired at Fort Sumter and had served as an artillerist in the Army of Northern Virginia until after the Battle of Antietam in September of 1862. He had then been transferred to the west and led an infantry brigade in Lieutenant General John C. Pemberton's army of Vicksburg. After Pemberton's surrender in July, 1863, Lee was exchanged and placed in command of all the cavalry in Mississippi. He had assumed responsibility for the department in May, 1864, after the previous commander, Lieutenant General Leonidas Polk, and most of Polk's soldiers, joined Johnston for the Georgia campaign.

Responding to Johnston's plea, Lee ordered Forrest and his cavalry to advance into Middle Tennessee and wreck the Nashville & Chattanooga Railroad. Forrest moved promptly. On June 1, he rode out of Tupelo, Mississippi, with two thousand hell-for-leather horsemen and a battery of artillery. Three days later, at Russellville in north Alabama, Forrest was overtaken by a courier with a message from Lee reporting that a powerful Union column had left Memphis to invade Mississippi. Forrest was told to forget the Middle Tennessee raid and to return to Tupelo.

In response to a call from Sherman, to send a formidable expedition toward Tupelo, or in whatever direction Forrest happened to be, Washburn ordered

Sturgis to advance from Memphis. Sturgis' force, which moved out on June 1, mustered forty-eight hundred infantry, thirty-three hundred cavalry, four hundred artillerists with twenty-two cannon, and a large supply train. The little army was organized into two divisions—one of infantry and the other of cavalry. Brigadier General Benjamin H. Grierson, a former music teacher from Jacksonville, Illinois, and now one of the North's best cavalrymen, led Sturgis' horse-soldiers, one regiment of whom were armed with seven-shot Spencer carbines. Colonel William McMillen, who had served with the Russian army as a surgeon in the Crimean War and had led the 95th Ohio Infantry during the Vicksburg campaign, commanded the infantry. McMillen was hot tempered and fond of whiskey.

Sturgis was to strike the Mobile & Ohio Railroad at or near Corinth and to destroy any force that might be posted there. He then was to proceed down the railroad, at least as far as Okolona, wreck it and to return to Memphis by way of Grenada. Forrest's corps, during this sweep, would be dispersed and destroyed and the countryside devastated.

At Lamar, Sturgis' scouts told him that the Confederates had evacuated Corinth and retired down the railroad. Sturgis changed his line of march to intersect the railroad farther south. On the 5th, Grierson, who had the lead, sent four hundred of his horse soldiers racing eastward to Rienzi. The Federals reached the railroad and did some damage and then rode northward until they found their way barred by rain-swollen Tuscumbia Creek.

Heavy rains pelted Sturgis' column as it bore southeastward through an area that had been ravaged by two years of raids and counter-raids. It was June 7 before Sturgis' infantry reached Ripley, seventy-five miles from Memphis. During the day, one of Grierson's brigades reconnoitered the New Albany Road and encountered a roadblock manned by two regiments sent out by Forrest to feel for the Federals. In the meantime, Sturgis advanced down Guntown Road. By nightfall on the 9th his command was concentrated and camped on Stubbs' farm, nine miles northeast of Brice's Cross Roads.

Forrest had returned to Tupelo from the aborted Middle Tennessee raid on June 5. Told about the general direction of Sturgis' march and that the Federals had broken the railroad at Rienzi, Forrest ordered two brigades to that point. Colonel Tyree Bell's Tennessee brigade stopped at Rienzi, and Forrest, with his artillery and escort and Colonel Hylan B. Lyon's brigade, took position at Booneville, where he was joined by Colonel Edward Rucker's brigade on the evening of June 9. Rucker's people had clashed with Sturgis' vanguard near New Albany, forty-eight hours earlier. Forrest also had one brigade—Colonel William A. Johnson's—at Baldwyn. Lee reached Booneville on the 9th and went immediately to Forrest's headquarters for a briefing.

After examining Forrest's troop returns and learning that his force numbered about forty-nine hundred cavalry and twelve cannon, Lee suggested that Forrest retire toward Okolona and let Sturgis push deeper into Mississippi and farther from his base before giving him battle. Forrest was to move out on June 10 in the direction of Brice's Cross Roads and then to continue on toward Okolona. Lee, accompanied by two batteries of artillery, then boarded a southbound train for Okolona.

That evening, June 9, Forrest called a number of his officers together. He told them that his spies had reported the Federals encamped at Stubbs' farm and that, while he would prefer to get them into the open country where he could "get a good look at them" as Lee desired, the Confederates might be drawn into a battle before that could be realized. Orders were issued for the brigade and artillery commanders to have their men ready to ride before daylight and to push forward as rapidly as possible toward Brice's Cross Roads.

Torrential rains, which did not cease until after midnight, turned the roads into ribbons of mud. When the sun rose, many knew that it would be one of those hot humid days which saps a man's energy. As Forrest traveled with Rucker's brigade, he told Rucker that he intended to attack Sturgis at Brice's Cross Roads and outlined his battle plan:

> I know they greatly outnumber the troops I have at hand but the road along which they will march is narrow and muddy; they will make slow progress. The country is densely wooded and the undergrowth so heavy that when we strike them they will not know how few men we have. Their cavalry will move out ahead of the infantry, and should reach the crossroads three hours in advance. We can whip their cavalry in that time. As soon as the fight opens they will send back to have infantry hurried up. It is going to be as hot as hell, and coming on a run for five or six miles over such roads, their infantry will be so tired out we will ride over them.

Forrest then pushed ahead to join his advance brigade of Kentuckians commanded by Lyon, an officer described by a Federal general as "a very rude and overbearing character." Unlike the Confederates, the Federals did not make an early start on June 10. It was 5:30 A.M. before Grierson's horse-soldiers swung into their saddles and started down Guntown Road; it was seven o'clock before the infantry marched.

Grierson's vanguard encountered, charged, and scattered a Forrest's scouting party, chasing the Rebels across the narrow bridge spanning Tishomingo Creek. By 9:45 the Union cavalry held Brice's Cross Roads, and one brigade had followed the retreating Confederates for a mile along Baldwyn Road. At the edge of a field, the Federals reined up their horses when they sighted Lyon's vanguard on the opposite side of a field, four hundred yards away. While two of his companies charged the surprised Yanks, Lyon dismounted and deployed his eight hundred-man brigade. Grierson did likewise, forming his thirty-two hundred horse soldiers to the left and right of the road. Like the Confederates, most of the Federals fought on foot.

Forrest knew that he would have to gain and hold the initiative, or the "bulge," as he called it. Lyon's Kentuckians were advanced. For almost an hour, the Confederates drove forward, then retired, and advanced again. A great quantity of powder was burned and a few men killed or wounded, but Grierson, unfortunately for the Union, had allowed himself to be bluffed by an inferior force.

Rucker's brigade now came up on a trot and formed on Lyon's left. Once again, Forrest waved his men forward. There was the sharp crack of small arms and the roar of artillery as the Confederates moved forward. On Forrest's left, one of his battalions advanced too far and was sent reeling. Johnson's 590-man brigade arrived from Baldwyn, and Forrest posted it on Lyon's right. As soon as the troopers had dismounted, they feigned an attack on Grierson's left.

It was now eleven o'clock, and although Bell's brigade and his artillery had not reached the front, Forrest decided to assault Grierson. He rode along his line and encouraged his men, telling them that he expected everyone to advance when the signal was given. At the sound of the bugle, the dismounted cavalry stormed across the field toward the Federals. Grierson's men held their ground and blazed away. At one point, Rucker's brigade penetrated Grierson's line, but the Federals called up two reserve regiments to close the breach. As the Yanks rushed forward, Rucker shouted for his men to draw "their six-shooters and close with them hand-to-hand." (Each man in Forrest's corps was armed with a rifled musket and two Colt revolvers. Forrest refused to arm his enlisted men with sabers, because he considered them useless in the type of fighting he favored.) After a desperate struggle, the Federals were forced to retire closer to Brice's Cross Roads. By 12:30 Forrest had whipped Grierson's cavalry.

Grierson, on encountering the enemy, had sent a courier galloping to tell Sturgis that he had found the Confederates and needed help. As Forrest brought up fresh units and increased the pressure, Grierson repeated his pleas for reinforcements with greater urgency. It was noon before Sturgis reached the field and after 1 P.M. before the advance columns of his infantry arrived, though they had marched as fast as road and weather conditions permitted. They had tramped nine miles since seven o'clock; the "last three miles had been made at a trot, and the final mile at a double-quick."

The thirty-two hundred infantry and their three supporting batteries struggled into position covering the crossroads, their left extending well north of Baldwyn Road and their right anchored about two hundred yards west of Guntown Road. West of Tishomingo Creek was Colonel Edward Bouton's reserve brigade of black soldiers and the army's trains. Covered by the infantry, Grierson sought to re-form his exhausted division.

Bell's Tennessee brigade and Captain John W. Morton's artillery now came up. The Confederate cannoneers, having traveled eighteen miles, rode up at a trot, threw their eight guns into battery, and hammered away at Sturgis' masses with telling effect. The Union artillerists replied. Placing himself at the head of Bell's brigade, Forrest rode to the left, dismounted, and formed the newcomers. While Forrest was positioning Bell, the fighting ebbed. The only sounds were the occasional crack of a sharpshooter's rifle-musket, the rustle of underbrush as men moved about, and the hushed commands of officers. The weather was stifling—there was not a cloud in the sky and the air was still. Several men had been felled by sunstroke.

Forrest attacked. Because of the thick undergrowth covering most of the area, the Confederates were able to close to within a few paces of Sturgis' infantry. A crashing volley, however, sent part of Bell's battle line reeling. The Federals called for a charge. Forrest's sixth sense had placed him at the key point. As he dismounted, he shouted for his escort to do likewise. Accompanied by these daring fighters and with revolver in hand, he rushed the Federals. Additional men came up, and the counterattack was repulsed. In the hand-to-hand fighting, the bayonets of the Union infantry were no match for the heavy Colt revolvers. The center of Sturgis' line crumbled, while the Confederate brigades on the right doubled back the Union left upon Ripley Road.

Off to the northwest in the direction of Tishomingo Creek, the 2d Tennessee Regiment, sent out by Bell to attack Sturgis' left and rear, had reached its objective "just as the fighting seemed heaviest in front." To deceive the Federals about their strength, the Confederates made a great commotion and a bugler galloped up and down the line sounding the charge. Not only did this show of force throw Sturgis' reserve brigade and the train guard into confusion, but Grierson sent off most of his cavalry to check the advance of the 2d Tennessee.

Forrest knew that the crisis had come and that now the battle must be won or lost. Riding along behind his line, he told his people that the enemy was starting to give way and that another charge would win the day. He told his young chief of artillery, Captain Morton, to be ready to advance four of his guns, double shotted with canister, to within pistol range of the Federals at the crossroads. When the bugle sounded, the Confederate battle line pressed forward. At the same time, Morton's cannoneers drove their teams up the narrow country road. At point-blank range, they unlimbered their pieces and fired double-shotted canister into Sturgis' infantry with frightful effect. After a brief but savage fight, the Federals were routed from the crossroads, with the loss of three cannon.

General Sturgis grimly described this phase of the fight:

> I now endeavored to get hold of the colored brigade which formed the guard of the wagon train. While traversing the short distance to where the head of the brigade should be found, the main line began to give way at various points. Order soon gave way to confusion, and confusion to panic. The army drifted toward the rear and was beyond control. The road became crowded and jammed with troops. Wagons and artillery sank into the deep mud and became inextricable. No power could check the panic-stricken mass as it swept towards the rear.

Several regiments, reinforced by two companies of the 55th U.S. Colored Troops that had crossed to the east side of Tishomingo Creek, attempted to check the onrushing Confederates; but, assailed on the flanks, with Morton's guns sweeping their front with doubled-shotted canister, the Northerners broke. To add to the Federals' embarrassment, a fleeing teamster's wagon overturned on the narrow wooden bridge over rain-swollen Tishomingo Creek and the men were forced to climb over the wreckage. In their frantic efforts to escape, soldiers pushed their comrades aside. Others, seeing it was hopeless to cross the bridge, attempted to wade or swim the creek. Many were drowned or shot as they floundered in the water.

On reaching the bridge, Forrest's men cleared it by pushing the wagons and the dead and wounded teams into the creek. Meanwhile, Forrest's escort forded the stream about four hundred yards south of the bridge and bore down on the flank of the panic-stricken Federals. A number of prisoners were taken, along with some wagons. Although the sun was about to set, Forrest brought up his horse holders and personally took charge of the pursuit. A mile beyond the bridge, some of Sturgis' infantry rallied, but Morton brought up two guns and smashed this pocket of resistance, and as dusk faded into darkness, Forrest and his hell-for-leather troopers overpowered another roadblock hastily manned by black and white Union soldiers. Forrest then halted his command to let his men and their mounts get a few hours rest. During their night-time crossing of Hatchie Bottom, Sturgis and many of his officers and men panicked, and they abandoned fourteen cannon and most of their wagon train.

Forrest had his people back in the saddle before daybreak and pressed the pursuit relentlessly. The Federals passed through Ripley, twenty-two miles from

Brice's Cross Roads. Here Sturgis attempted to re-form his command. But the Confederates came up too soon, and the Federals' retreat was resumed. Not until he reached Salem at dark did Forrest call off the chase. Sturgis' column, which had taken eight days to reach Brice's Cross Roads, retreated to Memphis in sixty-four hours. Union casualties in the fight and retreat were 2,612. Forrest listed his losses as 493 killed and wounded. The Confederates captured 250 wagons and ambulances, 18 cannon, and thousands of stands of arms and rounds of ammunition, as well as the Federals' baggage and supplies.

A noted British soldier, Field Marshal Viscount Garnet J. Wolseley, in commenting on Forrest's victory, called it

> a most remarkable achievement, well worth attention by the military student. He pursued the enemy from the battle for nigh sixty miles, killing numbers all the way. The battle and his long pursuit were all accomplished in the space of thirty hours. When another Federal General was dispatched to try what he could do against this terrible Southerner, the defeated Sturgis was overheard repeating to himself...: "It can't be done, sir: it c-a-n-t be done!" Asked what he meant, the reply was, "They c-a-n-t whip old Forrest!"

Mansfield Lovell

Arthur W. Bergeron, Jr.

Joseph E. Johnston called him one "of the best officers whose services we can command" and pronounced him "as fit to command [a] division as any [man] in our service."[1] Judah P. Benjamin described him as "a brilliant, energetic, and accomplished officer."[2] Braxton Bragg remembered him as "one of the best artillery officers in the old service."[3] His old and close friend Gustavus W. Smith praised him with these words: "Possessed of extraordinary physical strength, activity and endurance—with mental ability of a very high order—training and experience in military and civil service as well as in ordinary business pursuits— brave almost to the point of rashness—in conduct and character guided by the highest sense of right...."[4]

If you did not already know the subject of my paper, all of you might wonder to whom these compliments refer. Certainly, the name of Mansfield Lovell would be one of the last to occur to most Civil War buffs and scholars. The few of them who recognize his name know that he was a Northerner who joined the Confederate army after First Manassas and who tried unsuccessfully to defend the important city of New Orleans. In fact, about the only time his name even appears in writings about the conflict is when authors blame him for the fall of New Orleans. Criticism fell heavily on Lovell both during the war and in the years immediately thereafter. Professor Daniel E. Sutherland wrote in a 1983 article, "Lovell was a man condemned, and subsequent historians were slow to give him justice."[5]

Sutherland's article, entitled "Mansfield Lovell's Quest for Justice: Another Look at the fall of New Orleans," sparked my interest in the general. Sutherland expanded upon work begun by New Orleans newspaperman and historian Charles L. "Pie" Dufour. In his book *The Night the War Was Lost* and in an article written the next year, Dufour demonstrated that Lovell had been made the scapegoat for the loss of the Crescent City. He stated that President Jefferson Davis deserved the blame and criticized him for his "utterly unjust treatment of General Lovell."[6] Using sources unknown or unavailable to Dufour, Sutherland delved more deeply into the controversy. He concluded, "It is almost certain—as certain as it can be without a written confession—that Davis actively and consciously sought to make Lovell the 'victim' demanded by the Confederate people and history."[7]

The questions in my mind created by Sutherland's work had nothing to do with his or Dufour's assessment of blame for the fall of New Orleans or with

Major General Mansfield Lovell. *Courtesy of Library of Congress*

Davis' actions in making Lovell a scapegoat. I began to wonder about the general's background, how he came to receive command of the defense of the Confederacy's most important city, and what the rest of his Civil War career was like. No historian has ever attempted a biography of Lovell, so I planned to write one. When Larry Hewitt asked me to participate in this symposium, I had not yet begun to follow up on my desire to look more deeply at Lovell. The biography was just one of several of those "irons in the fire." My paper today is, hopefully, just the first step toward the completion of the project. With that caveat in mind, what follows is a tentative look at this little known Confederate general.

Born in Washington, D.C., on October 20, 1822, Mansfield Lovell was the first son of Dr. Joseph and Margaret E. Lovell. Dr. Lovell was the first surgeon general of the United States Army Medical Department and had received that appointment four years before his son's birth. He came from Massachusetts. His grandfather had served in the Continental Congress and had signed the Articles of Confederation, and his father had fought in the Continental Army during the American Revolution. Mansfield's mother came from an old New York family. Both of his parents died within a few weeks of each other in 1836, and he lived for two years with a guardian in New York.[8]

Lovell received an appointment to the United States Military Academy in 1838 and graduated ninth in a class of fifty-six on July 1, 1842. His classmates included twenty-one men who became generals during the Civil War. Among them were Earl Van Dorn, James Longstreet, John Pope, William S. Rosecrans, Martin Luther Smith, Abner Doubleday, and Gustavus Smith. After graduation, Lovell became a second lieutenant in the 4th United States Artillery. He continued to study while on active duty, and his friend Gustavus Smith said "he was soon recognized as one of the most prominent young officers in the artillery" service.[9] The 4th Artillery formed a part of Major General Zachary Taylor's army when the Mexican War began in 1846. Lovell fought in the Battle of Monterey and was wounded.[10]

Shortly after this engagement, Lovell became chief of staff to Brigadier General John A. Quitman of Mississippi. That volunteer general was commander of a brigade in Taylor's army. Gustavus Smith claimed that Quitman had asked the younger regular army officers in the army to recommend someone for the position on his staff and that "with great unanimity they named Mansfield Lovell."[11] Regardless of the circumstances of his appointment, Lovell and Quitman soon became very good friends. The latter's biographer wrote that they "established a close intellectual and personal relationship."[12] In the late 1850s, two of Lovell's brothers married Quitman's daughters. This relationship between Lovell and Quitman probably became like that between a father and son.

After Quitman's death, Lovell wrote a letter to one of his daughters. He said that the general had "inspired, 'especially in his younger friends a confiding reliance and affectionate regard, much akin to the holy feeling that should exist between child and parent.' "[13]

Lovell, now a first lieutenant, accompanied Quitman after he was transferred to the army of General Winfield Scott. Quitman eventually received command of a division, and his men played an important part in the campaign from Vera Cruz to the City of Mexico. In a reconnaissance with Quitman just before the battle of Chapultepec, Lovell performed bravely. Though several times exposed to heavy enemy fire, he succeeded in pinpointing important enemy positions and in leading to safety a small group of soldiers threatened with capture by the Mexicans. The next day, during the assault on the Belen Gate, Lovell received his second wound of the war. He and engineer Lieutenant Pierre G. T. Beauregard were sent by Quitman to investigate white flags raised over Mexico City. The officers left in charge surrendered the place to them. Lovell signalled the general that all was well, and Quitman's troops marched into the capital.[14]

At the end of the war, Lovell returned to his artillery company. He received a brevet as captain for gallantry at Chapultepec. Because the company's other officers had all been killed or wounded, Lovell became its commander when it was reorganized as a regular light artillery battery. He held this command until 1851. At that time, he was assigned to another company of the 4th Artillery stationed at Fort Hamilton in New York Harbor. Lovell married Emily M. Plimpton, the daughter of an army officer who had served in the War of 1812, Seminole War, and Mexican War. In 1854, Lovell resigned his commission and went to work for Cooper & Hewitt's Iron Works in Trenton, New Jersey.[15]

Lovell's friendship with Quitman continued after the Mexican War ended. The latter became involved in a number of filibustering schemes that had Cuba as their objective, and he brought Lovell into several of them. In 1850, Narciso Lopez planned an invasion of the island. He visited Quitman, then governor of Mississippi, and "offered Quitman command of the filibuster army and rulership over a Cuban republic if the invasion force...proved successful."[16] The governor wrote to Lovell and asked if he was interested in participating. Quitman tempted Lovell with the possibility of becoming either a Prime Minister or Secretary of War in the new government. Eventually, Quitman declined the command offered by Lopez but did assist him in his preparations.[17]

Several years after the failure of Lopez's campaigns against Cuba, Quitman again began looking toward acquiring the island for the United States. Lovell visited him at his plantation near Natchez in November of 1852 and talked about Quitman's plans. In July, 1853, Quitman spent several weeks in the North seeking support for an invasion. Not until late 1854 and early 1855 did he begin formalizing his command structure. Quitman's most recent biographer wrote: "Exact ranks and assignments within Quitman's invasion hierarchy remain unclear, but important spots went to Mansfield Lovell...Gustavus Woodson Smith, and Jones M. Withers....Lovell and Smith both resigned *their* commissions as of December 18, so that they would be free to go whenever Quitman gave the signal."[18] The opposition of President Franklin Pierce and Spanish reinforcements to Cuba caused Quitman to end his scheme in early 1855.[19]

This long and close relationship between Lovell and Quitman explains in large part, I believe, the former's support of the South and Southern rights during the 1850s. Smith pointed to the "rebel" tradition in the Lovell family as one reason for that support. He wrote that Lovell's "deep seated and firm convictions on [the] subject [of Southern rights] were based upon thorough knowledge of the history of the country from the time of the declaration of independence made by the thirteen British colonies."[20] Yet, since Professor Robert E. May describes Quitman as "the premier secessionist of antebellum Mississippi" and "one of the half dozen or so most prominent radicals and the most strident slavery imperialist in the entire South," his influence had to have been predominent in Lovell's life.[21]

The Lovell-Quitman friendship may also have been a factor in Lovell's future problems with Jefferson Davis. Quitman and Davis were personal and political rivals. This antagonism dated from the Mexican War when Davis had served under Quitman. According to one source, that relationship "provoked each of them to revile each other."[22] As Pierce's Secretary of War, Davis played a role in blunting Quitman's designs on Cuba. Davis undoubtedly knew that Lovell was one of Quitman's proteges and must have held that against him.

Lovell's association with filibustering created friendships with a number of army officers, some of whom would later recommend him for a position in the Confederate army and support him after the fall of New Orleans. One of these was Beauregard, for whom Quitman wrote a letter of recommendation when the Louisianian considered joining William Walker in Nicaragua. Another frustrated former army officer who toyed with the idea of going to Nicaragua was George B. McClellan. In an 1857 letter to Little Mac, Johnson K. Duncan, also one of Lovell's friends, voiced the frustrations many of these men felt after leaving the army: "You, Lovell, G. W. [Smith] and myself are anything but satisfied with our present occupations."[23]

Lovell apparently tried to recruit four thousand Americans for an army to support Benito Juarez and his liberal party in the Mexican civil war. In February of 1858, he wrote McClellan offering him a leadership role in the army and stated, "If we could raise money I would send you a call in less than 3 months."[24] Even Joseph Johnston became tempted to participate in this Mexican adventure. He had been friends with Smith, Lovell, McClellan, and other younger officers for some years. The group received no encouragement from the Juarez regime, and their plans fizzled out. When Johnston became quartermaster general in 1860, he received congratulations from Lovell and Smith. He wrote them an acknowledgement and said, "Filibusters are doing better, I think, than Filibustering."[25]

In April, 1858, Lovell became superintendent of street improvements for New York City. The following November, his old friend Smith named him to the higher position of deputy street commissioner shortly after Smith assumed the duties as street commissioner. During the next year, Lovell received command of a militia company known as the City Guard. It was "composed of about one hundred gentlemen of means and position" in the city.[26] Lovell trained the men in both infantry and artillery drill, making them particularly efficient in the latter. He opposed the election of Abraham Lincoln after the latter's nomination in the summer of 1860. Lovell supported the Crittenden Compromise and other measures that he thought would avert an armed conflict between the sections.[27]

Various Southerners began contacting Lovell and Smith about supporting their cause as early a December of 1860. In that month, Beauregard visited with them on his way to assume his duties as superintendent at West Point. He told them that if Louisiana seceded from the Union he would leave the army. Lovell and Smith apparently told him "that they would act in the same manner" if similar circumstances occurred.[28] Braxton Bragg wrote to the two after his appointment as commander of the Louisiana State Army in early February, 1861. He was seeking "experienced soldiers to command and train his volunteer army" and may have offered Smith and Lovell commissions. Bragg did ask their recommendations on other former army personnel whom he might also contact. Lovell replied to Bragg's letter without naming anyone, but he asked "what might [non-commissioned officers] expect in the way of rank?"[29] Bragg interpreted this letter to mean that Lovell wanted assurance of specific rank before he would join the Southern cause.

Jefferson Davis sent Raphael Semmes to New York in February of 1861 to purchase weapons and other supplies for the newly formed Confederate States of America. He instructed Semmes to contact Lovell and Smith while on his mission. Davis wanted him to tell them the South "would be happy to have their services in our army."[30] Later that month, Davis asked Beauregard to contact some of his friends about becoming bureau heads. One of Beauregard's letters went to Lovell and Smith, and he inquired when the Confederacy could expect them to offer their services. Smith replied that both he and Lovell sympathized with the seceded states though not citizens of any of them. He went on to say that he and Lovell thought that either Davis or his Secretary of War would make them a direct offer. Smith stated that if such an offer were made and "if [it were] up to our standard (as we understand it)" they would favorably consider it "and in all probability" accept it.[31]

Some of this correspondence makes it sound as if Lovell and Smith were trying to sell their services to the highest bidder. In fact, Bragg later criticized Lovell for his "mercenary" actions. This criticism was, I believe, unjustified. Though perhaps a biased account, Smith wrote after Lovell's death that the latter had "no shadow of doubt in his mind in regard to the legal and moral right of the course he pursued" in supporting Southern independence.[32] Smith and Lovell obviously wanted some kind of official assurance that Davis really wanted them in the Confederate army and an idea of what rank they would be offered. Considering Davis' hatred of Quitman and possible dislike of his friends, Smith and Lovell's wariness in understandable. Lovell's sentiments were expressed in a letter to McClellan after the surrender of Fort Sumter. He told Little Mac that he and Smith "had sworn they would never submit to 'throat-cutting' abolitionists who sought to give blacks 'political & civil equality with the white man,' a doctrine [that]...the South would resist to the death."[33]

Another criticism leveled at Lovell was that he did not go south until four months after the war started. His detractors doubted his dedication to the cause because he had waited so long to offer his services to the Confederacy. It is interesting that the same attack was not made on Smith. Of course, the latter was a native of Kentucky, and it could be argued that like that state he chose not to take sides until Kentucky's neutrality was violated. Because of illness, Smith could not leave New York City when war broke out, and he did not reach Lexington, Kentucky, until late July or early August. Perhaps Lovell chose not to make his way south until his friend could travel. He left his family in New York City and accompanied Smith to Lexington. The latter wrote after the war that Lovell had hoped that an armed conflict could be avoided and that he did not resign his job as deputy street commissioner until "he became satisfied that the Northern States would use all the resources of the general government...to keep the Southern States in the Union at the point of bayonet."[34]

Having learned that his two old friends had reached Lexington, Joe Johnston on August 19 recommended them to Davis as division commanders in his army around Manassas. Johnston wrote Davis that Lovell and Smith had "always wanted to serve us" but had "not come forward [before], because, not belonging to seceded states, they didn't know how [they] would be received."[35] The two did not get to Richmond until September 11. Confederate forces had violated Kentucky's neutrality by occupying Columbus seven days before and this undoubtedly prompted them to offer their services to the Confederacy. Smith received a commission as major general on the nineteenth and soon was leading a division in Johnston's army.[36] So far I have found no evidence why Davis did not make Lovell a general at that time or whether Lovell was considered for a command under Johnston.

Yet, Lovell was in the right place at the right time. The government in Richmond began receiving complaints about Major General David E. Twiggs, commander of Department No. 1. That military department consisted of Louisiana and the Gulf Coast counties of Mississippi and Alabama and had as its primary mission the defense of New Orleans. Former Louisiana Governor Andre B. Roman wrote Davis, "In spite of his good intentions the infirmities of General Twiggs, which confine him to his armchair, disqualify him completely for the situation he holds."[37] The seventy-two-year-old general realized that he needed assistance and asked the War Department to send two brigadier generals to the Crescent City as soon as possible. On September 25, Lovell was made a brigadier general and ordered to report to Twiggs. He would have charge of the coastal defenses of the department, an assignment that undoubtedly resulted from his recognized experience as an artillery officer. A week later, the War Department directed Brigadier General Daniel Ruggles to proceed from Pensacola, Florida, to New Orleans as an additional subordinate to Twiggs.[38]

Prominent Louisianians continued to ask Davis and Secretary of War Judah P. Benjamin to assign a competent officer to replace Twiggs. Finally, on October 5, the old general wired Richmond that because of his ill health he wanted someone sent to relieve him in command of Department No. 1. For some reason, Lovell had not yet left the capital. On October 6, he travelled to Fairfax Courthouse, Virginia, to consult with Beauregard on the defense of New Orleans. The next day, the War Department promoted Lovell to the rank of major general and named him as Twiggs' replacement. Twiggs received instructions to remain on duty until Lovell arrived. Lovell left Richmond on October 10 and made a brief stop in Norfolk, where his family had just arrived from New York under a flag of truce.[39]

Secretary of War Benjamin may have played a role in Lovell's assignment. In a letter to Joe Johnston, Benjamin called Lovell a "justly-esteemed officer."[40] Benjamin described Lovell to Louisiana Governor Thomas O. Moore as "a brilliant, energetic, and accomplished officer" when informing that official of Lovell's assignment.[41] John B. Jones, a clerk in the War Department, intimated in his diary that Benjamin was responsible for Lovell's and Smith's appointments as generals. Late in 1861, Davis considered removing the Mississippi counties along the coast from Department No. 1 and adding them to Bragg's department, but Benjamin persuaded him to leave the area under Lovell.[42] To date, I have found no pre-war connection between Lovell and Benjamin that would explain why the latter would have had any reason to favor Lovell. Benjamin was from Louisiana, and he may have seen Lovell's experience as an artillery officer as a good qualification for sending him to take over the defense of New Orleans.

Lovell's assignment greatly angered Bragg, commander at Pensacola. He had grown tired of his rather stagnant situation there and desired a more active field, so that he could prove himself as a commander. In a letter to a friend, Bragg stated that Davis had promised him command of the Gulf Coast from Pensacola to New Orleans. When Twiggs made it known that he would retire, Bragg expected the President to "show his sincerity and confer this command on me."[43] Bragg complained to Governor Moore after Lovell's appointment: "The command at New Orleans was rightly mine. I feel myself degraded by the action of the government...."[44] He spoke harshly of Lovell as an "eleventh-hour" convert who had been "purchased in the open market by the highest bidder."[45] While Bragg acknowledged Lovell's competence and energy, he told Moore that "but for his inordinate vanity [Lovell] would be a fine soldier."[46]

Thus, Mansfield Lovell received command of one of the most important points in the Confederacy despite his northern birth and recent appointment as a general. Why would Davis have given such a position to a man he obviously had little reason to reward? Lovell's presence in Richmond as complaints about Twiggs reached the capital may account for his initial commission as a brigadier. Yet, the President did not have to order him to take charge of Department No. 1 when Twiggs asked for relief.

Davis had at least two senior generals he could have sent to New Orleans. He might easily have placed Louisiana under Bragg, unifying the defense of the Gulf Coast. Instead, in the same order that had Lovell relieve Twiggs, the War Department extended Bragg's command to include Alabama (thus reducing Lovell's department).[47] This was obviously an effort to placate one of Davis' favorite officers. Two days prior to this order, Beauregard wrote to Benjamin asking for a transfer to his native state. Disgusted by Davis' refusal to reinforce the army at Manassas so that it could go on the offensive and fearful that the enemy would soon attack the Crescent City, Beauregard wished assignment there. The chief executive responded in a letter that said the Creole general "was too valuable in Virginia to be shifted to another theater."[48] I cannot help but wonder whether Beauregard's request had any effect on Davis' decision to promote Lovell and have him replace Twiggs.

That consideration aside, we still have no answer to the question of why Davis sent Lovell to take command at New Orleans. In the absence of evidence in Davis' writings, I have had to base my conclusion on the President's actions. It is clear that Davis thought that the forts below New Orleans would stop any enemy naval force that tried to ascend the Mississippi River. Thus, he felt that the only real threat to the Crescent City would come from the upper Mississippi River. I see good indications of Davis' low regard for Department No. 1 in his choices of Twiggs as its first commander and of Ruggles as one of the generals sent to aid Twiggs. The latter was obviously too old and infirm for his job. Except for leading a division at the Battle of Shiloh, Ruggles never held an important command during the war. Had Davis really feared for the safety of New Orleans, he would have placed it under Bragg's command or sent another experienced general there. Feeling that no significant fighting would occur in Louisiana, Davis saw little possibility of Lovell gaining any recognition as commander of Department No. 1. In short, it was a "safe" assignment.

Lovell reached New Orleans on October 17 by rail from Jackson, Mississippi, and formally assumed command the next day. The New Orleans press noted his arrival and spoke of him in approving terms: "General Lovell comes among us with a high character for energy and great administrative talents, and with an already distinguished military reputation."[49] He at once began trying to rectify the numerous deficiencies he found in the city's defenses. Pie Dufour has provided a fine summary of his activities. He wrote, "General Lovell's correspondence with Richmond in his first week in New Orleans shows how quickly and efficiently he sized up the situation, evaluating needs with the eye and knowledge of an experienced and energetic officer. Lovell's energy indeed was boundless."[50]

Davis tied Lovell's hands from the very first, making it virtually impossible for him to successfully defend the city against a strong naval attack. Before he left Richmond, Lovell spoke to both Davis and Benjamin about exercising command over the naval forces at New Orleans and on the lower Mississippi. The President refused to allow Lovell to have any control over the navy. He wrote,

> The fleet maintained at the port of New Orleans and the vicinity is not a part of your command; and the purposes for which it is sent there or removed from there are communicated in orders and letters of a Department with which you have no direct communication. It must, therefore, be obvious to you that you could not assume command of these officers and vessels, coming within the limits of your geographical department, but not placed on duty with you, without serious detriment to discipline and probable injury to the public service....[51]

In January, 1862, Lovell wrote Benjamin complaining about the lack of cooperation from the navy. He reminded Benjamin of his appeal the previous October: "I felt satisfied that if the protection of the navigable streams running up into the country was removed from my control it would in all probability not be properly arranged in connection with the land defenses,...This is just what has happened."[52] Lovell could not order available gunboats to positions where they could best aid the forts on the lower river in resisting an attack. Neither could he push the completion of ironclads under construction at the Crescent City. Although he gave the navy as much assistance as possible, Lovell received little support from its commanders. Davis would not change his original decision, however. As Dufour and others have noted, "the divided command at New Orleans was a vital factor in its fall."[53]

Despite the obstacles he faced, Lovell succeeded in improving the defensive posture of New Orleans. He had entrenchments constructed around the city and organized some fourteen thousand troops for its defense. The men mounted several hundred heavy artillery pieces that had arrived during Twiggs' tenure as commander. Powder mills began turning out several tons of gunpowder a day. Lovell accumulated small arms, medical stores, clothing, and other supplies for his men. Lovell's friend Gustavus Smith made a correct assessment when he wrote, "Within two months after General Lovell took command the military defenses of New Orleans were in condition to successfully resist any land attack that could probably be brought against the city."[54]

Lovell experienced somewhat less success in strengthening Fort Jackson and Fort St. Philip, the masonry forts ninety miles below New Orleans. He sent more men to the forts and supported his subordinates' efforts to improve the men's drill and discipline. Beauregard had suggested to Lovell that he have obstructions placed in the river between the forts. Lovell had his men construct a raft of cypress logs, schooners, and iron cable to block the river. As an artilleryman, he recognized the weakness of the cannons, most of them old smoothbores, mounted in the forts. He attempted unsuccessfully to obtain some columbiads and rifled guns to replace the outdated ordnance. Lovell hoped that with the more effective cannons his men could cause heavy damage to an attacking enemy fleet when it slowed down to try to get past the raft. He felt that such a bombardment, properly supported by the navy, would turn back the Federal vessels.[55]

In early February 1862, Davis and the War Department began stripping New Orleans of men, material, and naval vessels. Lovell received orders to send five thousand men to Columbus, Kentucky. A month later, Davis instructed him to hurry several thousand more men to Beauregard in western Tennessee. To reinforce the naval forces above Memphis, fourteen armed river steamers moved up river from New Orleans. Lovell had only about three thousand poorly armed and untrained militiamen left in the city. Benjamin informed Lovell that the government expected to defend New Orleans "from above by defeating the enemy" on the upper Mississippi. In early March, Lovell complained to the Secretary of War about how his command was being decimated. He wrote, "Persons are found here who assert that I am sending away all troops so that the city may fall an easy prey to the enemy."[56] Several weeks later, Lovell informed Benjamin that, despite the difficulties he faced, "I shall do my duty as I understand it."[57]

All of Flag Officer David G. Farragut's naval squadron had gotten into the Mississippi River from the Gulf of Mexico by early April. In spite of this obvious threat, Davis attempted to order away from New Orleans the ironclad *Louisiana*. That vessel was not yet completed, but Davis wanted it sent north to face the Union ironclads moving toward Memphis. Both Lovell and Governor Moore protested such an action. Lovell asked that if the *Louisiana* had to go he be allowed to keep her rifled guns so he could place them in Fort Jackson. Davis still thought the forts alone would destroy Farragut's squadron. He tried to persuade Moore of the correctness of his strategy: "The Louisiana [sic] may be indispensible to check the descent of the iron boats. The purpose is to defend the city [New Orleans] and valley."[58] Davis finally relented and agreed to leave the ironclad at the Crescent City.

Some of the mortar vessels under Farragut began shelling Fort Jackson and Fort St. Philip on April 15. Three days later, the bombardment began in earnest, with all twenty mortar boats participating. The Federals hoped to reduce the two forts with this fire so that the frigates could steam past without having to engage the Confederate guns. After five days, Farragut saw that this strategy would not work. The mortar vessels had caused little damage and few casualties, and only the morale of the forts' defenders suffered. Farragut decided to have his frigates run past the forts before daylight on April 24. One of his captains succeeded in cutting a gap in the obstructions. In a fight that lasted about four hours, all thirteen Federal gunboats succeeded in passing the forts and destroying almost all of the wooden Confederate vessels stationed near the forts. The next day, the advance elements of Farragut's squadron brushed aside some token opposition from batteries south of the city and dropped anchor before New Orleans. Rather than subject the civilian populace to a bombardment, Lovell decided to evacuate the city. He ordered as many troops and supplies as could get out to Camp Moore.[59]

Why had the most important city in the Confederacy fallen to the enemy so easily? In his official report, Lovell gave these three reasons:

> 1st. The want of sufficient number of guns of heavy caliber which every exertion was made to procure without success.;

> 2d. The unprecedented high water, which swept away the obstructions upon which I mainly relied, in connection with the forts, to prevent the passage of a steam fleet up the river; and

> 3d. The failure, through inefficiency, and want of energy of those who had charge of the construction of the iron-clad steamers *Loui-*

siana and *Mississippi* to have them completed in the time specified so as to supply the place of obstruction; and finally the decision of the officers in charge of the *Louisiana* to allow her, though not entirely ready, to be placed as a battery in the position indicated by General Duncan and myself.[60]

Pie Dufour has advanced two main reasons for the fall of New Orleans. First, as I quoted before, he said, "The divided command at New Orleans was a vital factor." Dufour went on to write, "Next to the divided command as a primary cause of the fall of the city comes the Richmond government's utter lack of appreciation of the realities of the situation at New Orleans."[61] In assessing the blame for this disaster, Dufour exonerated Lovell and concluded that "the responsibility for the fall of New Orleans rested squarely at the doors of the President of the Confederacy."[62] I agree completely with Dufour's conclusions on causes and responsibility. In no respect have I found any reason to criticize Lovell's performance as commander at New Orleans. He did everything within his power to defend the city and, with proper support from Richmond, might have succeeded in turning back Farragut's attack.

As I stated at the beginning of my talk, both Pie Dufour and Daniel Sutherland have adequately covered Davis' efforts to make Lovell the scapegoat for the Union capture of New Orleans. I do not intend to go over this ground again but instead invite you to read their works if you have not done so. I would like to quote Sutherland's conclusion on why Davis went so far in persecuting Lovell: "Davis obviously sought to avoid personal blame for what in retrospect could only be judged a terribly blunder. Yet he was too intelligent, too able a man not to realize that he and his cabinet were at least partly to blame. In this context, Lovell was simply a convenient scapegoat,..."[63] I hope that I have demonstrated that Lovell was a perfect candidate for being made a scapegoat. If Bragg, Beauregard, or any other Southern general had been in Lovell's place, Davis probably would not have even tried to lay all the blame on them.

Lovell did not remain inactive after the evacuation of New Orleans. He began immediately to reorganize his troops and to send them to Vicksburg, Mississippi. By fortifying the bluffs near that town, Lovell hoped to prevent the enemy fleet from ascending the river any farther. He had received a proposal for fortifying Vicksburg from a Mississippi militia officer in December of 1861 but could not provide any assistance to the project at that time. The Confederate defeat at Shiloh prompted Lovell to contact Beauregard about erecting heavy atillery batteries near the town. Lovell thought that this would serve a double purpose. First, it would protect the river. Second, it would provide an anchor for a defensive line running through Vicksburg to Meridian in case Beauregard's army had to retreat from Corinth. At that time, Lovell had no engineer officer to send to begin the work, so he asked Beauregard to send an engineer from his army. Once batteries had been erected, Lovell planned to transfer twelve to fifteen cannons from his works above New Orleans to be mounted at Vicksburg.[64]

The fortification of Vicksburg proceeded as quickly as Lovell could shift men, artillery, and supplies northward from Camp Moore. Additional heavy artillery pieces for the river batteries arrived from Mobile, Richmond, and possibly other points. Lovell sent Brigadier General Martin L. Smith, an experienced engineer, to assume command at Vicksburg and push construction of the fortifications. Smith reached the town on May 12 and found three batteries completed and a fourth almost ready. He soon had more than twenty-five hundred men under his command. On may 18, the leading ships of Farragut's squadron steamed up to the town. The Federals demanded the surrender of Vicksburg, but Smith refused. Unsure of the strength of the Confederate defenses, the Federals took no action but awaited the arrival of the remainder of the fleet. By May 20, the defenders had eighteen heavy guns mounted in seven batteries. Farragut ordered a bombardment of Vicksburg but decided not to risk an attack on the place. Lovell's promptness in providing defenses for Vicksburg prevented its fall in the spring of 1862.[65]

Lovell went to Vicksburg on May 21 to inspect its defenses. The next day, Ruggles arrived from Beauregard's army with orders to take command there. Lovell quickly protested to Beauregard and asked him to send Ruggles to northern Mississippi where he could do no harm. Beauregard responded by ordering Ruggles to Grenada. He then wrote Lovell that the War Department had added Vicksburg to his command and removed it from Lovell's The Creole general decided to allow Lovell to continue supervision of the Vicksburg defenses since all of the troops there came from his department. Lovell established his headquarters at Jackson, Mississippi, from which point he could move by rail to either Vicksburg or Camp Moore as circumstances dictated. He told Beauregard that he would maintain garrisons at both of those points to protect the railroads. Lovell hoped to be able to confine the Federals to a few garrisons along the Mississippi River. [66]

After Beauregard's army evacuated Corinth and retreated to Tupelo, Davis began a shake-up in the Western Theater. As part of the shake-up, he searched for someone to replace Lovell. Davis at first ordered Major General John B. Magruder to Jackson from Virginia, but that general could not go there immediately. Then Davis instructed Bragg to assume temporary command until Magruder could arrive. At that point, Beauregard informed the War Department that he was taking sick leave and that he needed Bragg to remain with the army in his absence. Davis accused Beauregard of abandoning his army and removed him from command. He named Bragg as Beauregard's replacement. Davis then decided to have Major General Earl Van Dorn replace Lovell.[67]

It appears that Davis' older brother, Joseph, had recommended Van Dorn, who was a native of Port Gibson, Mississippi, to take over Lovell's department. Joseph wrote his brother complaining of Lovell's evacuation of New Orleans and describing discontent with Lovell remaining in field command. Several months later, Lovell wrote to his wife that his brother had talked to Joe Davis and learned that the elder Davis had been instrumental in the change of command. Lovell also told his wife that at the time Joe Davis had been misinformed about what had actually happened at New Orleans but had since "seen the error of his ways[,] and would undo the mischief if the opportunity should offer."[68]

Neither Davis nor anyone in the War Department directly notified Lovell of the impending change in command. Lovell had learned by June 20 of Van Dorn's orders to relieve him. He sent a letter to Davis informing him of what he had heard and told the President that Beauregard had offered him "command of a fine corps in his army." He spoke of this opportunity as "a far better position for a soldier than one where he is incessantly striving to accomplish important objects with ridiculously disproportionate means."[69] Lovell also sent a request to the War Department asking for orders: "Would prefer to be sent to the field of immediate action. Will I be allowed a change of position to put an end to unfounded popular clamors?"[70] Though Davis had no intention of doing so immediately, he had the War Department tell Lovell that a court of inquiry would soon convene to look into the fall of New Orleans. For that reason, Van Dorn was being sent to relieve him.[71]

Van Dorn reached Vicksburg on June 27 and assumed command the next day. Lovell remained in the town to assist Van Dorn in the defense of the place. After the Federals broke off their bombardment of Vicksburg in late July, he went to Jackson to await orders for the court of inquiry. In Jackson, he learned that the inquiry had been postponed. He decided to go to Richmond and see what had happened. In a meeting with Davis, Lovell was told that a court would be convened soon. Davis also told him that he should return to Mississippi and serve under Van Dorn until the inquiry began. Lovell had no way of knowing that Davis had lied to him and was delaying as long as possible the court of inquiry.[72]

When Lovell returned to Jackson, Van Dorn assigned him to the command of a division still in the progress of organizing. Bragg had taken Major General John C. Breckinridge and part of his division with him on his invasion of Kentucky and recommended Lovell as a replacement to command the remnants of the division. Some of Breckinridge's men did eventually serve under Lovell. Bragg had left Van Dorn's and Major General Sterling Price's commands to tie down Union forces in northern Mississippi and western Tennessee so that they could not aid the Federals in Kentucky. Van Dorn planned an offensive into western Tennessee that would involve both his and Price's troops. He asked Davis for permission to organize and equip between twelve and fifteen thousand recently exchanged prisoners so that they could participate in the campaign. He intended for these men to form part of Lovell's command.[73]

While Van Dorn travelled to Holly Springs to make preparations for the campaign, Lovell remained in Jackson preparing Van Dorn's troops to move north. He entered into those duties enthusiastically and wrote his wife, "I could not have arranged it better if I had been allowed to fix it for myself." Once Van Dorn's and Prices' forces united and were reinforced by the exchanged prisoners, the combined army would be as strong as Sidney Johnston's at Shiloh. Lovell expected to be second in command of the army since he outranked Price. He went on to say to his wife, "Every one of my friends seems to think I have done a first rate thing in getting into position in this manner without any help from the War Dept...."[74] Lovell reached Van Dorn's army at Davis' Mill, eighteen miles north of Holly Springs about September 23. There Van Dorn formally organized Lovell's division by assigning to it three infantry brigades and one cavalry brigade. If the returned prisoners were forwarded to the army, they would form a second division under Lovell, who would then become a corps commander.[75]

Van Dorn planned to attack Major General William S. Rosecrans' army at Corinth and capture that place. The Confederate army outnumbered that of Rosecrans (twenty-two to fifteen thousand), but the Federals could quickly concentrate another eight thousand men from various outposts as reinforcements. Price cautioned Van Dorn to wait until the exchanged prisoners could join the army. Van Dorn did not want to wait until those men were armed and reorganized. The delay might give Rosecrans time to bring in reinforcements and strengthen his defenses. Lovell met Price for the first time on September 28. He informed his wife of his disappointment in Price's appearance and said, "He may be a very gallant man, but unless I am much mistaken is not a first rate soldier."[76]

Lovell's division led the advance toward Corinth. On the eve of the attack, he wrote that he expected the enemy to evacuate the town rather than try to defend it. He was in excellent spirits: "I feel as fine and hearty as a youngster of twenty and have had a better appetite than I have for the past ten years." He though that "with good generalship" the army could drive the Federals back to the Ohio River "without the loss of much life."[77] Rosecrans did not retreat without a fight, and Van Dorn's army fought a two-day battle, October 3-4, trying to take Corinth. Lovell apparently supported Van Dorn's decision to attack rather than carry out a war of maneuver designed to force Rosecrans to fall back. When one of his brigade commanders told him that an attack could not succeed, Lovell replied that "if we could not succeed we had better lay down our arms and go home."[78]

Lovell's division played an important role in the first day's fighting. His men routed the Federals on their front and captured an artillery piece. After the battle, he wrote his friend Gustavus Smith that the army had almost succeeded in taking Corinth. He stated, *"Had we known accurately the nature of the works and their positions we should have taken the place on Friday beyond all doubt."* Like Van Dorn, Lovell underestimated the strength of Rosecrans' army, thinking that most of it had fought the Confederates on October 3. Actually, a large portion of the Union army remained in reserve during that day's battle. Lovell's account to Smith went on to read,

> We lost time in 'groping' our way, and night came on before we could finish up our work which was in full tide of success. During the night fully 8000 men came in from the different outposts, and the enemy was saved—Two hours of daylight on Friday would have given us the most brilliant victory of the war, and disconcert[ed] all the enemy's plans for his offensive winter campaign. If the returned prisoners had been ready we should have succeeded.[79]

During the second day of fighting, Lovell was to push his division forward on the Confederate right and await word that Price's two divisions had broken through the Union lines. His men were then to join in the assault. The division commander on the left did not attack when scheduled, and then the center division went in prematurely. Both divisions suffered heavy casualties and had to fall back. Lovell awaited orders to advance but never received them. When his men finally began to prepare for an assault, he received word of the defeat of the other two divisions and orders to send a brigade to cover their retreat. This brigade helped check the pursuit by the Federals, and Lovell's division slowly withdrew from the field with the rest of the army. The next day, at Hatchie Bridge, Lovell's men acted as the army's rear guard and threw back an attack by Rosecrans, allowing the army to continue the retreat unmolested.[80]

Though the attack on Corinth had failed, Lovell felt good about his role in the campaign. He wrote his wife,

> If I am to believe all that I hear, my conduct throughout the operations has redounded much to my credit all through the Army. Hundreds of persons have come to me and said that although they began the campaign with prejudices against me, they would now rather serve under me than any one else....I did my duty bravely and nothing more....[81]

Some criticism of Lovell's conduct during the battle has been made. The Missouri troops under Price's command questioned Lovell's failure to attack on October 4.

They felt that if Lovell had sent his division into the assault, the battle would have been won.[82] Albert Castel, in his biography of Price, has picked up on this criticism. He said that Lovell "probably...had concluded that an assault on Corinth was hopeless, and therefore decided to have no share in it." Conceding that Lovell's assessment may have been right, Castel nevertheless pronounced him "guilty of betraying the confidence of [his] commanding general." Castel made this undocumented comment in a footnote: "Van Dorn probably was aware of this attitude on the part of Lovell...but dared not make an issue of it because it would reflect on his own ability as a general (it is just possible that Lovell, a member of his class at West Point, had some sort of personal hold over him, too)."[83]

There is absolutely no evidence to support any of this criticism and certainly none to back up Castel's allegations. That Lovell still hoped for victory on October 4 is shown in a conversation he had with a subordinate after he received Van Dorn's order to retreat. He told that officer, "I don't understand this, Colonel. I've got a position here, and I can whip anything that can come out of Corinth or hell and by G__d, I don't want to leave it."[84] Van Dorn praised Lovell's conduct during the battle, writing President Davis, "General Lovell has now the entire confidence of the troops and gained reputation in the late battle."[85] Though members of the same graduating class at West Point, Lovell and Van Dorn had had no contact with each other between 1842 and the Civil War except possibly during a brief period in the Mexican War. It is impossible for me to believe that Lovell could have had any kind of hold on the hot-blooded Van Dorn that would have prevented the latter from criticizing his role in the battle.

The Corinth campaign was Lovell's last active service in the Confederate army. Van Dorn reorganized his command after the battle and assigned Lovell to command one of his corps. Lovell remained with the army during its operations in northern Mississippi in October and November, but his men did no serious fighting. Davis urged Lieutenant General John C. Pemberton to relieve Lovell of command. Pemberton had assumed command of the newly organized Department of Mississippi and East Louisiana on October 14. Thus he became Van Dorn's superior. The War Department reorganized Pemberton's department of December 7. Those orders named Van Dorn commander of Lovell's corps and relieved Lovell. The orders directed Lovell to "await further orders" since he had not "been assigned to duty by the War Department."[86] When he learned of these orders, Van Dorn wrote Lovell, "Let it be your proud consolation that you have fought gallantly, skillfully at Corinth—persistently and bravely on the long retreat as rear-guard from the unfortunate field to Holly Springs—and subsequently from Holly Springs to Grenada....I am truly sorry to lose you from the Army."[87]

Davis kept Lovell in limbo by delaying the court of inquiry to look into the fall of New Orleans. Joe Johnston asked for Lovell's reinstatement in the army in Mississippi in December of 1862, but Davis turned down his request. In January, 1863, Lovell travelled to Richmond to testify in a Navy Department inquiry concerning New Orleans. He asked Davis at the end of that investigation to return him to duty, but again Davis refused. Lovell finally persuaded some friends in the Confederate Congress to initiate action that would force the calling of a court of inquiry. The War Department issued orders on February 18 for the court to convene in Jackson, Mississippi, but meetings did not begin until April 4. When Federal forces threatened Jackson, the court moved to Charleston, South Carolina. In June, the court moved again, this time to Richmond, and it finally issued its findings on July 9. Those findings included some criticism of Lovell's actions but did not lay responsibility at his door. As Davis had hoped, neither did the findings assign any responsibility to him or the Navy Department. The court concluded, "General Lovell displayed great energy and an untiring industry in performing his duties. His conduct was marked by all the coolness and self-possession due to the circumstances and his position, and he evinced a high capacity for command, and the clearest foresight in many of his measures for the defence of New Orleans."[88]

Though cleared by the court, Lovell still did not receive any orders to return to active duty. Because the proceedings of the court had not officially been published and sent to Congress, Davis and the War Department could continue to keep Lovell "on the shelf." Again, Lovell appealed to his friends in Congress to request a copy of the court's report, and the House of Representatives passed a resolution to that effect on January 15, 1864. Davis did not forward the copy until June.[89]

In the meantime, Joe Johnston had assumed command of the Army of Tennessee, and he asked the War Department in January of 1864 to assign Lovell to his army so he could command one of the three corps he hoped to organize. The War Department sent Johnston's request to Davis, who informed the general that he would not receive Lovell's services. Two months later, Johnston and Bragg corresponded about a new chief of artillery for Johnston's army. Bragg suggested several names, including Lovell's, and said, "Lovell was one of the best artillery officers in the old service, a good judge and fond of good horses...."[90] Johnston asked for Lovell's assignment as chief of artillery, but again Davis refused the request.[91]

Lovell volunteered his services to Johnston during the Atlanta campaign. Johnston wrote later that Lovell had done so because "prompted by a zeal in the cause which made him regardless of the claims of his rank."[92] Johnston assigned him to examine the crossings over the Chattahoochee River near Atlanta and to prepare defenses to prevent Federal cavalry raids from surprising the city and destroying the valuable depots located there. Lovell probably worked with Gustavus Smith, now commander of the Georgia militia, in placing state troops in the defenses constructed. He travelled back and forth between Johnston's army and Atlanta during the coming weeks. In late June, Johnston sent his chief of artillery to construct redoubts along the Chattahoochee at points selected by Lovell. When Lieutenant General Alexander P. Stewart succeeded to the command of Lieutenant General Leonidas Polk's corps in late June, Johnston recommended Lovell as the new commander for Stewart's division. The War Department rejected the request. General John B. Hood replaced Johnston on July 17 and asked for Lovell's assignment to command his old corps. Richard McMurry wrote, "Hood's suggestion that Lovell be given a corps was probably based on his ability to handle troops and his familiarity with the army and its situation...."[93] Hood had no better luck than had Johnston.

With this last refusal by Davis to allow him to return to field command, Lovell moved with his family to Columbia, South Carolina. Lieutenant General William J. Hardee inquired of the War Department in December of 1864 whether he could assign Lovell to some command at Savannah, Georgia. As everyone before him, Hardee received a rebuff to his request. Lovell volunteered his services to the governor of South Carolina late in December. He gave as his reason his desire "to contribute to the utmost of my ability to the success of the common cause."[94] After Joe Johnston took command in the Carolinas in March, 1865, he wrote to General Robert E. Lee asking him to order Lovell to report to him for duty. Lee persuaded the War Department to return Lovell to service, and, on April 7, Lovell received assignment to command of Confederate forces in South Carolina. The war was practically over, but Lovell remained on duty until late May, when he finally surrendered to Union forces.[95]

Lovell chose to remain in the South after the end of the war. He travelled to New York briefly to acquire capital that would enable him to establish and operate a rice plantation near Savannah. A tidal wave destroyed his first crop, and he was forced to return to New York City with his family. There he became a civil engineer and surveyor. Lovell served as assistant engineer under former Union general John Newton when the latter supervised the removal of obstructions in the East River at Hell's Gate. After a short illness, Lovell died June 1, 1884.[96]

It is difficult to assess Lovell's performance as a Confederate general since he held only two commands of any significance. He performed as well as anyone could have as commander at New Orleans and practically performed miracles in placing the city in a decent defensive position. He might have had more success with more support from Davis and the government in Richmond. As I have stated, his quick actions in May of 1862 prevented Union forces from capturing Vicksburg. Lovell participated enthusiastically in the Corinth Campaign and showed his abilities as a field commander. I think an examination of Lovell's war service shows him to have been a slightly above average general. If he had been given the opportunity, he would have made a good division commander in the Army of Tennessee. Despite all of the abuse heaped upon him by governmental officials, soldiers, and civilians, he remained loyal to the Confederacy to the bitter end. Dan Sutherland put it well when he wrote, "...wherever he served, Lovell won the praise of subordinates and superior alike for his courage, energy, and devotion."[97]

Endnotes

1 U.S. War Department, *War of the Rebellion: Official Records of Union and Confederate Armies*, 128 parts in 70 vols. (Washington, D.C.: Government Printing Office, 1880-1901), Series 1, Vol. V, p. 797, hereinafter cited as *O.R.*, all references are to Series 1 unless otherwise stated.

2 *Ibid.*, VI, p. 751.

3 *Ibid.*, XXXII, Pt. 3, p. 592.

4 Gustavus W. Smith, "Mansfield Lovell," *Fifteenth Annual Reunion of the Association of the Graduates of the U.S. Military Academy* (East Saginaw, Mich., 1884), p. 117.

5 Daniel E. Sutherland, "Mansfield Lovell's Quest for Justice: Another Look at the Fall of New Orleans," *Louisiana History*, XXIV (1983), p. 239.

6 Charles L. Dufour, "The Night the War Was Lost. The Fall of New Orleans: Causes, Consequences, Culpability," *Louisiana History*, II (1961), p. 174. See also, Charles L. Dufour, *The Night the War Was Lost* (New York: Doubleday & Company, Inc., 1960).

7 Sutherland, "Mansfield Lovell's Quest for Justice," pp. 258-59.

8 Ezra J. Warner, *Generals in Gray: Lives of the Confederate Commanders* (Baton Rouge: Louisiana State University Press, 1959), p. 194; Smith, "Mansfield Lovell," pp. 113, 117; Mary Gillett, "Joseph Lovell," *Dictionary of American Military Biography*, ed. by Roger J. Spiller, 3 vols. (Westport, Conn.: Greenwood Press, 1984), p.662.

9 Smith, "Manfield Lovell," p. 113.

10 *Ibid.*; Warner, *Generals in Gray*, p. 194.

11 Smith, "Mansfield Lovell," pp. 113-14; Robert E. May, *John A. Quitman: Old South Crusader* (Baton Rouge: Louisiana State University Press, 1985), p. 164.

12 May, *John A. Quitman*, p. 164.

13 Mansfield Lovell to Eliza Quitman, July 20, 1858, quoted in *ibid.*, p. 449n40; *ibid.*, pp. 164, 352, 359.

14 May, *John A. Quitman*, pp. 189, 194; John F. H. Claiborne, *Life and Correspondence of John A. Quitman*, 2 vols. (New York: Harper & Brothers, Publishers, 1860), Vol. II, pp. 308-310; T. Harry Williams *With Beauregard in Mexico: The Mexican War Reminiscences of P. G. T. Beauregard* (Baton Rouge: Louisiana State University Press, 1956), pp. 85, 97-98; Francis B. Heitman, *Historical Register of the United States Army, from its Organization, September 29, 1789 to September 29, 1889* (Washington, D.C., 1890), p. 644; Warner, *Generals in Gray*, p. 194.

15 Smith, "Mansfield Lovell," pp. 114-15; Heitman, *Historical Register of the United States Army*, p. 644; Warner, *Generals in Gray*, p. 194; Donovan Yeuell, "Mansfield Lovell," *Dictionary of American Biography*, ed. by Dumas Malone, 20 vols. (New York: Charles Scribner's Sons, 1928-1944), Vol. XI, p. 441.

16 May, *John A. Quitman*, pp. 236, 238.

[17] *Ibid.*, p. 238.

[18] *Ibid.*, pp. 274, 277, 290.

[19] *Ibid.*, p. 295.

[20] Smith, "Mansfield Lovell," pp. 117-18.

[21] *Ibid.*, p. xv.

[22] James T. McIntosh (ed.), *The Papers of Jefferson Davis*, Volume 2, *June 1841-July 1846* (Baton Rouge: Louisiana State University Press, 1974), p. 107n104; May, *John A. Quitman*, pp. 224, 263. 271.

[23] Quoted in Stephen W. Sears, *George B. McClellan: The Young Napoleon* (New York: Ticknor & Fields, 1988), pp. 52-53; Williams, *With Beauregard in Mexico*, pp. 106-108.

[24] Sears, *George B. McClellan*, pp. 56-57.

[25] Quoted in Gilbert E. Govan and James W. Livingood, *A Different Valor: The Story of General Joseph E. Johnston, C.S.A.* (Indianapolis: The Bobbs-Merrill Co., Inc., 1956), pp. 23-24, 26.

[26] "Mansfield Lovell," *DAB*, XI, p. 441; Smith, "Mansfield Lovell," p. 115; Gustavus W. Smith, *Confederate War Papers: Fairfax Court House, New Orleans, Seven Pines, Richmond and North Carolina* (New York: Atlantic Publishing and Engraving Co., 1884), pp. 360-61.

[27] Smith, "Mansfield Lovell," pp. 115-16.

[28] Alfred Roman, *The Military Operations of General Beauregard*, 2 vols. (New York: Harper & Brothers, 1884), Vol. I, p. 15.

[29] Mansfield Lovell to Braxton Bragg, February 25, 1861, quoted in Grady McWhiney, *Braxton Bragg and Confederate Defeat, Volume I, Field Command* (New York: Columbia University Press, 1969), p. 153.

[30] Dunbar Rowland (ed.), *Jefferson Davis, Constitutionalist: His Letters, Papers and Speeches*, 10 vols. (Jackson, Miss.: State Department of Archives and History, 1923), Vol. V, p. 55.

[31] *O.R.*, LIII, pp. 127, 129-30; Roman, *The Military Operations of General Beauregard*, Vol. I, p. 20.

[32] Smith, "Mansfield Lovell," p. 118.

[33] Lovell to George B. McClellan, April 15, 1861, quoted in Sears, *George B. McClellan*, p. 66.

[34] Smith, "Mansfield Lovell," p. 116; Smith, *Confederate War Papers*, pp. 363-64.

[35] *O.R.*, V, pp. 797-98; Govan and Livingood, *A Different Valor*, p. 73.

[36] *Richmond Whig*, Sept. 13, 1861; Warner, *Generals in Gray*, p. 281.

[37] *O.R.*, LIII, p. 739.

38 *Ibid.*, VI, pp. 738, 744, 745, 746, 751, and LIII, p. 743.

39 *Ibid.*, VI, pp. 643, 751: LI, Pt. 2, p 344; and LIII, pp. 742, 748, 748-49; Roman, *Military Operations of General Beauregard*, Vol. I, p. 154.

40 *O.R.*, V, p. 883.

41 *Ibid.*, VI, p. 751.

42 *Ibid.*, 786; John B. Jones, *A Rebel War Clerk's Diary, at the Confederate States Capital*, ed. by Howard Swiggett, 2 vols. (New York: Barnes and Noble, 1935), Vol. I, p. 89; Entry of Jan. 6, 1862, Thomas Bragg Diary, 1861-1862, Southern Historical Collection, University of North Carolina at Chapel Hill.

43 Major General Braxton Bragg to "My dear Doctor," undated, in the William P. Palmer Collection of Braxton Bragg Papers, Western Reserve Historical Society, Cleveland, Ohio, hereinafter cited as Bragg Papers, Western Reserve.

44 Bragg to Moore, Oct. 31, 1861, Moore Papers.

45 Bragg to "My dear Doctor," undated, Bragg Papers, Western Reserve; Bragg to Moore, Nov. 14, 1861, Moore Papers; *O.R.*, VI, p. 759.

46 Bragg to Moore, Nov. 14, 1861, Moore Papers; Bragg to "My dear Doctor," undated, Bragg Papers, Western Reserve; *O.R.*, VI, p. 759.

47 *O.R.*, VI, p. 751.

48 T. Harry Williams, *P. G. T. Beauregard: Napoleon in Gray* (Baton Rouge: Louisiana State University Press, 1955), p. 101.

49 New Orleans *Daily Picayune*, Oct. 17, 19, 1861.

50 Dufour, *The Night the War Was Lost*, p. 93.

51 *O.R.*, VI, pp. 645-46.

52 *Ibid.*, p. 798.

53 Dufour, *The Night the War Was Lost*, p. 340; John T. Scharf, *History of the Confederate States Navy* (reprint ed., New York: The Fairfax Press, 1977), p. 301.

54 Smith, "Mansfield Lovell," p. 119; *O.R.*, VI, pp. 754, 758, 760, 776.

55 Roman, *The Military Operations of General Beauregard*, p. 154; Smith, "Mansfield Lovell," pp. 118-19; Sutherland, "Mansfield Lovell's Quest for Justice," p. 236; *O.R.*, VI, pp. 646-47, 881.

56 *O.R.*, VI, pp. 561, 823, 847; Smith, "Mansfield Lovell," pp. 120-21; Smith, *Confederate War Papers*, pp. 71-75.

57 *O.R.*, VI, pp. 865-66.

58 *Ibid.*, pp. 646-47, 878; Dufour, *The Night the War Was Lost,* pp. 200-202.

59 *O.R.*, VI, 510-11, 514-15, 883; Dufour, *The Night the War Was Lost,* pp. 223-301.

60 *O.R.*, VI, p. 517.

61 Dufour, *The Night the War Was Lost*, pp. 340, 342.

62 Dufour, "The Night the War Was Lost," p. 174.

63 Sutherland, "Mansfield Lovell's Quest for Justice," p. 254.

64 *O.R.*, VI, pp. 567, 651, 783, 784, 877, 884, 885.

65 *Ibid.*, pp. 567, 585; XV, pp. 6-8; LII, Pt. 2, p. 316; U.S. Navy Department, *War of the Rebellion: Official Records of the Union and Confederate Navies*, 30 vols. (Washington, D.C.: Government Printing Office, 1894-1922), Series 1, Vol. XVIII, pp. 491-93, 507, 508.

66 *O.R.*, XV, pp. 739-40, 741-42, 746; LII, Pt. 2, pp. 318-19. The War Department order was dated May 26, 1862, several days after the Lovell-Ruggles confrontation. The author believes that Davis directed the War Department to remove Vicksburg from Lovell's department after he learned that the general was involved in the town's defense.

67 *Ibid.*, XV, pp. 758; XVII, Pt. 2, pp. 591, 599, 613; Robert G. Hartje, *Van Dorn: The Life and Times of a Confederate General* (Nashville: Vanderbilt University Press, 1967), pp. 182-83.

68 Mansfield Lovell to Emily Lovell, Sept. 20, 1862, Mansfield Lovell Papers in Keeler Collection, Henry E. Huntington Library, San Marino, Calif., hereinafter cited as Lovell Papers; Joseph Davis to Jefferson Davis, June 18, 1862, quoted in Clement Eaton, *Jefferson Davis* (New York: The Free Press, 1977), p. 154.

69 Lovell to Davis, June 20, 1862, quoted in Smith, *Confederate War Papers*, pp. 96-97.

70 *O.R.*, LII, Pt. 2, p. 325.

71 Lovell to Emily Lovell, June 26, 1862, Lovell Papers.

72 *O.R.*, XV, pp. 15, 769; Hartje, *Van Dorn*, 183.

73 *O.R.*, XVI, Pt. 2, p. 995; XVII, Pt. 2, p. 697; Lovell to Emily Lovell, Sept. 11, 19, 1862, Lovell Papers; Archer Jones, *Confederate Strategy from Shiloh to Vicksburg* (Baton Rouge: Louisiana State University Press, 1961), pp. 76-77.

74 Lovell to Emily Lovell, Sept. 20, 1862, Lovell Papers.

75 Lovell to Emily Lovell, Sept. 25, 28, 1862, Lovell Papers; *O.R.*, XVII, Pt. 2, p. 711.

76 Lovell to Emily Lovell, Sept. 28, 1862, Lovell Papers; Hartje, *Van Dorn*, pp. 214-15; Albert Castel, *General Sterling Price and the Civil War in the West* (Baton Rouge: Louisiana State University Press, 1968), p. 106.

77 Lovell to Emily Lovell, Oct. 1, 1862, Lovell Papers.

78 *O.R.*, XVII, Pt. 1, p. 417.

79 Lovell to "My dear G. W.," Oct. 26, 1862; *O.R.*, XVII, Pt. 1, pp. 404-405; Castel, *General Sterling Price*, pp. 123-24.

80 *O.R.*, XVII, Pt. 1, pp. 379-81, 405-406; Hartje, *Van Dorn*, pp. 228-32.

81 Lovell to Emily Lovell, Oct. 13, 1862, Lovell Papers.

82 R. S. Bevier, *History of the First and Second Missouri Confederate Brigades, 1861-1865* (St. Louis: Bryan, Brand & Company, 1879), p. 154.

83 Castel, *General Sterling Price*, p. 124 and note 40.

84 Quoted in Hartje, *Van Dorn*, p. 233.

85 *O.R.*, LII, Pt. 2, p. 381.

86 *O.R.*, XVII, Pt. 2, pp. 733, 745, 779, 786, 787; LII, Pt. 2, pp. 381, 729; Lovell to Emily Lovell, Nov. 4, 27, 28, 30, Dec. 12, 1862, Lovell Papers.

87 Quoted in Smith, *Confederate War Papers*, p. 98.

88 *O.R.*, VI, pp. 555-56, 600, 606, 639-42; Johnston to Lovell, Mar. 29, 1869, quoted in Dufour, *The Night the War Was Lost*, p. 349; Smith, *Confederate War Papers*, pp. 98-99; Smith, *Confederate War Papers*, pp. 99-108; Sutherland, "Mansfield Lovell's Quest for Justice," pp. 247-53.

89 *O.R.*, VI, p. 554.

90 *Ibid.*, XXXII, Pt. 2, pp. 563-64, 592.

91 *Ibid.*, p. 636.

92 Joseph E. Johnston, *Narrative of Military Operations* (reprint ed., New York: Kraus Reprint Co., 1969), p. 332.

93 Richard M. McMurry, *John Bell Hood and the War for Southern Independence* (Lexington: The University of Kentucky Press, 1982), p. 137; *O.R.*, XXXVIII, Pt. 4, pp. 749, 797; Pt. 5, p. 892; LII, Pt. 2, p. 681; Johnston, *Narrative of Military Operations*, pp. 332, 345, 572-73; Govan and Livingood, *A Different Valor*, p. 429n59.

94 Lovell to Governor of South Carolina, Dec. 24, 1864, quoted in Smith, *Confederate War Papers*, p. 115; C. Vann Woodward (ed.), *Mary Chestnut's Civil War* (New Haven: Yale University Press, 1981), pp. 626, 630, 671, 691, 692.

95 *O.R.*, XLVI, Pt. 3, p. 1339; XLVII, Pt. 2, p. 1454; Pt. 3, pp. 565, 688, 765, 817, 861, 862, 866, 872, 873.

96 Warner, *Generals in Gray*, p. 195; Smith, "Mansfield Lovell," p. 126; "Mansfield Lovell," *DAB*, XI, p. 442.

97 Sutherland, "Mansfield Lovell's Quest for Justice," p. 247.

"Jedediah Hotchkiss: Stonewall Jackson's Map Maker"

Archie P. McDonald

To Confederate soldiers in Virginia he was a familiar sight —

One leg cast over the pommel of his saddle, a tall man bending laboriously over his sketch book and drawing curious lines on a scrap of paper. Glancing at hastily taken notes, he skillfully formed a map which accurately located peculiarities of terrain, residences, and troop positions. When it was finished, this map would be used by General Thomas Jonathan Jackson; eventually, it would be returned to its creator, Jedediah Hotchkiss, Topographical Engineer of the Second Corps, Army of Northern Virginia. He was more than an engineer—companion to Jackson, courier, ofter a fighting soldier—but essentially he was an engineer and the best topographical engineer in the Confederate Army. He was the man more responsible than any other for Jackson's ability to always proceed in sure knowledge of the terrain, and he performed many services during the war that would have been a credit to officers of much higher rank.

Hotchkiss, the son of Stiles and Lydia Hotchkiss, was not a native Southerner. He traced his ancestry through New York and Connecticut to Stirling, Scotland. An older brother, Nelson Hill Hotchkiss, was born on December 3, 1819, and some time later a sister, Jenny, was born. Jedediah was born at the family home near Windsor, Broome County, New York, on November 30, 1828.

Young Jedediah was instructed by his parents in the Christian religion and contemporary methods of agriculture. His mother had been since her eighth year a devout Methodist, but she allowed her children to be reared in Presbyterianism, the faith of their father. Farming did not interest Jed. He much preferred to roam the New York countryside, examining plants and rocks and observing the land. Frequently chores prevented these wanderings, but sometimes while performing farm duties, the young boy could enjoy another diversion, books. While tending the cows or out of sight of his father, Jed would lie in the tall grass—preferably in a spot still warm from a sunning cow—and pore over the printed pages.

This paper is drawn from my introduction to *Make Me A Map Of The Valley: The Civil War Journal of Stonewall Jackson's Topographer*, published by Southern Methodist University Press (Dallas, 1973), paperback edition, 1988, and is reproduced with the permission of SMU Press.

Stiles Hotchkiss decided that his son's fondness for study should receive proper direction. After attending the local public school, Jed was enrolled in Windsor Academy. He celebrated his graduation from the Academy in 1846 by joining a group of young men in a walking tour in Lyken's Valley, near Harrisburg, Pennsylvania. The Valley's coal mining operations interested him, and he secured a teaching position among the German miners for one year. His leisure was spent profitably in the study of the geology of coal deposits and in the business of extracting the fuel.

When the term was completed, Hotchkiss began another tour in the company of a fellow teacher. They explored the Cumberland Valley of Pennsylvania and the western portions of Virginia. Stopping briefly in Page County, Virginia, Hotchkiss met Henry Forrer, one of the owners of an iron furnace near Luray, Virginia. Forrer invited him to Mossy Creek to meet his brother, Daniel, who was looking for a young scholar to tutor his children. Jed accepted the position. His pay was to be $300 annually, plus board, room, washing, and a horse. He had plenty of time for reading and study, and during this period he taught himself the principles of map making and engineering. A great deal of native talent and desire made this possible; formal education in these subjects was available only at military schools.

Forrer was pleased with Jed's work, and in conjunction with other Mossy Creek residents he initiated a movement to build the Mossy Creek Academy. On August 26, 1852, a building committee of seven met and pledged $100 each for the construction of the school. Hotchkiss was to head the building committee and remain as principal of the school.

These activities in Virginia turned Jedediah Hotchkiss into an established young man. By 1853 he had an education, a community position, and a promising future as a teacher. Mossy Creek was good for him; it gave him honest labor in the instruction of the young, pleasant diversion in a beautiful lake, and a field laboratory for his geological and engineering interests. It was here that he took the two most important steps in his life—church membership and marriage. Trained in the theology of the Presbyterian church, he was already imbued with the religious convictions which remained throughout his life. On May 22, 1853, he went before the board of the Mossy Creek Presbyterian Church to confirm his affiliation with that congregation. Reverend William B. Brown presided over the examining committee, and satisfied with Hotchkiss' faith in Christ, they received him as a member of the church. He was soon characteristically in harness, teaching a men's Bible class which pridefully boasted of one hundred members.

In December Hotchkiss traveled north to Lanesboro, Pennsylvania, to claim Miss Sara Ann Comfort as his wife. He had met Sara in 1846 while touring

Pennsylvania. Born on February 14, 1833, Sara Ann was the daughter of John and Anna Hunt Comfort. Educated at Kingston Seminary, she was an intelligent woman, proficient in languages, and fully capable of aiding her husband in his school. They were married on December 21, 1853, and returned to Mossy Creek. They quickly settled in a home at the foot of a hill near the Academy. On May 6, 1854, Sara was received by letter into the church of her husband.

Hardly a year had passed before the family was enlarged by the birth of Nellie. In two years Anne, the second and last child, was born. Anne's birth was difficult for Mrs. Hotchkiss, and the ordeal left her in poor health for several years. In 1858, Hotchkiss sold his interests in Mossy Creek to Thomas Moore and moved his family to Stribbling Springs, Virginia, where Mrs. Hotchkiss drank the healthful waters and regained her strength. Jed joined his brother-in-law, William McKune, in business, and he also taught one term in a small local school, but with Sara's improvement he decided to move on.

In 1859 Jed was joined by his brother Nelson H. Hotchkiss. Together they purchased a farm near Churchville, Virginia. Here the brothers erected several buildings and in the fall they began the Loch Willow Academy. Jed, assisted by his wife and a small staff, had charge of the administration and instruction. Nelson attended to the farm and the boarding of the scholars. Loch Willow proved very successful; for the 1860-1861 term 54 students enrolled, bringing to the school a total revenue of over $1,700. The Hotchkiss family changed their church membership to Union Church in anticipation of a long residence at their new home.

Jed and Sara Hotchkiss concerned themselves little with the national crisis during the late 1850s. Absorbed in the new school, Jed spent most of his time close to his work. His brother Nelson, however, was an outspoken Unionist; but both were cemented to their new home. Jed had lived in Virginia for fourteen years and was tied economically to that state. His roots were in New York—both parents still lived in Windsor—and undoubtedly he lamented a situation which would separate him so completely from them; but Virginia was his home, and it was to Virginia that he turned when forced to choose.

Despite the political storms at the close of the decade, Hotchkiss tried to keep Loch Willow in operation as long as possible. But when Virginia seceded from the Union on April 17, 1861, an assistant teacher organized an infantry company and several pupils joined him. Shortly afterward several more students enrolled in a cavalry company. In June Hotchkiss acknowledged the inevitable. He dismissed the remaining students and offered his services to the Confederate Army.

Hotchkiss reported to Lieutenant Colonel Jonathan M. Heck at Rich Mountain in western Virginia on July 2, 1861. The first Federal thrust was rolling the Virginia forces back and Brigadier General Robert Selden Garnett hurried to stop the invasion. On July 3 Hotchkiss began his service to the Confederacy by initiating a survey of "Camp Garnett" and its vicinity preparatory to making an accurate topographical map. In the matter of maps the Confederacy had to begin from scratch; the few maps they had were inaccurate and out-of-date. Hotchkiss had almost completed his survey when the enemy arrived in force, and he was forced to remain in the entrenchments during attacks on July 10 and 11. The situation was serious for the Confederates—"Camp Garnett" became separated from the main force by Rich Mountain. In order to re-establish communication it would be necessary to cross the mountain—under enemy fire if detected. At midnight on July 11, Colonel John Pegram ordered Heck to assume command and to rejoin Garnett. Heck selected his engineer to lead the march over the mountain.

Led by Hotchkiss and the Augusta-Lee Rifles of Captain Robert Doak Lilley, the hurriedly formed column began its slow trek. After proceeding some distance in the stillness a whistle brought the marchers to their knees. Hotchkiss managed a low reply. It was later learned that a Federal regiment had occupied ground parallel to their line of march and only the whistled reply had enabled them to complete their escape. The summit of the mountain and the safety of the other slope was reached as the first streaks of dawn appeared. The light revealed that Hotchkiss led but fifty of Lilley's men instead of the much larger column that had begun the march. It was later established that the others had been halted by a courier from Pegram. The messenger had traveled only as far as the rear of Lilley's company, and his caution and the need for silence had prevented the order from being passed to the head of the column. Only those men who had not received the order made it to safety.

In the hasty departure Hotchkiss had been forced to leave behind his valuable engineering equipment. As soon as possible he filed a claim with the Confederate Government for "1 Barometer (Aneroid), 1 set of Mathematical instruments," and two sets of compass and chain for a total value of $83.

Back in camp, Hotchkiss was made acting adjutant, but he wrote to his wife that he expected to relinquish the post when Brigadier General Robert E. Lee arrived to take command. When Lee arrived, he put Hotchkiss to work on a map of Tygart's Valley. By working furiously Hotchkiss finished the map by early August. But the effort to complete the work sapped his strength, and he became easy prey for typhoid fever. For five days he suffered with severe headaches, pains in the limbs, and insomnia. He decided to return to Loch Willow to convalesce and to finish the map in the leisure of home. In October while still at home, he was notified that he would receive the monthly pay of a lieutenant of engineers, $93.33, for services rendered to date.

By March 1862, Hotchkiss considered himself again fit for service. When Governor John Letcher called out the militia of the Shenandoah Valley, Hotchkiss decided to return to the army if he could obtain engineering duty. He wrote to Colonel W. S. H. Baylor, a member of Major General T. J. Jackson's staff, to inquire if the colonel could secure his appointment. Baylor replied that the prospects seemed good, but he urged Hotchkiss to apply in person. Hotchkiss obtained letters of introduction and left with the Augusta County militia on March 17 for Jackson's camp. The militia was commanded by Colonel William S. Sproul, and its officer corps also included Colonel John H. Crawford and Major William M. Wilson. These officers were as inexperienced as their men, and Hotchkiss accepted a position as adjutant to help clear up problems of the march.

Soon after he arrived at Jackson's camp, Hotchkiss was dispatched on a preliminary reconnaissance of Woodstock and vicinity. He was accompanied by Lieutenant James Keith Boswell, Chief of Engineers, who ultimately became Hotchkiss' closest friend. On March 21 Hotchkiss helped Boswell muster the militia into the regular service. On that day he also received the happy news that Jackson would detail him for engineering duty, and he had important work for him to begin immediately.

But the momentary joy of Hotchkiss' appointment to staff duty was shattered by grave news from home. An epidemic of scarlet fever was sweeping the Valley, and already Nellie and Anne were its victims. For many days Hotchkiss lived with the fear that his children were dying, if not already dead. He became resigned to their loss and put his faith in God. At last word came that his daughters were spared, and Hotchkiss found time to comfort Major John A. Harman, Jackson's Chief Quartermaster, who lost two children and expected the death of others.

And there was hard work to fill his mind. Jackson summoned Hotchkiss to headquarters on the morning of March 26, and after a general conversation about engineering, Jackson spoke the words that made Hotchkiss his topographical engineer: "I want you to make me a map of the Valley, from Harper's Ferry to Lexington, showing all the points of offence and defence in those places. Mr. Pendleton will give you orders for what ever outfit you want. Good morning, Sir."

Lieutenant A. S. "Sandie" Pendleton detailed William Humphreys as Hotchkiss' assistant and secured a wagon and supplies for the reconnaissance. Thus was formed a partnership between general and engineer. The engineer, with his quick perception of terrain, could swiftly supply the general, who had no real facility for grasping the lay of the land, with accurate sketches in a short time. Hotchkiss, realizing this lack of ability in his chief, was always prepared to explain his maps. Before movements of the army he was called in frequently to give advice on terrain. He made it a point to be able to furnish graphic representations of any point on which Jackson was not clear. He used different colored pencils for greater clarity in the definition of surface features.

In April 1862, Hotchkiss received permission to visit his home while on a trip to confer with Brigadier General Edward "Allegheny" Johnson, who was encamped near Staunton. Hotchkiss was tired of war already, and the pleasantness of home made the front porch rocking chair twice as hard to leave. But he hurried back to camp, for Jackson needed specific maps of the Valley. During the famous Valley Campaign of 1862 Hotchkiss was engaged in reconnaissance and map making. From mid-June through July he spent nearly a month in Staunton drawing maps of the campaign. On July 15, he was ordered to meet Jackson at Gordonsville with full equipment, and he joined the Second Corps in time for the engagements at Second Manassas and for the Maryland invasion. As in the past, his duties were limited mainly to reconnaissance and the sketching of field maps. It was while in Maryland near Frederick City that Hotchkiss performed a curious service for Jackson; he bought his commander a new hat. Hotchkiss requested permission to go into town to purchase a head piece, and Jackson asked his engineer to buy him one as well. The correct size was determined by the General trying on Hotchkiss' hat: "What fits you will fit me." When Hotchkiss returned with Jackson's new cover, "a tall black hat," he took the General's old grey cap and put it into his saddlebags for safekeeping. The cap was on another occasion a subject of conversation between them. Just before the battle of Fredericksburg in December 1862, Jackson inquired of Hotchkiss as the whereabouts of his old cap, and remarked that it had fit him better than any other he had ever owned. When he suggested that he might have it destroyed, Hotchkiss grew bold enough to ask for it as a souvenir. Jackson was pleased and after a while said, "I reckon you may have the cap." Before Hotchkiss sent the cap home he gave a button from the headband to S. Howell Brown, a fellow engineer.

In December Hotchkiss was again ill. Plagued by colds, he suffered from fevers and was yellowed by jaundice. He stayed at the job and spent most of January 1863, making detailed maps of the Battles of Kernstown and McDowell. On February 3 he applied for leave of absence to attend to the sale of the farm in Augusta County, and "...to attend to business which has been neglected since June, 1861." An added incentive was his wife Sara's birthday, only seven days away on the 10th. He left on the 5th for Loch Willow and arrived there three days later. The journey was delayed by a broken locomotive, but the talkative Hotchkiss had little trouble passing the time with the other passengers.

The explanation of the sale of the farm was a rift between the brothers Jed and Nelson Hotchkiss. Just what caused the misunderstanding is not known, but their political differences would seem a good guess. Whatever their disagreement, they were still in sufficient accord to reject the price offered at the sale on February 10. Another sale was scheduled for the 28th. While he was home Jedediah settled other outstanding business. For instance, he paid his taxes,

$26.61. The tax receipt lists five slaves among his assets. In addition he had Christian Beer sign his note to Mrs. Jane Kiger for the annual hiring of William Gearing, a servant boy.

The trip back to camp proved difficult. Hotchkiss' watch was a half hour late, and he arrived at the station just as the train was leaving. Jumping aboard, he found that his luggage was too heavy to pull aboard the moving car. Hotchkiss got off the train at Waynesboro and rode a freight back to get the box. The following day the engine derailed. Back on the track, the train was delayed overnight by another stalled carrier. The one pleasant event of the trip was an offer from a fellow passenger, a Mr. Van Meter, for Hotchkiss to teach school in Hardy County. He would have fifteen students and receive $100 per student. He declined the offer, saying that Hardy County was too far north for the safety of his family.

But the family bonds seemed to weaken further. Nelson wrote to Jed on February 27, informing him that he had purchased a farm near Howardsville. In March, Nelson sold the farm at Loch Willow. Jed's house and laboratory were not included and he was to retain half of the vineyard. Hotchkiss was pleased; he wrote to his wife that "...no better way exists than to take different roads when the one travelled does not suit the disposition of brethern—and we can only pray that each may, in God's fear, deal justly and righteously with the other...."

As winter thawed into spring, Hotchkiss thought of home and wrote to his wife of camp life. He subscribed to the *Central Presbyterian* and the *Southern Literary Messenger*, and had them mailed to Loch Willow for Sara. Hotchkiss wrote to his wife that he had at last been able to take a warm bath and put on clean clothes, since William did the washing, and now felt "quite civilized." Occasionally his letters revealed the grim side of army life. On March 1 he wrote of a deserter being shot. "Discipline," he wrote, "is going on—a good many have been shot, some whipped, some drummed out of the camp and then put to labor with a ball and chain, some branded on the backsides with letters of D. or C. for desertion or cowardice...." Hotchkiss was mortified to find Samuel Forrer, the son of his Mossy Creek benefactor, charged with desertion. Forrer had been apprehended while crossing the lines, but contended that he was going for medicine. Hotchkiss visited Forrer and spoke to the military court on the youth's behalf. Whether Hotchkiss was responsible or not, Forrer did escape the death penalty, and he was thereafter grateful to his old friend. As late as 1908 he wrote to the family, on the occasion of Mrs. Hotchkiss' death, of his gratitude to Hotchkiss.

In early April Hotchkiss found a small farm for sale that he liked. It was perfect for his needs—large enough for subsistence agriculture and a small school. He wrote to the owner, a Mr. Lindsay, to inquire his terms. They were apparently to his liking, for he considered borrowing the money to purchase the farm if he could obtain a good interest rate. Sara was unwilling to move, however, and in the end Jedediah bowed to her wishes. Later in the month he sent the hired slave, William, home for supplies. The servant brought the news that all was well at home, and his glowing accounts made Hotchkiss homesick.

But reverie of home was soon snapped by the cold reality of battle. As April passed into May a major engagement was imminent. On May 2, 1863, a Federal force under Major General Joseph Hooker fought the Battle of Chancellorsville against the Confederate units of General Robert E. Lee and his "right arm," Lieutenant General T. J. Jackson. During the day the battle went well for the Confederates. By a flanking movement Jackson took his whole corps to Hooker's rear, and after hard fighting, won the day. As night fell the troops began to secure their positions. Jackson rode out with members of his staff on a personal reconnaissance. Just beyond Major General A. P. Hill's position he learned from Federal prisoners that Hooker was throwing up obstacles to the advance. Wheeling at an alarm signal, the little band trotted back toward the safety of their own lines. It was a dark nine o'clock, and the random firing had created tension. As Jackson and his staff approached the positions of the North Carolina regiment they were mistaken for a Yankee cavalry charge, and a nervous line of men opened fire. Jackson held up both hands and ordered the men to cease firing. He was struck in the right hand and again in the left arm. Jackson's racing horse was caught by Captain R. E. Wilbourn and the limp general fell into his arms.

Hotchkiss and Pendleton arrived on the scene shortly after the firing ceased. Seeing the general on the ground, Hotchkiss turned his horse and raced for Dr. Hunter Holmes McGuire, Jackson's medical director and personal physician. He then hurried on to find a stimulant. When he returned, Hotchkiss was dispatched to General Lee to inform him of the development. Lee had heard already the news from Wilbourn, who had preceded Hotchkiss by thirty minutes.

Hotchkiss rested for a while and then went to look for James Keith Boswell. He found the place where Jackson had been wounded, and there, too, he found his friend's body sprawled about twenty paces from where Jackson fell. Boswell lay by a side road, pierced through the heart by two rifle balls and also was wounded in the leg. Hotchkiss started to get his personal effects for his family, but found that the body had been "...riffled of hat, glass, pistol, daguerreotype, &...." He secured an ambulance and took Boswell to Wilderness Tavern where Jackson had been taken. Here he employed two men to dig the grave in the Elwood family cemetery near the spot where Jackson's amputated arm was buried. The Reverend Tucker Lacy offered "...a feeling prayer."

Hotchkiss was deeply affected by Boswell's death. The two had been more than superior and subordinate; they had been friends. Sharing the same tent and mess, they had the kind of association known only to soldiers. Now the friend was gone, taken away by the war that brought them together, and it was all happening too fast for Hotchkiss to understand. Jackson still lived, and that helped for a while. But he had to be taken to the rear for recovery. Lacy aroused Hotchkiss early on May 4 to select the route and lead the way to the home of Thomas Coleman Chandler near Guiney's, where Jackson was to convalesce. Hotchkiss selected a route to Todd's Tavern, through Spotsylvania Court House and thence to Guiney's Station. He preceded the ambulance with a small party to clear the rocks from the road and to order the wagons out of the way. A few of the waggoners were obstinate until they were informed of the identity of the patient. Then, with hat in hand, some weeping, they gave way. The party arrived at Chandler's about eight o'clock. Hotchkiss soon hurried back to headquarters to resume his topographical duties. Jackson's last words to him promised that he, too, would soon be returning to duty. Within a week Jackson was dead.

Shaken by the loss of Boswell and Jackson, Hotchkiss wrote to his wife that "...the charmed circle in which General Jackson and his staff moved is broken & the break is a heavy one." When he learned that Jackson was not expected to recover, he was resigned; "...but I do pray Heaven to spare him, unless, in the wise council of eternity, he has accomplished the end for which he was created...." He missed Jackson very much; headquarters was dreary, to him most of all, "...for my tent mate is gone as well as my General...."

Major General A. P. Hill was appointed temporary commander of Jackson's corps. Hotchkiss welcomed him as a good military man, but he was worried because Hill was not a "Man of God," and did not wear the "...Sword of the Lord and of Gideon." Shortly afterward, a general reorganization of the command structure placed Lieutenant General Richard S. Ewell in command of the Second Corps, and Lieutenant General Jubal A. Early eventually replaced him. But Hotchkiss always missed Jackson: "I was in no great battle subsequent to Jackson's death in which I did not see the opportunity which, in my opinion, he would have seized, and have routed our opponents...."

Yet Hotchkiss had scant time to reflect on his losses. He soon was busy helping to prepare for Lee's second northern invasion. As the army marched toward Pennsylvania and Sara's home, Hotchkiss saw scenes which probably filled him with nostalgia and with fear. Stopping to talk with a woman who had been robbed three times by Federals and left with one dress and nothing to eat, he heard her vindictive prayer: "...that there might never be another Yankee child born & that not one of the race might be left on the face of the earth the first day of next June...."

Hotchkiss travelled with the army as far north as Carlisle, Pennsylvania. Taking over the United States Barracks there, the Confederates raised their flag and listened to the Reverend Mr. Lacy deliver an appropriate sermon. As the army neared Gettysburg, Hotchkiss was engaged in reconnaissance, serving Ewell much in the same way as he had Jackson. During the first day of the battle he acted as a courier, but he was soon ordered to the ridge to observe the troop positions so he could draw an accurate map of the battle. On July 4 he was up at two in the morning working on a map of the country that had to be crossed on the return to Virginia. On the retreat to the Potomac River he helped move the wagons and took careful notes on the terrain. On July 14 the army recrossed the river into Virginia.

Being back in Virginia made Hotchkiss anxious for Sara and for Loch Willow. On July 14 he wrote that he longed for the "repose and quiet" of home, but could see no chance of getting there. In early August Hotchkiss applied for his first leave in six month. His request took about a month for final approval, and the nearness of home made army life even more distasteful. Food, consisting mostly of corn, beans, and stewed peaches, was limited and monotonous. When not working, Hotchkiss passed the time by reading and conversing with fellow soldiers, doubtless finding solace in their mutual complaints. From the Reverend Mr. Lacy he bought Nellie and Anne each "...a set of the Gospels, four pretty little volumes..." and a "...nice...Testament..." for Sara. But still the leave was delayed.

In early September the Reverend R. L. Dabney visited headquarters collecting information for a forthcoming biography of Jackson. Hotchkiss guided him over the battlefield at Cedar Run. He was pleased that Dabney was writing the biography: "I think he will make a good life of Gen. J. and still leave room for another work...." Apparently Hotchkiss already was nurturing the ambition to write about Jackson himself.

Hotchkiss became bitter as the furlough continued to be postponed. His health was declining while able-bodied men sat out the war at home. He angrily wrote to his wife that she would make a better soldier "...than 75 percent of the-stay-at-home-and-won't-organize people...." By September 8 his health was such that he was granted an emergency medical leave by order of Hunter McGuire. He had to ride from Staunton to Loch Willow in an ambulance. Dr. Wilson, a local physician, called daily for five days after Hotchkiss' return and prescribed "some active Medicine" to treat a condition diagnosed as dysentery. The case was assumed by Dr. Robert S. Hamilton on September 13, and Hotchkiss rapidly improved. But by late September he was not considered sufficiently recovered to return to service, and he was granted an additional ten days for convalescence. On the 28th he went to Court Day in Staunton and greeted his friends. Louis T. Wigfall and William "Extra Billy" Smith made political speeches.

Before he returned to the field Hotchkiss received a curious letter from Governor Letcher's aide, S. Bassett French. French wrote on behalf of Mrs.

Anna Jackson, who requested that Hotchkiss send her the Generals' old grey cap. It had been a present from her, and she was willing to trade him Jackson's gauntlets for its return. The following day James Power Smith wrote to him for Mrs. Jackson, "...I really can see no other way to do than to give it up." Hotchkiss decided perhaps ungallantly, to retain possession of the cap, and it was preserved by his family until October 25, 1939, when it was presented to the Virginia Military Institute. No reason for this denial of a widow's request, except a soldier's affection for his commander, can be advanced.

Hotchkiss returned to camp on October 5, 1863, disgusted with war, and although only a few hours removed, already anxious for home. Matters were complicated by the theft of his horse, but fortunately a Mr. Harnsberger, a former pupil, supplied him with another mount. Gradually Hotchkiss settled down to the map work that was to become his routine during the fall of 1863. In early December he and Pendleton made an extensive reconnaissance to select winter quarters. But Hotchkiss did not like the idea of winter in the field. On December 20 he requested and received a 25-day leave to "...attend to business and copy a map of the Valley." The business he transacted demonstrates wartime inflation in Staunton. The price of hiring the servant William Gearing for another year had risen to $300, and Hotchkiss sold a horse for $600.

After nearly a month at home, Hotchkiss was, on January 18, 1864, ordered to report to Major General Jubal A. Early in Staunton with his assistants and baggage. Early wanted a map of all the approaches to Staunton and Lexington from the west. Beginning work on the map, Hotchkiss requested Early and Brigadier General John D. Imboden to detail a guide and a courier to him. Early sent A. D. Moore, a cousin of Major William Allan, to be his courier, and Imboden ordered that "...Private James L. Williams, Company 'G,' 18th Va. Cavalry...will report to Capt. Jed. Hotchkiss...in the capacity of guide."

Hotchkiss grew mindful of home as winter passed to spring. In late January he had to write to Nelson of the death of their sister, Jenny, who died in New York, from childbirth; and from home a toothache complaint brought forth an old soldier's remedy. He became apprehensive when letters from home were delayed, and he gently chided his wife to "...be sure to write to me often, if only a few words at a time—that I may not fail to know of your welfare."

In mid-summer Hotchkiss was with Early on his famous raid on Washington. Penetrating to the suburbs of the Federal capital, the Confederates came to within six miles of the White House, close enough to worry President Abraham Lincoln. Early had promised his men that he would take Washington, but the hot July sun and the dusty roads had taken their toll, and he was forced to retreat with only a moral victory. As the army slowly pulled back, Hotchkiss took advantage of the low prices and abundant supplies in the north. He bought some bonnet ribbon and forty yards of calico for Sara and a fresh Maryland horse for himself. Suprisingly he had no difficulty in using Confederate currency for these purchases. He also wrote a letter to his parents, who still lived in Windsor, New York.

Hotchkiss remained with Early until after the Battle of Cedar Creek in October. Early and Philip Sheridan were fighting for supremacy in the Valley, a contest which was, of course, won by Sheridan. On the eve of the battle, Early sent Hotchkiss and Major General John B. Gordon to the summit of Massanutton Mountain on reconnaissance. Hotchkiss made a field sketch showing heavy defenses on the Federal left; it also revealed the relatively unguarded right wing. When the attack came the Confederates were victorious initially, but they failed to follow up this advantage. Gordon blamed Early for the failure, while Early laid it to Gordon's lack of readiness. Hotchkiss was dispatched to General Lee with the news of the action, but he was instructed by Early not to mention the halted advance to the commander.

When he had delivered the report to Lee, Hotchkiss was able to get home for a visit. For some time he had maintained an office in Staunton, and he needed to attend to affairs there. On November 30 he celebrated his thirty-sixth birthday, sorrowed that the rapidly passing years brought only more war: "God grant that they may not have been spent in vain."

Hotchkiss was home again for Christmas, as he had been each year of the war. It was again time to pay accounts and to hire his servants for the coming year. This time, however, he determined to purchase William Gearing from his owner. He felt an obligation to William, who, like many another that went away to war, had acquired a taste for spirits. Hotchkiss was able to raise $2,000 and borrow $3,000 more to purchase William from Mrs. Kiger.

Returning to the field in January, Hotchkiss was used more frequently now for reconnaissance and in supervising a small staff in the making of maps. He and his assistants worked with the same devotion and patriotism as before, but the years of war were beginning to tell in economic loss and in the appearance of an understandable apprehension about the future. This was evident, when in late February 1865, he wrote to Sara that he had traded his Webster's Dictionary to Christian Beer for a barrel of flour: "I thought you would like the bargain—it is a good one & you can hide the flour & keep it—I think...."

During the final spring of the war Hotchkiss was engaged in reconnaissance duties for Brigadier Generals Thomas L. Rosser and Lunsford L. Lomax. He was with Lomax at Lynchburg on April 9 when the first rumors of Lee's surrender reached there. Lomax rode to Danville to confer with Secretary of War John C. Breckinridge, and then returned to dismiss his command.

Hotchkiss arrived at Loch Willow at dusk on the 18th. A meeting of the Soldier's Aid Society of Churchville, held in his home, had just adjourned. His family was surprised to see him; they thought that he might go to North Carolina to join General Joseph E. Johnston. He found many soldiers already home, bewildered as to what course to follow. Theoretically still soldiers, they lacked leadership and initiative. Lincoln's proposition that Virginia come back into the Union without conditions "...worked a revolution in sentiment..." that helped them make up their minds to stay in their homes. Another factor in this decision was maurauding Federal troops who rode over the countryside stealing anything that struck their fancy.

April 20 brought the first rumor of Lincoln's assassination. Indignation and regret greeted confirmation of the news. There was fear, for "...Johnson, of Tennessee, has become President and breathes out wrath against the South."

A Federal provost marshall arrived in Staunton on May 1 and began parolling Confederate soldiers. Hotchkiss' parole fortunately is preseved in the collection of his papers, and it furnishes a description of him at war's end. He stood five feet ten inches, was probably a little thin, and he had a fair complexion, with dark hair and brown eyes. His lower lip was slightly extended. His eyes were a little sterner, a little deeper than they had been—but their view was forward. Jedediah Hotchkiss was a man of determination whose faith in Virginia was boundless. He never forgot the past, and in memory found strength for the present. The past was a tool to be used in the building of the future: it was not a model to be reconstructed but a lesson learned so that a better future might be realized.

Hotchkiss remained in Virginia in the post-war period, and his contributions to the recovery of that state were many. He became an important developer of the western Virginia coal fields, and he was also a noted educator. His service as a collector and publisher of Confederate military history was noteworthy. His death on January 17, 1899 was mourned by a variety of friends—capitalists, educators, soldiers, and engineers. His exalted place in all areas was earned by hard work, but in no area did he deserve a higher reputation than in topographical engineering. As Stonewall Jackson's Map Maker his services to the military efforts of the Confederacy were ideally suited and well performed.

"Stephen D. Lee and The Guns at Second Manassas"

Herman Hattaway

It is now twenty-seven years since I first began investigating the life and career of Stephen D. Lee, and thirteen years since my biography of him initially appeared in print! The book was the first, and I would imagine in all likelihood forever to be the only, full-length biography of this remarkable man to be published—him the *last* Civil War general of his rank to be biographed. There are a number of reasons that Lee was so long-passed over by scholars, and eventually not even noticed by a host of students and buffs, and I went into some explanation of those reasons in my book. One of them was *not*, I am sure (nor is it even true, although I often was tempted to begin my narration—in a mock opposite to the way that my mentor T. Harry Williams began his colorful work on that most colorful figure, P. G. T. Beauregard) that S. D. Lee was the dullest of all the Confederate generals! What happened that allowed Lee to be all-but-forgotten, until my biography, was, I honestly think, mainly accidental.

I always have been so glad that T. Harry Williams had an interest in having some graduate student work on S. D. Lee and that it became my job to do so. Whatever else Lee may have been, and however good a general he was—he certainly has been good for me! His life did make an acceptable book, and not only that, it became a book which won the Confederate Memorial Literary Society's coveted Jefferson Davis Award given at the Museum of the Confederacy, and now—so many years later, and to my tremendous gratification—has been reissued in a fine paperback edition by the University of Mississippi Press, an edition which attracted the History Book Club and induced its officers to feature it as an "HBC Classic." And I'm especially pleased with my good friend Jack Davis' praise-worthy critique which he did for the Club.

Well, I knew some time ago that this book was going to be reissued, and so when the good folks here in Louisiana who produce this annual Deep Delta Civil War Symposium asked me again this year to appear on the program—which involved preparing a paper ultimately to be published in the annual volume which results from this Symposium's proceedings—it seemed that perhaps it would be nice and even symbolically appropriate to commemorate the reissue of *General Stephen D. Lee* by taking another look—now, at this more mature point in my own career—at one of the high points of Lee's military career. I wondered if I might now conclude anything differently or, if I could find any fresh material which had eluded me before, that might shed any new light on some still-shady element in the story.

S. D. Lee's activities at Second Manassas, I always have felt, *made* his reputation initially, and in the long period of his not being much noticed by Civil War enthusiasts, if he was recalled for even one thing only, it usually was for this episode. And I myself never until this April 8th just past had gotten around to visiting this battlefield! I'm sorry, I know that my dear and respected friends—among them Dick Sommers and Albert Castel—believe it is reprehensible to write about military actions if one has not personally visited the ground where they took place; and indeed I agree with them: its just that in the old days my wife and I simply did not have enough time or money to afford getting to *everyplace* that S. D. Lee saw action. One of the things that made Lee so much fun, but also hard, to study was that he got practically everywhere: from Fort Sumter, to the Virginia battlefields, to Mississippi, and subsequently all over the Western Theater, and finally to a corps command in Georgia, Tennessee, and North Carolina. It's been just an unfortunate coincidence, in my life's travel itinerary thus far, that Manassas got short shrift; and I'm awfully glad to have had the opportunity at last, as a result of my being one of the featured speakers at a meeting there of Jerry Russell's Confederate Historical Institute. It *is* true that actual visits to the terrain provide insight that can be obtained in no other way, and I profited from my experience.

The author at the site of Stephen D. Lee's battery during the Battle of Second Manassas.

Stephen Dill Lee was born September 22, 1833. Thus, he was twenty-seven-and-one-half years-of-age as the Civil War began and he accepted commission as a Confederate captain and served as P. G. T. Beauregard's aide during the operations against Fort Sumter. Lee had graduated from West Point in 1854, seventeenth in a class of forty-six, and had served for the ensuing seven years as a lieutenant of artillery in the United States Army. And so, Lee would be twenty-eight years-eleven months old at Second Manassas—where, incidentally, he later recalled he had his first serious religious thought in his life. Before he met and married his wife, late in the war, he never belonged to any church, though he had turned during the conflict from his youthful indifference. At Second Manassas he had looked out across the field just before the Yankee hordes had charged across it, and he said, "Well there is hell to play here, for sure, and...nothing but some unseen and superintending power, can tell where this thing is going to end."[2]

Shortly after the capitulation of Fort Sumter, Lee transferred to the Hampton (South Carolina) Legion to be its artillery battery commander, and that unit moved to the vicinity of Manassas to join the Confederate army in Virginia, eventually to be an element of Major General James Longstreet's division. Lee participated conspicuously and well during the various minor episodes of the fall and winter of 1861-62. Thus, when the Hampton Legion's artillery was reorganized into a two-battery battalion, Lee was named battalion commander, and was promoted to major on November 8, 1861.

Lee and the battalion won John Bell Hood's praise for gallant service in support of the latter's brigade during the battle of Eltham's Landing on May 7, 1862, and at Hood's urging, Lee was promoted two days later to lieutenant colonel. (Hood, incidentally, was a fellow member of S. D. Lee's 1854 West Point graduating class.) Lee remained with his battalion within the Hampton Legion for the rest of the Confederate retreat up the Virginia peninsula, but at the end of May, when the Southerners made a defensive stand near Richmond, Lee joined Brigadier General William H. C. Whiting's division staff, even though retaining command of the battalion. In this new capacity Lee served as liaison officer between Whiting and his division's two brigades. Lee's artillery battalion did not become engaged in the Battle of Fair Oaks (also called Seven Pines), May 31, 1862, a fateful episode that resulted in the army commander, General Joseph E. Johnston, being wounded and having to be replaced on the next day by General Robert E. Lee.

General Lee at once commenced reorganization, renaming his force the Army of Northern Virginia, and uniting it with previously detached troops under Major General Thomas J. Jackson. R. E. Lee had inherited a cumbersomely construed command, composed of quasi-independent divisions, sometimes called "wings." Major General Daniel H. Hill had the left, James Longstreet the center, and John B. Magruder the right. Gustavus W. Smith, who had been army second in command, previously had the reserve, but—after initially succeeding Johnston to head the army—had suffered a nervous breakdown.

During early June, Magruder became much impressed with S. D. Lee's performance, and requested S. D. Lee's transfer to his wing. R. E. Lee acquiesced, and Magruder named S. D. Lee to be chief of artillery for the right wing.

As wing chief of artillery, Lee exercised a degree of supervision and advisory responsibility over the various batteries which were assigned to brigades, forty-four guns served by 815 men, and he personnally commanded the reserve, twenty-two pieces.

S. D. Lee's artillery participated in a number of hard fights during the Seven Days Campaign, June 25-July 1, 1862, but Magruder's conduct—and the overall conduct of his wing—was assessed unfavorably at General Headquarters. Shortly after the campaign concluded, R. E. Lee accomplished some drastic restructuring, and arranged for the transfer of Magruder to the Western Theater. Indeed all four of the officers within the Army of Northern Virginia who outranked Longstreet were soon transferred, leaving Longstreet the senior major general and second in command.

During August of 1862, both the northern and the southern armies in Virginia made organizational changes; the Confederates restructured into two corps, a larger one of five divisions under Longstreet, and a smaller one of three divisions under Jackson, and made significant change in artillery distribution. Thenceforth Confederate artillery was to be doled out much less than before to units of brigade or smaller size; now it was more typically to be concentrated—in battalion-size units—at division or corps level, and kept well toward the front, with the exception of an army reserve.

S. D. Lee acquired command of an artillery battalion, a new one still incompletely organized and formed. [Eventually it had six batteries; for Second Manassas it was understrength; it fought that battle with only four of its batteries present, plus whatever reinforcement—and there is some becloudedness as to just how much reinforcement—that joined it.] The reorganizations occurred rapidly, and took place only a short time before the Second Manassas Campaign began, and as a result the sources are a bit garbled, some are contradictory, and some are surprisingly brief; so it is that I have not been able to prove beyond all doubt the precise types nor exact numbers of guns that Lee's battalion had for the campaign. A Civil War artillery battery typically had four guns, but they often had as many as six—indeed it was determined by artillery leaders that this larger number was a wiser one, but logistical limitations usually precluded this—and batteries might sometimes, because of losses or other circumstances, have fewer than four guns.[3] [A seriously understrength battery likely soon would be either reinforced or combined with another.] Numerous sources say Lee's battalion for the Second Manassas campaign had eighteen guns—and Lee himself so recalled in 1878: that he had nine howitzers and nine rifles—but one contemporary news release—an article written by one of the battalion's battery commanders, Captain William W. Parker—asserted that the battalion consisted of sixteen guns, supplemented for the Second Manassas Campaign by four others, two from Norfolk and two from Lynchburg, the supplemental pieces being mostly long-range rifles.[4]

S. D. Lee's battalion was the army artillery reserve, and as such he reported directly to R. E. Lee, not to Longstreet, although the battalion moved with an element of Longstreet's corps, Major General Richard H. Anderson's division, the army's infantry reserve. Lee's battalion was referred to as "light artillery" and the objective was, obviously, for the army reserve artillery to be highly mobile. Until Lee took over the unit, it briefly had been commanded by its executive officer Major Delaware ("Del.") Kemper; and Kemper remained in the battalion thereafter. The unit was comprised as follows:

1. The Bath Virginia Battery commanded by Captain John L. Eubank. This well prepared outfit was one of seventy-five artillery batteries which, between November 1, 1861, and June of 1862, were equipped and trained at Camp Lee, a basic training center located on the Hermitage Fair Grounds near Richmond.[5] The unit was armed with four smoothbores.

2. One section of the Portsmouth (Grimes') Virginia Battery with two Parrotts, under Lieutenant Thomas J. Oakham.[6] The state had furnished this socially prominent unit's original pieces, and later one of them was put on display at the U.S. Navy Yard;[7]

3. The Bedford (Virginia) Battery under Captain Tyler Calhoun Jordan— himself later an artillery colonel;[8] no source has been found to ascertain what the unit had for armament at Second Manassas. It took four rifles into the 1863 Pennsylvania campaign;[9] but S. D. Lee's Second Manassas Report indicated that the unit had at least one howitzer.

4. The Richmond Virginia Battery under Captain William Wing Parker. A few of the personnel of this later-famous battery were teenagers, though subsequent myth has suggested that almost all of them were. Actually the average age in the battery was 25.2 years, and one of the men was forty-eight.[10] Nevertheless, and not totally without reason, it was called the "Boy Battery," and at first was a source of grief for S. D. Lee, who was angry at having any extremely young boys in his battalion, and, more importantly, concerned over the unit's inadequate training and total lack of experience. It joined Lee's battalion only ten or twelve days before the Second Battle of Manassas, and in those days, Lee made himself quite unpopular with the cannoneers by working them ex-

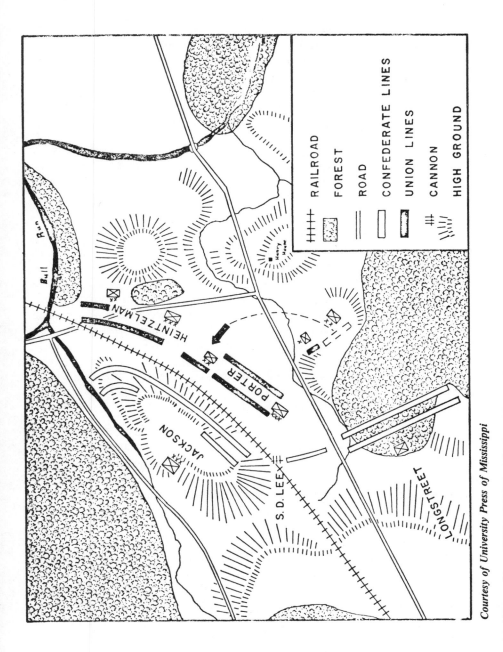

Courtesy of University Press of Mississippi

tremely hard in forced training,[11] but that paid off and they performed well in the battle, their first combat. Lee mentions in his report of Second Manassas that this unit had two howitzers, and Robert Krick in his careful study of the Parker Battery not only confirms that but also identifies the rest of the battery's armament at Second Manassas as being two Parrott rifles.[12] Parker later recalled that his battery had four 3-inch rifles, which had been captured from the Federals (doubtless in McClellan's Peninsula Campaign), and it is confirmed that this was true at least at some later date by chronologically later notations in the *Official Records*;

5. Rhett's South Carolina Battery, under Lieutenant William Elliott. S. D. Lee's Second Manassas report mentions two of the unit's pieces as being howitzers; one article which mentions the unit[13] implies that the battery had (at least some) short-range guns: at Antietam it fired at short range; and

6. Taylor's Virginia Battery, under Captain John Saunders Taylor. This battery is one of the foggier elements in the picture. It *is* listed in the table, "Organization of the Army of Northern Virginia during the battles of August 28-September 1, 1862,"[14] as being part of Lee's battalion, and E. Porter Alexander, who later succeeded Lee in its command, penned in his recollections that the battalion did then have five batteries, twenty-two guns in all,[15] but the truth seems to be that this battery did not in fact actually join the battalion until long after Lee had departed from its command. Robert Krick first mentions it as being in the combat near Chancellorsville in May of 1863. If Taylor *was* present earlier, what armament did he have? Again, with certainty and specificity, I do not know, but it probably was the four 12-pounder Napoleon's— which constituted the unit's armament later in the war.[16]

I conclude that Krick is correct (although there may be a bit more to the story): that at Second Manassas Lee had only four of his regular batteries present, plus Oakham's Section, and the correct official total number of guns was eighteen: nine howitzers and nine rifles.[17] [The two other batteries officially assigned to Lee's battalion joined it near Frederick, Maryland, for the Antietam Campaign: Pichegru Woolfolk's Ashland Battery from Virginia and George Moody's Louisiana Battery. Hence, for Antietam—but not Second Manassas— Lee's battalion had six batteries.] But, good evidence suggests that, Lee's failure to recall so notwithstanding, at some moment, very shortly before the Battle of Second Manassas, Lee's battalion was further reinforced. Two rifle guns and their crews, were detached from one of the batteries in Jackson's corps— probably Captain W. T. Poague's—and united with Lee's other guns. This, then, would harmonize with Captain Parker's contemporary account which indicated twenty guns, not eighteen. The general's son, Robert E. Lee, Jr.—later a Confederate captain, but now serving in the ranks—was "number one" crewman for one of the pieces, and it is his later published recollections that reveal this little part of the story.[18]

*　　*　　*　　*　　*

So, Lee's longest-range guns were Oakham's two Parrotts, probably the smaller 3-inch type which could hurl a 9¾ pound projectile approximately 3,000 yards (the larger 20-Parrott, which, of course, these pieces could have been, had about the same range).

The 3-inch Ordnance Rifle, or the 3-inch Rodman Rifle (whatever Jordan and Parker may have had) could fire 10-pound projectiles approximately 2,800 yards.

Although howitzers were not *always* smoothbored, they generally were. Howitzers typically were made of bronze and were manufactured in standard projectile weight classes: 12-, 24-, and 32-pounders. They had short tubes with chambered interiors that allowed a light power charge to lob a shell on a high trajectory and, thus in employment, were very similar to mortars—very effective against personnel, and in covering "dead spaces" in a field of fire. Basing a "best guess" on Lee's battalion's rapid mobility, his howitzers probably were the 12-pounders, which had a maximum range of 1,070 yards.[19]

Other known officers in Lee's battalion included Lieutenant William H. Kemper, adjutant, and Lieutenants Taylor [I never have been able to learn his first name], Stephen Capers Gilbert, J. T. Brown—[apparently J. Thompson Brown, Jr.; himself later an artillery battery commander], and W. W. Fickling [also later promoted to captain and given command of a battery]. [Their names are known because S. D. Lee cited them for good conduct in his report to Second Manassas. There doubtless were other officers.]

*　　*　　*　　*　　*

Strategic maneuvers preceded the Second Battle of Manassas. R. E. Lee ordered an advance to commence from Gordonsville on August 20. Longstreet's corps on the right was to cross the Rapidan River at Raccoon Ford; Jackson's on the left, was to cross at Sommerville Ford. Anderson's Division, to which was attached S. D. Lee's battalion, constituted the army reserve.

The to-be-short-lived Federal Army of Virginia, forty-seven thousand strong, under Major General John Pope had begun moving on July 14 toward Gordonsville. As the campaign proceeded to unfold, R. E. Lee gained intelligence that Pope soon would be reinforced. To prevent that, and in hopes of "striking a blow," as Lee liked to phrase it, the Army of Northern Virginia effectuated a turning movement, Jackson's corps thrusting ahead and succeeding in getting between Pope's force and Washington, D.C.

Jackson concentrated north of the Warrenton Turnpike, just above Groveton, and waited. Pope's forces approached and on August 28 clashed with Jackson's men in very fierce little skirmish, called the Battle of Groveton, which lasted until nearly midnight. Assessing the situation, Pope erroneously concluded that Jackson was attempting to withdraw into the Valley.

That night the head of Longstreet's columns reached Thoroughfare Gap; and during the same night, the Federal forces previously guarding the gap were ordered to move toward Manassas, for the concentration that Pope believed would spell Jackson's doom. On August 29, Longstreet's troops gradually approached Jackson's position, the first of them contacting Jackson's right flank by 11 A.M., and the bulk of them uniting by mid-afternoon. S. D. Lee and his artillery still remained in the mountain passes.

Blindly confident of imminent success, Pope ordered his entire force to concentrate for a decisive assault. Actually, Jackson had selected an admirable defensive position behind an unfinished railroad bed. The grades and cuts provided ready-made entrenchments while the ties and rocks afforded cover for the men. Pope conducted a series of piecemeal, uncoordinated frontal assaults, all of which failed. Jackson's men followed up the various repulses by advancing to seize positions forward of the main defensive line.

Night brought a temporary end to the fighting, while the Union troops regrouped into a single mass and the Confederates made some important movements. Jackson's men abandoned the advanced positions they had won, and all returned to the strong defensive line along the unfinished railroad. Longstreet's corps stretched out next to them, at an angle bending to the front so that the Confederate army occupied a four-mile-long line shaped like an open V, facing the enemy to the east.

S. D. Lee's artillery battalion, with the last of Longstreet's forces, received orders late in the evening to march toward the front. Lee and his men moved in darkness, and after a tiresome trek, encamped just before dawn on the thirtieth, not knowing precisely where they were in relation to Jackson's corps, only that they were somewhere on the Warrenton Turnpike. At daybreak Lee discovered that his bivouac occupied exactly some of the positions involved in the previous day's fights, the Battle of Groveton.

Lee consulted with Major General John B. Hood, one of Longstreet's division commanders and closest to Jackson's corps, and then decided to put his battalion on the same spot that had been occupied the day before by the Washington Artillery of New Orleans. [This fact is important, for later in determining who should receive credit, and how much, for the great Confederate success, it would be pointed out that the position was an obviously excellent one, and that S. D. Lee certainly needed to expend little or no mental energy in selecting it.] In this position, Lee's battalion could fire across Jackson's front, in direct support of Colonel Stapleton Crutchfield, Jackson's artillery chief. Lee's artillery, adjacent to Hood's brigades, constituted the exact midpoint of the Confederate lines.

Interestingly, only recently has the National Park Service become aware of the precise location of Lee's guns—and indeed knows the gun emplacement spots for only about one third of them. A mere small part of the Manassas battle area was set aside for commemorative purposes during the nineteenth century; with the passing of time, only gradually have various additional parcels of land since been acquired and added to what is now the Manassas National Battlefield. Quite by accident, relic hunters turned up at Park Headquarters, sheepishly to admit that they had found—and opened—a Confederate gravesite, but also had found several concentrations of friction primer remnants—the archeological evidence of the gun emplacements. Before that time, the Park experts had guessed that the location was some twenty-five or more yards forward of where it actually was.[20]

The position hardly could have been better; the guns pointed northeast and were nestled along a commanding ridge about a quarter of a mile long. They *may* have been situated just behind a stone wall (which of course would have offered cover to the gunners, helping to protect them from any enemy assault upon the position.) No sources mention that stonewall, but remnants of one are there to this day. If it was not there at the time of the battle, then it would have had to have existed though been leveled before that time, or built and subsequently leveled since. No one now knows. Whichever as to the wall, the gunners overlooked a field of fire embracing some two thousand yards—over a mile to the front! Immediately opposite Jackson's lines stretched an open field, of which Lee's fire could sweep any part. Beyond that, to the east, was farmland with corn fields, orchards, and fences—an inviting expanse for enemy skirmishers—and still farther to the east was timberland, an obvious assembly area for a Union assault force. Gen. R. E. Lee himself inspected Colonel Lee's position and declared, "You are just where I wanted you; stay there...."

Remembering S. D. Lee's unhampered field of fire, one battalion member recalled that "we had a grand view of the plains of Manassas, reaching as far as Centreville." While no major strike occurred until noon, the first Federal infantry became visible at 7 A.M., some two thousand yards away. Lee's guns opened fire, forcing the enemy, even at that distance, to scurry for cover. The Federals returned the volley with long-range guns.

During the morning the act was repeated many times. At every appearance of Union infantry, Lee's artillery harassed them. They answered with fire from their own big guns, but did no damage to Lee's emplacements. One of Lee's men recalled that "the enemy had a 36 pounder," certainly a large artillery piece, "but fortunately he did not get our range."[21] Lee himself, helped with some of the firing. Once he sighted a gun for thirty-five hundred yards, aimed at a Federal caisson, and killed two of the wheel horses with his second shot. Meanwhile, the Federals continued preparations for a massive charge.

Throughout the morning Lee's artillery engaged only a far-distant enemy, some of the other nearby Confederates almost growing complacent. One regimental commander actually sat under the shade of a persimmon tree, eating his breakfast of dry crackers and boiled bacon, watching Lee direct fire at a line of troops too far away to recognize as soldiers until sunlight glinting off their bayonets betrayed them. Around noon the Federals tested the position with an advance, driving in the few Confederate skirmishers. The artillery drove them back, and then suddenly all firing ceased. An ominous silence prevailed.

Then, suddenly, at about 3 P.M., a huge concentration of Federals which had massed behind the timber opposite Lee's position, advanced in heavy force against Jackson's left, "glittering lines of battle in magnificent array," one Southerner recalled. Accompanied by crash after crash of musketry, regiment after regiment of bluecoated soldiers moved toward the extreme left of Jackson's lines. One of the men in Lee's battalion later penned a news release for the Richmond *Dispatch*:

> The shells burst above, around, and [seemingly] beneath us. Every man is at his post, no talking—no ducking of heads now. An intense, silent earnestness. It was an hour big with every man's history. It was a struggle for life. The face of every man was flushed, his eye full,...It seemed like the very heavens were in a blaze, or, like two angry clouds surcharged with electricity and wafted by opposing winds, had met terrific in battle.[22]

The Confederates fought back furiously, some quickly running out of ammunition. At intervals, Southerners scrambled out and stripped the dead and wounded of cartridge boxes. At some points along Jackson's front, crouching Federals were huddled so close that some Confederates resorted to throwing rocks at them.

Momentarily fearful of a break-through, Jackson sent a desperate message to General Lee, requesting reinforcements. Lee immediately ordered Longstreet to send a division; but by the time Longstreet received the order, huge masses of Federal troops, the main assault force, aimed toward Jackson's center, were crossing the field of fire of S. D. Lee's guns. Henry Kyd Douglas, one of Jackson's couriers, later recalled that Longstreet had replied to the request for reinforcements that before any could reach Jackson, "that attack will be borken by artillery."[23] It was about 4 P.M., as one of the men present later phrased it, Lee had "planted artillery so thick...that cannoneers almost elbowed each other."

[It is fair, and perhaps important, to observe though that Stapleton Crutch-field and Jackson's corps artillery emplaced within the lines, and eighteen of his guns also helped repulse the assaults. They fired frontally into the attacking troops, supported by the effective enfilade fire which Lee's position allowed.][24]

The assault force, despite two attempts to rally it, was thrown back. Douglas, who witnessed it, recalled that the first "assaulting line halted,..thrown into confusion, and they fled. In their place came another line, with the same disastrous result. And then again a splendid column of attack, compact and determined, came grandly up to their endeavor." But S. D. Lee's artillery stood ready, and "when the blue line was within proper range, these hoarse hounds of war were unleashed and the destruction they did was fearful. Deep rents were torn in the enemy's ranks, their colors went down, one after another." "The heavens rocked with the roar of the Confederate batteries," wrote one soldier, and "such a blaze of artillery as I never heard," another recalled. For thirty full minutes, regiment after regiment—thousands of Federal troops—charged into the open. Lee's guns belched an incessant fire. Thousands of reserve troops, ready to exploit any success by the main assault, never moved up—intimidated by Lee's effective fire.

Suffering tremendously from the continuing artillery bursts, three Federal regiments slashed desperately forward, in a futile attempt to assault Lee's guns. The howitzers belched canister, pinpoints of flame jutting forth. All finally were repulsed, some of their dead falling within two hundred yards of Lee's guns.

*   *   *   *   *

Here is one minor point that I have been persuaded to change from which I believed when I first published *General Stephen D. Lee*: I said then that in capitalizing on Lee's successful fire, Longstreet ordered up the other batteries, which had been attached to his corps, to the position, making thirty guns in all which[25] joined in the enfilade fire that wrought the final destruction of the Federal assault, sweeping the last blue waves from the field. Longstreet did order the other guns forward, but they were far to the right of Lee's position, and never got to within effective range. At the crucial moment, it *was* S. D. Lee's show.

Lee had his short-range guns moved to within five hundred yards of their targets, and they did severe damage until finally having to quit firing because the thick smoke created a blinding curtain over the battlefield. This smoke also hampered the feeble Federal effort at counterfire. Only two Union batteries even fired on Lee, and these overshot their mark.

The Union "charge was turned into a retreat," Henry Kyd Douglas recalled, "and they soon broke over the field in a wild rout. The avenging shot and shell scattered the fleeing mass and their flight became a panic." And Longstreet's grey host at last counterattacked, inflicting severe punishment on some units of the disorganized Federals, the kind that R. E. Lee had attempted unsuccessfully to achieve all during the Seven Days Campaign. For more than a mile and a half, well into the old battlefield of First Manassas, the Confederates, who "came on like demons emerging from the earth," one Federal observer said, the grey-clad men pushed the demoralized Northerners. One Federal regiment, Duryee's Zouaves from New York, suffered in killed and wounded the greatest losses of any Civil War Regiment on any day in the entire war.[26]

*　　*　　*　　*　　*

Much credit belonged to S. D. Lee and his guns. In addition to having had a perfect position from which to fire, their performance had been magnificent. In repelling the charges Lee's men had worked incessantly; six of them sustained wounds, including the executive officer Kemper who was hurt badly in the arm. For two of the batteries this was their first battle action. The enormous expenditures of each gun—estimated by one careful student at not less than one hundred fifty rounds apiece—ranked this as one of the greatest muzzle-loading artillery conflicts of history. It also made Lee something of a hero. His name, was on the lips of every soldier in the army. Some even said, with obvious extravagance, that "never, in the history of war, had one man commanded so much artillery, with so much skill and effect as he did."

Apparently, however, Lee did not receive as much credit and adulation from his superiors as he did from his admirers. In later years many persons cited Second Manassas as one of Lee's two or three truly outstanding Civil War accomplishments. Even R. E. Lee had said to him, the first time they met after the battle, "Young man, come here! I want to thank you for what you did yesterday. You did good work." And the following December, President Jefferson Davis, referring to S. D. Lee, said, "I have reason to believe that at the last great conflict on the field of Manassas he served to turn the tide of battle and consummate the victory." But the general had given Lee no special personal credit in his official report. He mentioned only that Lee occupied the same position as Walton's Washington Artillery the day before and that under Lee's "well directed fire, the supporting lines were broken and fell back in confusion." That was all: no high praise.

Longstreet exhibited an even cooler attitude. In his official report, he blandly stated that "Colonel S. D. Lee, with his reserve artillery placed in the position occupied the day previous by Colonel Walton, engaged the enemy in a very severe artillery combat. The result was, as on the day previous, a success."

And, years later—in 1877 and 1878—Longstreet and Lee fought a bitter literary debate.[27] Perhaps they always had been cool toward one another, maybe even enemies, it is impossible now to prove one way or the other. We do now know that after 1870 Longstreet increasingly had come under personal attack, and his enemies tried to besmirch his war reputation. Among several episodes about which he was harried was *his* conduct at Second Manassas. At times, in attempting to defend, he was goaded into intemperance.[28]

What Longstreet did with respect to S. D. Lee's performance and contribution at Second Manassas was to damn him and it with faint praise: Longstreet did not say anything really negative; he simply did not say much at all, and he grossly exaggerated the importance of the artillery he had moved in the end to S. D. Lee's support. As Gary Gallagher recently put it in an article published in *Civil War History*, "Lee had much the better of the exchange."

Longstreet's post-war bitterness notwithstanding, it is difficult to assess his and R. E. Lee's apparent restraint at the actual time, concerning S. D. Lee's performance at Second Manassas. Contrasted with many assessments by other writers, both participants at Second Manassas as well as students of the battle, they were remarkably matter-of-fact about S. D. Lee's contributions.

To be sure, S. D. Lee had enjoyed good luck! True to his sometime nickname "Pet of Fortune," he just wandered by default onto a position that Walton's Washington Artillery already had selected, but abandoned, because it was too debilitated even to continue in action. Indeed, luck may well have been the principal factor in the outcome: luck that S. D. Lee's guns stood where they happened to be; and luck that Pope's Federals were hurled in such massive numbers and so persistently into S. D. Lee's enfilading fire zone. Yet Second Manassas was a great Confederate victory. Undeniably, S. D. Lee's luck and his skill both had entered into the picture. Suppose Lee had not gone to the trouble of trying to train his youthful and inexperienced gunners; suppose they had broken, or been over run? [As a matter of fact, one modern expert in infantry assault tactics suggested to me recently that by using cavalry to assault S. D. Lee's position, and then thrusting troops just to the right of it, breaking through the Confederate lines there, rolling laterally into Longstreet's minions, was the most obviously desirable way out for Pope's forces.] Lee had been the man of the moment. Many more such moments, and the outcome of the war might have been different.

Endnotes

1 Herman Hattaway, *General Stephen D. Lee* (Jackson: University Press of Mississippi, 1976, republished in paperbound edition, 1989). It seems pointless to repeat the documentation from the book, in this paper, hence for this paper I shall footnote only the passages which are not specifically documented in the book.

2 Partially identified Charleston, South Carolina, newspaper clipping, 1908, in Scrapbooks of Stephen Dill Lee, Lee Museum, Columbus, Mississippi, Book three.

3 Edward Porter Alexander, "Confederate Artillery Service," *Southern Historical Society Papers*, 11: p. 99. This collection of papers is hereinafter referred to as *S.H.S.P.*

4 See Joseph Mills Hanson, *Bull Run Remembers* (Manassas, Virginia: National Capitol Publishers, 1953), p. 124; Partially identified newspaper clipping, dated 31 August 1862, in Scrapbooks of Blewett Lee, Lee Museum, Columbus, Mississippi; Robert K. Krick, *Parker's Virginia Battery C.S.A.*(Second edition revised, Wilmington, North Carolina: Broadfoot Publishing Company, 1919), especially Chapter III.

5 *S.H.S.P.* 26: p. 244.

6 *S.H.S.P.* 6: p. 250. Oakham's last name is OAKUM in *S.H.S.P.* 34: 148 & 150, but OAKHUM in the index to the *S.H.S.P.* as well as in Stephen D. Lee's report, in *War of the Rebellion: A Compilation of the Official Records of the Union and Confederate Armies* (70 volumes in 128 parts, Washington, D.C.: Government Printing Office, 1880-1901), Series I, Volume 12, part 2, pp. 577-78. Hereinafter cited as *O.R.*

7 *Confederate Veteran* 14: p. 390.

8 *O.R.* 1, 51, Pt. 2, p. 900.

9 *O.R.* 1, 25, Pt. 1, p. 877.

10 Krick, *Parker's Virginia Battery*, second edition, pp. 6-9.

11 *S.H.S.P.* 35: pp. 103-05.

12 Krick, *Parker's Virginia Battery*, second edition, p. 35.

13 *Confederate Military History* VI: p. 158.

14 *O.R.*, I, 12, Pt. 2, pp. 546-51.

15 Edward Porter Alexander, *Fighting for the Confederacy* (ed. by Gary W. Gallagher, Chapel Hill, The University of North Carolina Press, 1989), p. 134. Alexander and Lee had been close friends ever since Lee had been cadet lieutenant in Alexander's plebe company at West Point, and later they carried on a chummy correspondence. I think Alexander was referring to Oakham's section as the fifth battery, but I do not know what to make of Alexander's recollection of twenty-two guns at Second Manassas.

16 *O.R.* 1, 42, Pt. 3, p. 1339.

17 Krick, *Parker's Virginia Battery*, second edition, p. 50.

18 Robert E. Lee, Jr., *Recollections and Letters of General Robert E. Lee, by His Son, Captain Robert E. Lee* (New York: Doubleday, Page, & company, 1904), p. 76.

[19] I have extrapolated my technical data from L. Van Loan Naisawald, *Grape and Canister* (New York: Oxford University Press, 1960); Fairfax Downey, *The Guns at Gettysburg* (New York: Collier Books Edition, 1962); and Jennings Cropper Wise, *The Long Arm of Lee* (2 vols. Lynchburg, Virginia: J. P. Bell, 1915).

[20] John Hennessey, former historian at the park, is writing what doubtless will be the definitive history of the Second Manassas campaign. I got all of this information from him verbally during my visit to the battle site in 1989.

[21] Newspaper clipping, dated 31 August 1862, in Scrapbooks of Blewett Lee.

[22] Newspaper clipping, dated 31 August 1862, in Scrapbooks of Blewett Lee.

[23] Henry Kyd Douglas, *I Rode With Stonewall* (Chapel Hill: University of North Carolina Press, 1940), p. 140.

[24] See William Thomas Poague, *Gunner With Stonewall* (Monroe F. Cockrell, ed., Jackson, Tennessee: McCowat-Mercer Press, 1957), p. 38; Hanson, *Bull Run Remembers*, p. 124.

[25] See Lenoir Chambers, *Stonewall Jackson* (2 volumes, New York: William Morrow & co., 1959), II, p. 170, this being the source I used at the time.

[26] Frank Vandiver, *Mighty Stonewall* (New York: McGraw Hill, 1957), pp. 370-71; Inscription on monument to Duryee's Zouaves, at the battlefield.

[27] See *S.H.S.P.* 6: pp. 59-70; 215-17; and 250-54.

[28] For a good explanation of this particular matter, see Gary W. Gallagher, "Scapegoat in Victory: James Longstreet and the Second Battle of Manassas," *Civil War History* 34: December, 1988, pp. 293-307.

John C. Breckinridge and the Confederate Defeat

William C. Davis

The Civil War presents a fertile field of forgotten men, and nowhere need one search to find a group more overlooked than in the office of the Secretary of War. No other individuals of comparable station in this war have been so neglected by scholars. When one looks at them from the standpoint of Confederate military leadership it is not hard to see why. No others of comparable station exerted so little real influence.

The one exception is John C. Breckinridge of Kentucky. The least studied of all the Secretaries of War, he proved to be the most capable and efficient of the lot. Chronologically the last in the succession of war ministers, he was in fact the first and only functioning Secretary of War the South ever had, the only one to leave the stamp of his personal influence upon the military course of the Confederacy.

The reasons for the failure of Breckinridge's predecessors have been oft repeated at great length. In sum they reduce to a name, Jefferson Davis. Convinced of his own military omniscience, yet placed in a high civil rather than military post, he solved his dilemma by appointing as Secretary of War a succession of men of mediocre talents and, more importantly, of totally domitable will. All of these men had been, as Burton Hendrick so aptly characterized them, "alternating ghosts [who] might flutter through the executive building in Richmond, but it was Jefferson Davis who organized armies, appointed officers, supervised military campaigns, and attended even to the details of the office."[1]

Considering this, the appointment of Breckinridge as Secretary of War on February 6, 1865, represented a major shift in Davis' attitude toward that office and a redefinition of the role it would play in Confederate military leadership.

Of all of the statesman who joined the southern ranks, Breckinridge was at once the most illustrious and the most popular. Davis himself was believed by some to be jealous of the Kentuckian's popularity.[2] Envious or not, Davis did esteem and respect Breckinridge. He had been Vice President of the United States, and in 1860 his presidential candidacy carried all but two of the states now comprising the Confederacy. Nearly half a million men who were now Confederates had voted for him, and the trust thus expressed had been greatly enhanced by the Kentuckian's three years service as one of the most popular and capable major generals in the army.[3] Furthermore, he had the confidence of the irascible Confederate Congress, which had once voted him its thanks, and on another occasion voted to allow him a special seat on its floor.[4] Expressions were abroad that if the Confederacy should survive to the expiration of Davis' Presidential term, Breckinridge would be his possible successor. Noted Southern historian Clement Eaton has even declared that Breckinridge, and not Davis, was ideal choice for Confederate President.[5]

Davis could not impose upon or neglect a man of this stature. At the same time, Breckinridge's own background made him an ideal war minister, possessed of every qualification which his predecessors lacked. An eminent statesman, with extensive military experience, he served in and knew every major theater of the war. He was intimately acquainted with every major commander except Richard Taylor. He had planned his own campaigns and suffered the administrative torture of departmental command in southwest Virginia, emerging with enhanced reputation from a responsibility which had eclipsed every commander before him. And of all of those who held his portfolio, he was the only one—save perhaps George Wythe Randolph—who neither feared nor stood in awe of Davis.

Breckinridge made Davis feel his independence immediately. Despite ample display of incompetence, Brigadier General Lucius B. Northrop had been retained as Commissary General by Davis for nearly four years. Breckinridge made it clear when Davis offered him the cabinet post that he would not accept unless Northrop were removed. It was a test of just how much authority Breckinridge would be able to wield in office. A week before Davis sent Breckinridge's nomination to the Senate, the Kentuckian's old friend Eli M. Bruce temporarily relieved Northrop. Two weeks later Breckinridge personally selected a permanent Commissary General, the capable I. M. St. John.[6]

Davis would declare that the function of assigning officers to command was "exclusively executive."[7] Now, however, Breckinridge took over much of the direction of general officers, their transfers and assignements.[8] Robert E. Lee consulted him rather than Davis in the matter of replacements for generals.[9] It was Breckinridge, not Davis, who ordered John B. Hood transferred to the Trans-Mississippi in March 1865. Henceforward all recommendations for promotion of general officers were made by the Secretary of War.[10]

The conduct of military operations and the movement of troops were functions formerly denied to Secretaries of War. Breckinridge engaged in both without interference. He advised Lee on the proper course to follow in southwestern Virginia and proposed grand strategy for the defeat of William T. Sherman.[11] To P. G. T. Beauregard he dispensed counsel and orders for the evacuation of Columbia, South Carolina.[12] In mid-March 1865, as Ulysses S. Grant's line threatened to encircle Richmond, the secretary personally managed the movements of portions of Fitzhugh Lee's cavalry in attempting to hold open a route to the south.[13] He ordered a union of the forces of Daniel Adams and Howell Cobb to defend Columbus, Georgia, in April.[14] Following the surrender of Lee, he authorized all soldiers not surrendered with the Army of Northern Virginia to attach themselves to units of their choice in the Army of Tennessee, and directly ordered Brigadier General John Echols, commanding the Department of Western Virginia and Eastern Tennessee, to move his command to link with Joseph E. Johnston in North Carolina.[15] Breckinridge, on his own authority, gave Wade Hampton orders exempting him from Johnston's surrender and allowing him to take his command away in hopes of reaching the Trans-Mississippi.[16] By mid-April, as the armies were surrendering, it seems to have become generally understood that Breckinridge was now fully in command of the War Department and all its functions. When Jefferson Davis denied Virginia Governor William Smith's proposition that he be given command of all remaining Virginia troops, Smith took his case to the Secretary of War.[17]

The Commissary General's office provides a worthy case study in how the new Secretary of War seized and maintained direction of the affairs of his department. "When I arrived at Richmond," he later wrote, "the Commissary department...was in a very deplorable condition."[18] With the appointment of St. John as Commissary General, Breckinridge made the revitalization of this bureau his first priority. The two conferred daily and at great length. To alleviate the immediate shortage in Lee's army, they devised a system of collecting supplies by appealing to farmers and shipping the proceeds directly to the army, bypassing Northrop's old bottleneck central depots.[19] Seeing the success wrought in the Old Dominion under this plan, Breckinridge personally persuaded Governor Zeb Vance to make the same appeal in North Carolina.[20]

The results were dramatic. Three weeks after Breckinridge and St. John began their work, Lee sent a letter stating that his army had not been so well supplied in months. By April 1 they had collected in Virginia and North Carolina three million rations of bread and two and one half million rations of meat. Breckinridge and St. John were producing supplies in quantities which outstripped the transportation facilities available.[21]

It was only a war minister who felt confident of his authority who could venture into some of the delicate areas traversed by Breckinridge. When complaints reached his ears from Nathan B. Forrest and others that men raising companies in the mountains of Kentucky refused to join the regular service when ordered, and were instead plundering the local citizenry, Breckinridge sent his own cousin into the state with orders that all Confederates who did not come out and join the regular service would be handed over to the enemy as guerrillas.[22]

More potentially volatile was the matter of censorship of the press. Voluntary censorship by newsmen and editors had worked successfully early in the war, but as the conflict progressed the government felt increasing need to regulate news. The attendant outcry was predictable. Yet, when Breckinridge took office he agreed that continued censorship was necessary. As a result, an almost total embargo on war news was enforced by the secretary. Yet Breckinridge found himself complimented by the press for his conduct. The Richmond *Whig* declared that "if anything of interest transpires which can be published, we are confident that the intelligent Secretary of War will cause the news to be promptly communicated to the press."[23]

Under authority from Congress, the government was empowered to take over railroads and direct their operation. As soon as the law was passed, Breckinridge notified Braxton Bragg that he would use the power if necessary, and almost immediately a case presented itself.[24] As a military necessity for the movement of supplies, Beauregard wanted the track gauge of the Piedmont and North Carolina Railroads between Salisbury and Danville widened to that of the major Virginia roads. Vance objected, but Breckinridge told him bluntly that "under the late law, I may be compelled to take possession of some of the roads."[25] Under authority from the Secretary of War, instructions had earlier been given for Joseph Johnston to take over all rail facilities within his command, and while Breckinridge was negotiating with Vance orders went out taking over the western portion of the South Side Railroad. The war ended before the work was fairly begun, but it is one more indicator of the self confidence and security which the new secretary felt in office.[26]

As all of this was taking place, Breckinridge had been busy organizing what must be described as a small scale campaign—the evacuation of Richmond. On February 23 Assistant Secretary John A. Campbell had advised Breckinridge to make plans for the almost inevitable evacuation, but the Kentuckian was, in fact, considerably ahead of him.[27] From first taking office he had seen what must happen, and had already been in correspondence with Lee on a possible route of retreat from the capital, at the same time making preliminary arrangements to have supplies waiting for the retiring army at its destination.[28] Breckinridge gathered intelligence from southwestern Virginia, through which Lee would probably retreat, held stores in some depots in North Carolina, and quietly but firmly alerted commanders along Lee's route to "gather every thing up, hold it well in hand and not let the enemy advance." Confidentially he told them, "The country towards the S west may soon become of vast importance."[29]

Breckinridge and Lee conferred frequently. The secretary tried to pinpoint how much time was available for preparation. Even before receiving a reply he ordered his bureau chiefs to prepare their archives and public stores. At the same time he brought the matter before Davis and the cabinet on February 25, to no avail. "Nothing has been done," he lamented to Lee. "Do you advise that I go to work at once?"[30]

Breckinridge conferred with representatives of the general assembly, saw to the strength of the Richmond reserves, and made tentative plans for the destruction of material that could not be taken away. In two days the secretary had the evacuation planned and all arrangements made for its execution. In an interview with Lee he promised that the movement could be completed within ten or twelve days.[31] On April 1 the Kentuckian was at the War Department all day and all night still packing. On April 2, when word came that Lee could hold out no longer, it took Breckinridge less than twenty-four hours to complete the evacuation of the government. Whereas in former days Davis would certainly have taken a major role in organizing and conducting such an important operation—particularly important should the Confederacy survive—now he played no part at all. From first to last it was the Secretary of War who managed the evacuation.

With this operation barely concluded, it was the Secretary of War, who further conferred with the retreating Lee, and who counselled him in the matter of a linkup with Johnston.[32] Leaving Lee on April 7, Breckinridge began yet another minor campaign, this time managing the flight of the Confederate Cabinet through North and South Carolina, into Georgia. The story is one well known. A salient feature, however, is the increasing amount of authority that he assumed after Lee's surrender. As Davis took less and less part in making the decisions, Breckinridge took more and more. It was to the Secretary of War that Johnston turned for advice and counsel in his surrender negotiations with Sherman. It was Breckinridge who, on his own initiative, disbursed to the remaining Confederate troops the last of the treasury specie. And it was the Kentuckian who, in effect, disbanded the War Department at Washington, Georgia, on May 4.[33] Indeed, among those who were with the fleeing government in its last weeks, the general feeling was, as Brigadier General Basil Duke put it, that only Breckinridge "knew what was going on, what was going to be done, and what ought to be done."[34]

As far back as September of 1861, before Breckinridge joined Southern ranks, he had confided to friends his belief that the Confederacy would ultimately be overthrown.[35] What he met when taking over the War Department hardly changed his mind. On his first day in office a report of the unsuccessful Hampton Roads peace conference was submitted by Assistant Secretary Campbell, and shortly afterward the secretary got a firsthand account of it from Robert Ould.[36] Two days later came Lee's complaint of lack of supplies, and with it the warning that "you must not be surprised if calamity befalls us."[37] Replies to a circular he sent to all bureau chiefs asking the condition of their departments—Breckinridge was the first secretary to bother making such a survey—were uniformly disheartening.[38] The generals, as always, were still squabbling, and there was no money to pay the troops or buy needed supplies.[39] Barely two weeks after taking office Breckinridge first voiced to the President his feeling that the cause was lost. Explaining all of the above, he declared "It is plainly impracticable for this Department to carry on any of its operations under such a condition of things."[40]

Taking an honorable peace as his goal, Breckinridge seized every opportunity to persuade the President. When Lieutenant General James Longstreet presented tentative plans for meetings between himself and Union Major General E. O. C. Ord, having the cessation of hostilities as their object, the Secretary of War vocally approved the plan before Davis.[41]

On March 8, after reflecting on recent conversations with Lee, Breckinridge asked the general in chief for his written views on the military situation.[42] After receiving Lee's gloomy reply, Breckinridge addressed another circular to his bureau chiefs. These replies, too, were pessimistic.[43] Then on March 13, he submitted the entire correspondence to Davis, voicing his own concurrence in Lee's portent of calamity. Ostensibly the material was submitted for Davis to pass on to Congress before it adjourned.[44] In fact it had quite another purpose, one divined by Vance and others. The secretary actually hoped to persuade Davis that further resistance was futile.[45]

Vance's suspicion is confirmed by the fact that Breckinridge began meeting privately with Senators such as R. M. T. Hunter, discussing Lee's letter with them.[46] A few days after sending the papers to Davis, he called a conference at the hotel room of Kentucky Senator Henry C. Burnett. Present were Wigfall of Texas, Hunter and Allen Caperton of Virginia, and Waldo Johnston and George G. Vest of Missouri. As Vest later recalled it, "Breckinridge stated his conviction that the Confederate cause was hopeless and in a very few days all would be lost."

> I have wished for some time to confer with the members of the Confederate Senate...as to the effect of the final collapse....
> What I propose is this: That the Confederacy should not be captured in fragments, that we should not disband like banditti, but that we should surrender as a government, and we will thus maintain the dignity of our cause, and secure the respect of our enemies, and the best terms for our soldiers.

When someone asked, "How about the President?" the Secretary of War replied that "that gives me more concern than anything connected with the plan." The meeting concluded, Breckinridge gave the Senators a final plea: "This has been a magnificent epic; in God's name, let it not terminate in a farce."[47]

Neither Davis nor the Congressmen were yet persuaded to act. Even Lee's surrender did not change the President's mind and, when Breckinridge rejoined the cabinet at Greensboro, North Carolina, after leaving Lee, Davis was determined to fight on with Johnston.[48] By prearrangement, Breckinridge obtained for Johnston and Beauregard an opportunity to present their view of the hopelessness of the situation before an April 13 cabinet meeting. They wanted to ask Sherman for terms. Davis disapproved, supported by Judah P. Benjamin, but Breckinridge, Stephen R. Mallory, and John H. Reagan argued for the plan, and the President gave in.[49]

But still Davis hoped to continue the fight. When the cabinet moved south to Lexington, North Carolina, and was joined by Governor Vance, Davis took up in a cabinet meeting the idea of retreating west of the Mississippi to continue the war with Edmund Kirby Smith. It was obvious that Davis wanted Vance to lead the North Carolina troops out of the state with him. One or more of the cabinet members agreed with the President and then, wrote Vance,

> General Breckinridge [sic] spoke.
>
> I shall never forget either the language or the manner of that splendid Kentuckian. With the utmost frankness, and with the courage of sincerity, he said he did not think they were dealing candidly with Governor Vance; that their hopes of accomplishing the results set forth by Mr. Davis were so remote and uncertain that he, for his part, could not advise me to forsake the great duties which devolved upon me in order to follow the further fortunes of the retreating Confederacy....With a deep sigh Mr. Davis replied to General Breckinridge: 'Well, perhaps, General, you are right.'[50]

That same evening began the Secretary of War's involvement in the Sherman-Johnston surrender negotiations. Johnston specifically requested Breckinridge's presence in the negotiations because he felt that the Kentuckian could overcome Davis' objections and persuade him to accept whatever terms resulted.[51] Breckinridge, having already approved in cabinet a preliminary list of surrender provisions, spoke for several minutes in advocacy of them before Sherman.[52] One of his chief concerns was the political rights of paroled Confederates, and the influence of his "concise and statesmanlike mind" clearly showed in the finished document in the provision for reestablishment of Federal courts in the South, and the stress given to protection of the legal rights of former Rebels.[53]

Breckinridge personally put a copy of the agreement in Davis' hands, but the President, still clinging stubbornly to his hopes, asked for the opinions of his cabinet members in writing. Breckinridge gave his bluntly. "Prompt steps," he wrote, "should be taken to put an end to the war."[54] This time the cabinet was unanimous, and finally Davis agreed to Sherman's terms. When Washington rejected the cartel and directed Sherman to treat only of Johnston's army alone, Davis and escort continued their journey south, to the last so-called cabinet meeting at Abbeville, South Carolina, on May 2. Yet again Davis tried to persuade his military men to continue the fight west of the Mississippi. Yet again Breckinridge and others opposed him, thinking his views were, as Colonel W. C. P. Breckinridge put it, "wholly erroneous."[55] Even here it was observed by members of the escort that of the remaining cabinet, only the Secretary of War did not stand in awe of the President.[56] After making good his escape to Cuba, the Kentuckian made yet one more plea for honorable surrender, advising all remaining Confederates to throw themselves on the clemency of President Andrew Johnson and ask for pardon. He wanted no more blood shed for an extinct cause, and so expressed himself to the press.[57] It is clear that Breckinridge regarded his efforts to bring about an honorable surrender for the Confederacy as the most important contribution of his cabinet service. "Should my friends ever know my part in the occurrences of the last three months," he wrote this May, "I venture to think it will give me an increased claim on their confidence and regard."[58]

Of course the South would have fallen with or without Secretary of War John C. Breckinridge, but that it fell as it did, as a nation rather than as piecemeal bands led by Davis and others, owes much to this Kentuckian and his vision of the Confederacy in posterity. It is also indicative of the role that this war minister played in Confederate leadership. Unlike any of his predecessors, he exerted a major influence on civil and military policy and, equally important, upon the president. This does not necessarily mean, however, that the outcome of the war might have been otherwise if Breckinridge had been appointed earlier. Davis had considered him for Secretary of War back in October of 1861 when Breckinridge first joined the Confederacy.[59] But then the Kentuckian had almost no practical experience at warfare and would have been an able, but unknowledgeable administrator. When he took office in 1865, however, his appointment was received as a breath of fresh air.[60] His energy inspired hope in many, among them the ever-quotable Mrs. Chestnut. "If we had had Breckinridge in Walker's place at the beginning," she wrote, "what a difference it might have made."[61] Others more expert than she agreed, among them Robert E. Lee. William Preston later recalled that, upon hearing of Breckinridge's appointment, Lee said that he was the ablest general in the Confederacy to assume such a post. "If I had an army I would at once put it under his command."[62] Three years after the surrender Lee made it clear to William Preston Johnston that he regarded Breckinridge as the ablest of the War Secretaries. "He regretted that Breckinridge had not been earlier made secretary of war," Johnston recorded. "He is a great man," said Lee. "I was acquainted with him as Congressman and Vice-President and as one of our Generals, but I did not *know* him till he was secretary of war, and he is a lofty, pure strong man."[63]

This last is the real point. Breckinridge was a *strong* man, and his tenure in the War Department built the office of secretary into a strong one. Many factors contributed to this, not the least of which was Lee's assuming some of Davis' former powers when he accepted the post of general in chief. It is also evident that Jefferson Davis in 1865 was physically and mentally weakened by four years of his terrible burden, not as formidable an opponent for a war secretary as in earlier days. But still there is no doubt that the chief ingredient that finally brought the office of Secretary of War into its own, to the near-realization of its intent and potential in the process of military decision making, was the character of its last incumbent, John C. Breckinridge.

Endnotes

[1] Burton J. Hendrick, *Statesman of the Lost Cause* (New York, 1939), p. 324.

[2] New York, *Turf, Field and Farm*, May 21, 1875.

[3] John H. Reagan, "Flight and Capture of Jefferson Davis," *Annals of the War* (Philadelphia, 1879), p. 152; Jefferson Davis to L. P. Connor, October 7, 1860, in Robert McElroy, *Jefferson Davis, The Unreal and the Real* (New York, 1937), I, p. 221; Arthur M. Schlesinger, Jr., ed., *History of American Presidential Elections 1789-1968* (New York, 1971), II, p. 1152.

[4] House of Representatives to John C. Breckinridge, August 23, 1862, January 11, 1864, John C. Breckinridge Compiled Service Record, Record Group 109, National Archives, Washington, D.C.

[5] John B. Jones, *A Rebel War Clerk's Diary at the Confederate States Capital* (Philadelphia, 1866), II, p. 425; New York, *Herald*, October 20, 1863; Clement Eaton, *A History of the Old South* (New York, 1966; 2d ed.), p. 499.

[6] Augusta, Georgia, *Tri-Weekly Constitutionalist*, February 8, 1865; Jones, *Diary*, II, pp. 395, 403; Henry S. Foote, *Casket of Reminiscences* (Washington, 1874), p. 297; Thomas R. Hay, "Lucius B. Northrop: Commissary General of the Confederacy," *Civil War History*, IX (March 1963), pp. 19-20; Breckinridge to Davis, February 14, 1865, Chapter IX, Volume 99, Record Group 109, National Archives.

[7] U.S. War Department, *War of the Rebellion: Official Records of the Union and Confederate Armies* (Washington, 1880-1901), Series I, Volume 47, Part II, p. 1303.

[8] *Ibid.*, I, 46, III, p. 1339, I, 47, II, pp. 1174, 1284, 1313, 1347, 1398; Breckinridge to P. G. T. Beauregard, February 28, 1865, P. G. T. Beauregard Papers, Duke University, Durham, N.C.

[9] *O.R.*, I, 46, III, p. 1362, I, 49, II, p. 1166.

[10] *Ibid.*, I, 53, p. 1041; Breckinridge to Davis, February 7, 8, 14, 17, 21, 22, 27, March 2, 3, 8, 9, 13, 17, Chapter IX, Volume 99, RG 109, National Archives.

[11] *O.R.*, I, 49, I, p. 970, I, 46, II, p. 1245.

[12] *Ibid.*, I, 47, II, pp. 1201, 1207-1208, 1238.

[13] *Ibid.*, I, 46, II, pp. 1292, 1311-12.

[14] *Ibid.*, I, 49, II, p. 1255.

[15] Breckinridge to Alfred Iverson, April 15, 1865, Beauregard Papers; *O.R.*, I, 47, III, pp. 795-96.

[16] *O.R.*, I, 47, III, pp. 813-14, 829-30, 836, 845, 851.

[17] *Ibid.*, I, 51, II, p. 1069.

[18] Breckinridge to I. M. St. John, May 16, 1871, in Dunbar Rowland, ed., *Jefferson Davis, Constitutionalist, His Letters, Papers and Speeches* (Jackson, Miss., 1923), VII, p. 356.

19 *Ibid.*, p. 357, St. John to Davis, July 14, 1873, pp. 351-52; Clement A. Evans, *The Civil History of the Confederate States* (Atlanta, 1899; Volume I of Clement A. Evans, ed., *Confederate Military History*), p. 622.

20 *O.R.*, I, 51, II, pp. 1063-64, I, 47, II, p. 1312.

21 St. John to Davis, July 14, 1873, Breckinridge to St. John, May 16, 1871, Rowland, *Davis*, VII, pp. 349-52; Evans, *Civil History*, p. 622; *O.R.*, I, 51, II, pp. 1063-64.

22 *O.R.*, I, 49, II, pp. 1124-25; Richmond, *Whig*, March 31, 1865.

23 J. Cutler Andrews, *The South Reports the Civil War* (Princeton, 1970), pp. 529-33; *O.R.*, I, 46, II, p. 1279, I, 47, II, p. 712.

24 *O.R.*, I, 47, II, pp. 1312, 1376, 1425.

25 *Ibid.*, pp. 1311, 1312, 1313, 1425; Breckinridge to Zebulon Vance, March 23, 31, 1865, Secretary of War, Telegrams Sent March 1863-April 1865, Chapter IX, Volume 35, Record Group 109, National Archives.

26 *O.R.*, I, 47, II, p. 1313, I, 46, III, pp. 1335-36.

27 *Ibid.*, I, 46, II, pp. 1252-53.

28 *Ibid.*, pp. 1242, 1244-45.

29 *Ibid.*, I, 49, I, p. 1006; Jones, *Diary*, II, p. 441; Breckinridge to J. Stoddard Johnston, February 23, 1865, J. Stoddard Johnston Papers, Filson Club, Louisville, Ky.

30 *O.R.*, I, 46, II, pp. 1254, 1257.

31 *Ibid.*, pp. 1257, 1259-60, 1264-65, I, 46, III, p. 1370; Jones, *Diary*, II, p. 454.

32 Joseph Packard, "Ordnance Matters at the Close," *Confederate Veteran*, XVI (May 1908), p. 228; St. John to Davis, July 14, 1873, Rowland, *Davis*, VII, pp. 354-55; Breckinridge to Chiefs of Bureaus, May 4, 1864, Jeremy F. Gilmer Papers, Museum of the Confederacy, Richmond, Va.

33 See William C. Davis, *Breckinridge: Statesman, Soldier, Symbol* (Baton Rouge, 1974), pp. 518-40 *passim* for a full account of the escape.

34 Basil W. Duke to W. T. Walthall, April 6, 1878, Breckinridge Family Papers, Library of Congress, Washington, D.C.

35 Cincinnati, *Commercial*, November 15, 1887; Louisville, *Courier-Journal*, May 30, 1900.

36 *O.R.*, I, 46, II, p. 446; "Interesting Statement of Judge Robert Ould," *Confederate Veteran*, XV (October 1907), p. 455.

37 *O.R.*, I, 46, pp. 1209-10.

38 *Ibid.*, IV, 3, p. 1064; Jones, *Diary*, p. 416.

39 *O.R.*, I, 49, I, pp. 978-79, I, 38, III, p. 697.

[40] Breckinridge to Davis, February 18, 1865, Jefferson Davis Papers, Louisiana Historical Association Collection, Tulane University, New Orleans.

[41] James Longstreet, *From Manassas to Appomattox* (Philadelphia, 1896), p. 504.

[42] John A. Campbell to Breckinridge, March 5, 1865, John A. Campbell Papers, Southern Historical Collection, University of North Carolina, Chapel Hill; R. E. Lee to Breckinridge, March 9, 1865, Davis Papers.

[43] *O.R.*, IV, 3, p. 1137; Richard Morton to Breckinridge, March 10, 1865, A. R. Lawton to Breckinridge, March 10, 1865, Josiah Gorgas to Breckinridge, March 11, 1865, Louis T. Wigfall Papers, Library of Congress.

[44] Breckinridge to Davis, March 13, 1865, Frederick M. Dearborn Collection, Houghton Library, Harvard University, Cambridge, Mass.

[45] Breckinridge to Vance, March 25, 1865, Zebulon Vance Papers, North Carolina Department of Archives and History, Raleigh.

[46] R. M. T. Hunter to William Jones, October 1877, Rowland, *Davis*, VII, p. 577.

[47] George G. Vest, "John C. Breckinridge: Recollections of One Who Knew Him in the Prime of His Manhood," Louisville, *Courier-Journal*, June 8, 1875.

[48] *O.R.*, I, 46, III, pp. 1382-83, 1393.

[49] Joseph E. Johnston, *Narrative of Military Operations* (New York, 1874), pp. 396-98.

[50] Clement Cowd, *Life of Zebulon B. Vance* (Charlotte, N.C., 1897), pp. 485-86.

[51] Johnston, *Narrative*, pp. 404-405.

[52] John H. Reagan, *Memoirs, With Special Reference to Secession and the Civil War* (New York, 1906), p. 200; Johnston, *Narrative*, pp. 404-405.

[53] William T. Sherman, *Memoirs of General William T. Sherman, by Himself* (New York, 1875), II, pp. 252-53. J. Stoddard Johnston, "Sketches of Operations of General John C. Breckinridge, No. 3," *Southern Historical Society Papers*, VII (October 1879), p. 389; *O.R.*, I, 47, III, p. 243.

[54] *O.R.*, I, 47, III, pp. 830-31, 834; Breckinridge to Davis, April 23, 1865, Johnston Papers.

[55] W. C. P. Breckinridge to Walthall, May 3, 1878, Rowland, *Davis*, VIII, p. 192; John W. Headley, *Confederate Operations in Canada and New York* (New York, 1906), p. 435.

[56] William H. Parker, *Recollections of a Naval Officer, 1841-1865* (New York, 1883), p. 366.

[57] New York, *Herald*, June 27, 1865.

[58] *O.R.*, I, 49, II, p. 719.

[59] Richmond, *Daily Dispatch*, October 28, 1861.

60 Sallie Putnam, *In Richmond During the Confederacy* (New York, 1961; 2d edition), p. 365; Jones, *Diary*, II, p. 435; Frank E. Vandiver, *Ploughshares Into Swords; Josiah Gorgas and Confederate Ordnance* (Austin, Tex., 1952), p. 261; Frank E. Vandiver, ed., *The Civil War Diary of General Josiah Gorgas* (University, Ala., 1947), p. 169.

61 Mary Boykin Chestnut, *A Diary from Dixie* (Boston, 1949), p. 473.

62 Louisville, *Courier-Journal*, May 18, June 18, 1875.

63 W. G. Bean, ed., "Memoranda of Conversations Between General Robert E. Lee and William Preston Johnston May 7, 1868 and March 18, 1870," *Virginia Magazine of History and Biography*, LXXIII (October 1965), p. 479.

"The Speakers of the State Legislatures' Failure as Confederate Leaders"

Jon L. Wakelyn

The political leaders of the Confederacy often have been unfavorably describ-ed and evaluated as failures. One contemporary analyst of the Confederate political system, Robert Garlick Hill Kean, confided in 1864 to his *Diary* that the Confederate civilian command suffered from the "absence of a represen-tative man, a Leader..." In *The Statesmanship of the Civil War,* Allan Nevins agreed with Kean as he claimed that those leaders lacked "the power to com-prehend exactly the forces that affect the minds of the people and to discern what they desire and will support." He also insisted that no Confederate political leader displayed the ability to plan and to conduct that revolutionary govern-ment. In his essay, "Died of Democracy," David Donald attempted to explain such harsh judgements. Donald speculated that the Confederate leaders could not overcome the many problems of political democracy. He suggested that the home folks "insisted upon retaining their democratic liberties in wartime," and that their political leaders on all levels lacked the talent and perhaps the devo-tion to persuade them to remain loyal to the Confederate cause.[1] These judgements on their loyalty and ability have grasped the central issues of the Confederate leaders' failure.

Many other works have condemned the Confederate civilian leaders in the same way. Only a few have praised any of those men. For example, there have been numerous studies critical of President Jefferson Davis' ability to sustain civilian morale, and at last count at least six more works on his leadership qualities are in process. The Davis cabinet members have been analyzed for their support or opposition to the President, and the verdict on their perfor-mances is mixed. "Little Aleck" Stephens has just become the victim of a six-hundred page, closely reasoned, exhaustive day by day defense of his dissent from the administration. Almost all of the governors, especially the bombastic presenters of self, have claimed their modern defenders or detractors.

A recent excellent comparative collection on the governors' roles in the war concluded that they stridently defended their homeland. Less studied have been the state judges, although a seminal work on their decisions showed that they usually supported the demands of the government.[2] The civilian political leaders' performances in behalf of the Confederate war effort thus appear to have been studied in depth.

But the activities of one group of Confederate state politicians, the legislative leaders, most particularly the speakers of the state houses or assemblies, has gained little attention. Yet those leaders of the legislatures made important contributions to the political process.[3] The lower houses originated all tax measures and appropriations bills, controlled the direction of internal improvements, regulated banks, and elected and gave instruction to many political officeholders, including the United States and later the Confederate States senators. Powers to appropriate, exempt, and confiscate meant that the state houses and their leaders also had major wartime governance roles. Most importantly, as J. Mills Thornton maintained, the legislature "typified the society which elected it..."[4]

Perhaps this oversight is connected to the confusion about the legislators' authority during the Civil War. A few scholars have asserted that wartime powers actually shifted to the state governors, because those executives commanded the state militias and held office when the legislatures were not in session. But since the governors had to await the assembly sessions before they could process any legislation their jobs too had periods of inactivity. The governors claimed to have struggled continuously with the legislature leaders over control of finances and other matters. In the states of South Carolina and Florida, the secession conventions continued to meet during the war's early stages and thus assumed legislative and executive authority. But the lower houses soon disbanded the conventions and reclaimed their proper duties. Others believe that the central government dominated all branches of state government, and that the legislators simply carried out executive orders. Yet, the Confederate Constitution clearly outlined the relationship between central and state governments, and those divisions of authority gave an inordinate amount of power to the state legislatures and to the speakers.[5]

County government officials also clashed with the legislators. In those struggles power often slipped to the local leaders. For if the assemblies authorized expenditures, the local officials delivered the goods and services. The county leaders dealt directly with food shortages and other personal problems of the people. If the legislators influenced key decisions on local quotas, and even local defenses, the county officials actually raised the troops. Thus, those disorganized, incompetent, and sometimes crooked local officials at times disrupted the flow of material and personnel. But some legislative leaders believed that they actually supported the local power structure.[6] Possibly their own relationship to the home constituents was reflected in those battles with the county functionaries.

The laws which codified state government revealed shared power. Thus, all state leaders had to make compromises. For example, the governor, the upper house, and the local authorities often challenged the prerogatives of the powerful lower houses.[7] The leaders also had to satisfy an electorate which resisted outside interference and was jealous of its local powers.[8] The legislative leaders themselves were raised and trained in that localistic political environment which questioned all power.[9] At times their commonly-based political views would make them appear weak despite their authority and in opposition despite their professed loyalty to the Confederate nation. Historians' questions about legislative power, no doubt, contributed to their verdict on whether or not those leaders failed during the Civil War.

In the only systematic study of the Confederate state houses, May Spence Ringgold claimed that the legislators provided for the folks back home, as they appropriated funds necessary to care for the soldiers' loved ones. She insisted that most of the legislators supported the needs of the national government, although toward the end of the war their leaders' defended localistic priorities against the Davis government. Ringgold also suggested that the legislative leaders never really gained the experience necessary to deal with wartime financial matters, especially taxation and bond issues. Those men just were unable to overcome popular resistance to the draft, to exemptions, and to the government's use of slaves. She stated that by "1863 lack of confidence in legislative capacity to solve wartime problems was widespread and increasing." But Ringgold concluded that the legislators failed primarily because "the southern states could only build with straw."[10] In the long run, for her nothing the leadership did could have saved the Confederacy.

However, participants during the war years and other scholars have focused their criticism on the legislative leadership's lack of political skills. Reuben Davis, wartime judge and former member of the Mississippi house, in his memoirs criticized the leaders as inadequate to their tasks. North Carolina politician A. J. Roper, in a letter of 1862 to Governor Zebulon B. Vance, fumed, "don't wait for the legislature, that body indulges in unimportant discussions and delights in delay." Perhaps the best student of the war behind the lines, Charles W. Ramsdell, found those leaders ineffectual though earnest. In the introduction to a collection of edited essays on the Confederate governors, Wilfred B. Yearns stated that the legislative leaders interfered with the governors' duties, and thus sabotaged the states' support for the war. Most pithily, Nash Boney claimed that "Virginia's Confederate legislature was an unimpressive body which seldom responded adequately to the governor's pleas for quick action."[11]

There then seems little reason to question the verdict that legislative leaders, which included the speakers, in large part failed because of their inability both to prescribe adequate legislation to sustain military defense and to persuade the citizenry to sacrifice for the homeland. But save for Donald's brilliant "died of democracy" theme, which concentrates on the voters rather than the leaders, few accounts have discussed why the speakers lacked political skills. Thus, many questions remain about the reasons for leadership failure.

Analysis of the careers of the speakers of the Confederate state legislatures may provide some explanations for their failure. This is a difficult task because of the paucity of available information on the lives of the thirty-two men who led their respective assemblies from the outbreak of hostilities until Appomattox Courthouse. Because of the lack of usable data on the wartime careers of the four Louisiana speakers, their lives have been excluded from this study.[12] Enough material on the remaining twenty-eight speakers exists to attempt an individual and collective review of their career patterns. Concentration will center on how they prepared for wartime office, their recorded words and deeds during the war, and the public duties the citizens gave them in the postwar years.[13]

Most of those future speakers would bring years of political preparation to their wartime positions. In what capacities had those men served? Thirteen of the twenty-eight at one time had been in the lower houses of their respective legislatures, and four of those had held the speakership. Virginia's Oscar Minor Crutchfield and South Carolina's James Simons, Sr. had spent the ten previous years as speakers of their assemblies. A number had served as county judges. Only three had been in the federal congress. Many had gained election to their states' secession conventions. Only two had attended the Confederate states Constitutional Convention, including Mississippi's Josiah A. P. Campbell who drafted part of the Constitution.[14] The pattern of political officeholding, then, seems weighted toward county and district representation, with few of the wartime speakers having had previous national political experience.

Prewar interstate or even statewide business careers might have compensated for their lack of political stature. Allan Nevins stated that those civilian leaders who made wartime legislative decisions should have had prior training in financial and corporate management.[15] Of the twenty-eight future speakers, twenty-one had practiced law. Only a few of them had argued before the state courts, since most had been small-time lawyers. At least one understood the value of political propaganda, for he had risen in business and in politics as editor of a small town Democratic party newspaper. Two farmed and one for a short time practiced medicine. Three owned and operated large businesses. Florida's Phillip Dell and Thomas Jefferson Eppes directed railroad companies and managed banks in Tallahassee, and thus had experience with loans, taxes, and large payrolls. Virginia's Hugh White Sheffey used his family connections and his Staughton law practice to become a leading Shenandoah Valley banker.[16] Thus, only a few of those future leaders fulfilled Nevins' desire for them to have had important prewar business experience

Although no clear predictor of political or analytical skills, the speakers' level of education reveals something about their political opportunities made through school connections as well as their exposure to outside influence. Fourteen of those men were known to have attended college or university. As did many of his predecessors in the speakership, Robert Boylston went to the home-state College of South Carolina, a training ground for public office. The other South Carolina wartime speakers attended their more parochial hometown College of Charleston. After university, the wealthy Washington T. Whitthorne of Tennessee read law in the office of his kinsman James Knox Polk. Walter H. Crenshaw of Alabama went to the state university, where he met a number of bright young men whom he brought to his father's law office, a center of local political activity. Two of the four future North Carolina speakers began their political careers just after they had left the state university, where they had used family connections to make friendships with other young wealthy men. But those future political leaders' college experiences hardly expanded their geographical horizons. Only two travelled outside the South for their education. Sheffey of Virginia attended Yale College and Law School, and the Maryland-born William A. Lake of Mississippi went to Jefferson College in Pennsylvania.[17] It appears, then, that those future speakers' college careers showed the value of local connections and the limitations of parochial schooling.

What of those future speakers who had not attended college? At least three went to primary or "old field" schools near their fathers' farms, and four of them attended preparatory schools. Three of those whose higher education is unknown grew up on plantations, perhaps had home tutors, and eventually took over the family business. One private school graduate, William T. Dortch of North Carolina, came from a small farmer family. His father, realizing that young Dortch would inherit little property, sent him to study law in the office of a prominent judge. As with most of the former college students who studied law, many of those young men who did not go to college read law in a local lawyer's office. Two studied for the bar on their own while working as farmers and teachers.[18] For the non-college men, then, the lack of higher education seemed no impediment to their business careers. But their education hardly spread their horizons beyond the locale in which they had been reared.

As with their education, the future speakers' mobility patterns reveal their localist upbringing. Of the twenty-eight studied, sixteen served during the war in the legislatures of their native states. Eleven of those sixteen remained throughout their lives in the county in which they had been born. Richard S. Donnell of eastern North Carolina eventually moved one county over because the local Whig majority had declined. Twelve moved either at an early age with their parents or emigrated as adults to the states where they rose to the speakership. Especially was this true of migration to the newer southwest, which included the one certain northern-born speaker, as well as at least six others.[19] Thus, the majority of those future leaders learned their politics and gained office within their birth states.

The types of communities in which those men grew up and developed their political values, succeeded financially or sustained family wealth, and launched their political careers may also help understand what to have expected of them as leaders. Eleven of them lived in rural counties where they either farmed or had small legal practices. Ten came from small towns and belonged to law firms. Only seven lived in large towns where ostensibly they had opportunities for trade, financial, and corporate law practices.[20] Those seven future speakers lived in cities such as Charleston, Huntsville, Murfreesboro (near Nashville), and Tallahassee, environments that could have allowed them to adjust to the new demands placed on legislatures during wartime. But the largest number lived in rural settings or in small towns that may have limited their ability to grow.

Political attainment, professional careers, educational level, mobility, and even size of community also point to the important issue of class background. A number of scholars have suggested a class basis for leadership disloyalty to the Confederacy.[21] Others, such as Emory Thomas, maintained that the Civil War provided the opportunity for able and ambitious young middle class southern men to become leaders.[22] Seven of the future speakers, William T. Dortch, Bradley Bunch, Horace B. Allis, J. F. Lowry, James Scales, M. D. K. Taylor, and Nicholas H. Darnell, came from either the middle class or from poor farmer backgrounds. All of those leaders except for Dortch moved to new states in order to enhance their professional and political careers. There is no evidence that any of those future speakers used their class background to rise in office, although both of the Texans certainly prided themselves on being self-made men.[23] Only two future speakers' careers suggest in any way a relationship between class and wartime reconstructionist attitudes. Twenty-one came from well-to-do families.

Taken together the prewar patterns reveal much about what to expect from the future speakers. Most of those men had been raised in affluent families. Some of them ventured outside their states, perhaps because of ambitious fathers or because of their own political motivations. Many grew up in rural or small town environments. As might be expected, most of them practiced law. Few had gained the skills that came from ownership of large businesses. They rose in public life through family connections, business practice, and party loyalty. Most of them remained cosseted in the political, economic, and social values of their home communities. Those local talents would indeed face a new challenge in their wartime legislative careers.

The speakers' behavior in office in part might have been related to the stamina and the health which they enjoyed. Although medical records are unavailable, the ages when they attained office could tell something about the wartime speakers' stamina. Certainly past generations have placed different emphasis on what age was considered fit for political office. For example, during the 1850s the southern house speakers' ages averaged about thirty-eight years when they entered office. Perhaps the duty had been thought most proper for relatively young men. But in 1861, most of the Confederate state speakers were in their fifties. Virginia speaker Crutchfield was sixty-one. The youngest, Mississippi's Scales, became speaker in 1862 at the age on thirty-one.[24] The older ages of most of them suggests a stamina problem and perhaps, more importantly, a lack of patience and receptivity to new ideas. But this is speculation, and other factors in their careers, as well as the actual functions of the office, are certainly more crucial to explain their failed performance.

One sure obstacle to speaker success was the lack of time to gain experience in that position. This was because of the historical precedent of turnover in office and the wartime pressures of divided loyalties as to where their talents could best be utilized. Two of the speakers, one of whom had been in the federal Congress and the other who had served twenty years in public office, died a few months after the war had begun. One of those was Mississippi's Lake, who quarrelled with Governor John J. Pettus, resigned his office to join the army, and died as a result of a duel fought in the late spring of 1861. A few, including Simons of South Carolina who had been house speaker since 1851, and that enormous legal talent Campbell of Mississippi, left office soon after the fighting had commenced. In all, nineteen of those men served one year or less as speaker, and three of them, including the Republican unionist Allis of Arkansas, served only a few months. Eight held office for two years, and part of that time they appeared distracted by military duties. Only Alabama's Crenshaw held the speakership throughout the Civil War.[25]

Fifteen of the speakers resigned from office or refused re-election in order to enter military service. Perhaps the most important of these was Virginia's James Lawson Kemper, who served and afterward attained the rank of major-general in the Army of Northern Virginia. This well-educated lawyer had spent the ten previous years in the state assembly, had led the state out of the Union, and had held the key chairmanship of the military affairs committee. As speaker he supported the creation of a strong military defense for the Richmond government. Even while speaker, Kemper presided over the Board of Governors of the Virginia Military Institute and devoted his energies to organize a regiment.[26] This absent leader became a noble warrior, but Virginia's legislature was the poorer.

Two other speakers who left office entered the Confederate Congress, while one became an important state supreme court justice. Georgia's Warren Aiken's departure for Richmond meant that few men of stature in that state remained to cooperate with the Confederate government. Aiken became a staunch Davis administration ally and eventually clashed with Governor Joseph E. Brown and the legislature because of their non-compliance with national interests. The highly respected Mississippi secession leader, Campbell, also went off to the Confederate Congress, then rose to colonel in the army, and was wounded at Corinth. Governors of Mississippi came to lament the loss of his talents as they attacked later speakers for incompetence and non-support of the Confederate war aims.[27]

Another group of speakers' tasks were made more difficult due to forced disruption from Yankee invasion of their states. Louisiana's legislature moved so often that today even its journal records are difficult to trace. The northern conquest of parts of Arkansas resulted in the election of two unionist speakers in that state, neither of whom served the southern cause. The Mississippi legislature moved often during the last two years of the war. Most upsetting was the demise of Tennessee's legislature in 1862 due to Yankee control of the state. The talented Whitthorne responded to the northern invasion by resigning his speakership and joining the Confederate army. His replacement, the equally able Edwin A. Keeble, brought excellent legal and rhetorical skills to the speakership. After 1862 he defended Tennessee as an army staff office.[28]

Thus, turnover in the office as well as the disruption of warfare and invasion exacerbated the tasks of achieving legislative leadership continuity. Perhaps those speakers who had other important wartime careers would have been strong and able leaders in their respective state legislatures. Certainly, the nine who held office for two or more years had the opportunity to make their presence felt in behalf of a separate Confederacy. Comparison of all of the speakers' wartime legislative records provides further explanation for why they failed.

Analysis of their abilities as leaders relates to the powers they had in office. The unwritten informal rules of governance reveal what the legislators expected of the speakers. To govern required personal decorum, knowledge of procedure, and the ability to persuade, both with political manipulation and rhetorical skills. The prewar assemblies had the reputation for raucous behavior, constant interruptions of the speakers, and the presence of outsiders on the house floor. But the wartime printed proceedings and the few accounts of witnesses described that body as orderly and serious in its purpose. The traditional closing statement thanked the speaker for his services and always included comments on how well he had kept order and presented himself to his peers.[29] With such emphasis placed on personal conduct and presence, lack of respect for the speaker's abilities could have affected the activities of the entire legislature.

The speakers' formal duties which gave them enormous authority were often printed boldly and forthrightly in the first sections of house journals. The speaker controlled the organization of the house. He decided who to seat if there were multiple claims to office, and he could excuse the lengthy absences which occurred quite frequently due to the disruptions of war. The speaker ruled on seating non-members on the floor and decided who of them could address the body. Most important, the speaker appointed all committee members and chairs. Since bills originated in the committees, the speaker's power to name the membership in effect gave him policy control. Chairmen of key committees, such as judiciary and military affairs, often became speakers themselves, which meant that the speaker could select his successor. The speaker controlled debate, because he decided its order and time limits. Because he introduced all petitions and memorials, the speaker could persuade his followers with the powers of his discourse. In most states the speaker voted first, which perhaps influenced the acceptance or rejection of a measure.[30]

These procedures which gave the speaker such powers point to the importance of the opening of the legislative session. The words those leaders used to express loyalty and dedication to the cause meant much to those men who were so taken with the power of the spoken word. But most of the speakers had little talent in that direction, or at least they have not been remembered for such skills. Keeble was an exception. After his close election to the speakership in early 1862, he urged his fellow legislators to support the Confederacy by continued resistance to the Northern army. He affirmed the principles of free speech, free press, and the consent of the governed as the central values for which he was fighting. He proclaimed his own duties to "aid in sustaining our armies in the field, and to expel the dark shadow of want from the hearth of the absent soldiers."[31] Keeble knew that assistance to those behind the lines was crucial to keeping the soldiers in the field.

That Tennessee speaker also understood the importance of symbolic gestures to gain support for his desired bills. Keeble sponsored the measure to create another Confederate congressional district for Tennessee in hopes of strengthening his state's position in Richmond. The limits of his devotion were tested, when, during the debates, he was called home to watch his son die. Overcome with grief, he nevertheless returned to the legislature after only five days at home so as to cast his vote for the redistricting bill.[32]

The house records reveal that a number of other speakers achieved some successes through use of their legislative powers. For example, speakers Dell and Eppes, both of whom knew finances, led Florida's legislature to create an adequate currency to fund the war effort. They wrote the bond bills and asked for taxes on the profits from those bonds. Alabama's Crenshaw drafted his legislature's impressment bill and conducted it through the house. When confronted with the need to extend Florida's draft ages to 15 and 55, at first Dell rebelled. But at the war's end he asked the legislature to require even older men to take part in local defense. South Carolina speaker Simons hurried an election to admit to the assembly the talented future speaker, Boylston. Over the objections of Governor Brown, Georgia's Thomas Hardeman, Jr., spoke out in favor of a repeal of the state's habeas corpus law. Eppes introduced a bill to punish all citizens who planted tobacco rather than the corn so needed for the troops and the ill-fed citizenry. Crenshaw supported confiscation measures, but asked for adequate compensation. The speaker of the Georgia house at the end of 1864 went so far as to advocate confiscation of the property of deserters who lived near the east Tennessee border.[33]

But even those able leaders' actions seemed more reactive than active. The legislative journals reveal that most of the speakers, despite their enormous authority, appeared to respond to outside pressure rather than to originate measures for the conduct of their states' war effort. Enemy army attacks, Confederate national government's expressed needs, governors' instructions, house factional politics, and the appeals of their constituents seemed to dictate the speakers' actions. Most of them, then, usually supported the legislative initiatives of other leadership groups.

What made those speakers followers rather than leaders? Scales of Mississippi explained that the many ballots required for his election deprived him of a mandate for leadership. Scales implies that the absence of party loyalty meant that he had no constituency in the house to facilitate the passage of legislation. Perhaps David Donald's charge that, because of the absence of party leaders were unable to exercise control over the many conflicting factions in the Confederacy, obtains also for the speakers.[34] The majority of wartime speakers had once belonged to the Democratic party and had risen in public life as loyal party followers. But during the War their partisanship gave way to near anti-party animus, probably due to the desire to launch a united struggle in behalf of a new nation.

The speakers also registered concern over the contest for power among branches of the state governments. They often clashed with their states' executive branches. Speaker Lake resigned because of his quarrel with Governor Pettus. Virginia's speakers believed that their governors tried to interfere with the house's financial authority. The Virginia legislators even fought with North Carolina's Governor Vance over the extension of railroads into that state. Georgia speakers and Governor Brown argued over local loyalties and Confederate needs. At one stage of their dispute, Brown accused the speaker of lack of support for national interests. When the speaker asked for copies of all correspondence between the governor and the Richmond government, Brown refused to comply. Speaker Aiken then demanded the governor give him a report on coastal defenses. Brown accused Aiken of partisan feelings against him, and insisted that the state Constitution gave him the right to refuse information. On another occasion the governor claimed that the house wanted illegal control over state troops so as to turn them over to the Davis government. When speaker Hardeman offered censure and moved to print Brown's untoward remarks as an appendix to the house journal, the governor exploded. But he soon backed off and called for concord and unity between the house and himself. The speaker closed further discussion when he stated that he "would report such action as may be necessary to vindicate the independence, dignity, and privilege of the House."[35]

In the exchanges between Georgia governor and the speakers much is reveal-ed about those leaders' defense of their wartime authority. The tensions also expose leadership uncertainty over just how to facilitate legislation in behalf of the Confederacy. The speakers seemed sensitive to local issues and interests, perhaps even at the expense of national needs. Were those internal disputes, meant to support the folks at home as well as to protect their fellow legislators? A look at their speeches and written communications to the legislatures dur-ing the secession movement and during the war captures how the speakers view-ed limitations on authority, their ambivalence about their own powers, and even the contradictions in their own loyalties to the cause.

In those state legislatures which met to debate secession and in the seces-sion conventions themselves, the speakers lectured their fellow leaders about loyalty. Taylor of Texas described his support for secession in the same way that he would later explain his duties as speaker. Taylor "mourned the loss of equality in the government which was bequeathed to me by a revolutionary ancestry." Just as the war broke out he claimed authority to act "in the name of a free people, whose very liberties are endangered,..." Speaker Crenshaw drew up the Alabama Declaration of Rights which the secession convention sent to the legislature. In it he stated, "No human authority ought, in any case whatever, to control or interfere with the rights of conscience." Former speaker Simons sent the South Carolina legislature an impassioned defense of his role in the firing on Fort Sumter. He stated that indeed he had led the house in an action contrary to the desire of the chief justice of the state supreme court. Simons proclaimed, "I will ever claim and exercise, as a freeman of this commonwealth, the privilege of forming my own conclusions, according to my convictions of reason and honor, irrespective of the favors of official power, however exalted."[36] As the Civil War began, these harangues from such supposedly powerful men sounded almost anarchistic.

They used much of that same language throughout the war. When Eppes became speaker at the end of 1862, he promised to commit himself totally to the cause of the Confederacy, which meant to give complete support to the ar-my that would protect an invaded Florida. Eppes nevertheless reminded his peers that at all costs "an idle or careless legislature" must "battle in the cause of liberty and in defense of all that is sacred and dear to freemen." When elevated to the speakership, Alfred P. Aldrich of South Carolina lectured his peers on the delicacy of his task, his determination to hold them to a code of honor, and of his personal duty. He began, "representatives, we are now engaged in a great revolution," but concluded, "we are fighting for our liberty and our civilization." Speaker Darnell revealed his local attachments when he attacked the Texas legislature for freezing the pay of soldiers from his own county. The speaker of the Mississippi house in 1864 summed up the meaning of all those expressed values when he opposed the Confederate States Congress' suspension of the writ of habeas corpus as dangerous to liberty, because it put civil power under the military and "establishes a precedent of a doubtful and dangerous character..."[37]

These conflicting loyalties also appeared in much of the speakers' legislative political activities, which led to charges that they failed to display the proper devotion to the cause of the new nation. But what did those accusations of disloyalty mean? Surely the speakers desired to assist the people behind the lines in order to retain popular support for the Confederacy. Despite their fears of excessive military power over civilian life, the speakers helped to pass bills to aid those in the front lines. Even when they argued over how best to support the cause, they usually claimed to speak for a separate nation. Perhaps the types of disloyalty which Georgia Lee Tatum discussed in *Disloyalty in the Confederacy*, still the only full-length monograph on the subject, could focus the meaning of leadership dissent. Tatum identified three categories of disloyalty: those who refused to aid the government and worked against it; the disaffected, who only passively opposed the war effort; and the unionists, who from the beginning opposed the idea of a separate nation.[38]

A number of speakers at one time or another represented a citizenry which resented, resisted, and refused support to Confederate government activities. Popular allegiance to the Confederate government seemed to decline in Arkansas, Mississippi, North Carolina, and Georgia. Speaker Allis of Arkansas actually led a northern-controlled house. Both Allis and his successor, Lowry, actively opposed the Confederate government and supported early reconstruction of their state. Sheffey of Virginia came from a unionist section of the Shenandoah Valley, and he consistently opposed Confederate States measures. But most of the accused speakers behaved like Donnell of North Carolina, whom President Davis believed opposed the government. Donnell represented the large slaveholding and Yankee army beleaguered eastern section of the state, and he certainly desired an early end to warfare. When it counted, Donnell supported all appropriations for troops, as did most other speakers from communities under Union fire.[39] It appears that many of the speakers who refused to support the central government hardly believed themselves disloyal.

Almost all of the speakers registered disaffection with the government. They were guilty of lack of enthusiasm, or passive support, for the Confederate nation. During the last years of the war, speakers displayed impatience with the Richmond authorities, expressed real fears that neither they nor the central government were able to alleviate the suffering of their home constituents, and made errors in judgement concerning their assistance to the military. Most of those leaders resisted outside force, whether it be from Richmond, the state capitol, or Washington. When former Whig Lake fought with Governor Pettus over how best to spend taxes, he appeared as an anti-war advocate. Speaker Scales at times vacated his chair out of disgust and frustration. Speaker Hardeman of Georgia named the unionist Linton Stephens as head of the judiciary committee, but Hardeman also supported President Davis' attempt to raise more troops. Alabama's Crenshaw often warned of the governor's efforts to control the state house, but he led in the impressment of fellow planters' goods to feed the troops and the people behind the lines. North Carolina's Donnell, whom President Davis wanted removed from office, opposed his legislative peers' movement for early reconstruction.[40] One asks, what did disaffection mean?

Tatum's last category of disloyalty suggests that some southerners opposed a separate Confederacy from the beginning. Was this true of any of the speakers? Arkansas' Allis and Lowry, one of whom had fought in the Union army, and both of whom probably came from outside the South, obviously never supported the Confederate nation. Perhaps the Virginia Whig speaker Sheffey, who had opposed secession, might have been a secret unionist. Because of the activities of Allis, Sheffey, and other Whigs, a number of later historians have charged that few Whigs or anti-secessionists ever showed enthusiasm for a separate nation. But Thomas P. Alexander and William J. Cooper, two excellent students of southern politics, dispute this charge.[41] My information on these twenty-eight speakers tends to support them. Eight of the speakers had been Whigs, and five of those men opposed secession. One former Whig joined the secessionists, and the two who supported cooperation later decided in favor of single state secession. Aiken of Georgia became a staunch ally of President Davis, Lake died too early for us to know his true feelings, and Crenshaw served as a tower of support for the war effort.[42] That meant that twenty-five of the twenty-eight speakers, which included five former Whigs, do not deserve the classification unionist.

Unless further evidence surfaces, for most of the speakers the charges of disloyalty remain on the whole unproved. There is, however, some reason to doubt their undivided devotion to the Confederate nation. The speakers' incompetence with complex tax measures, inability to work well with executives, frustrations over the failure of the local delivery system of goods and services to the people, and anger over Richmond's seeming insensitivity to state and local needs and prerogatives, at times made them appear disloyal to the cause. Given their prewar career patterns and political values, protection of their freedoms seemed to take precedence over their support for the new nation. At times they appeared willing to sacrifice the whole for the part. Perhaps it was the speakers' fierce defense of community against all outside threats that has been misread as disloyalty.

One further test of speaker disloyalty is how their constituents rewarded or punished them once the war had ended. After the war, Donnell helped to draw up the Black Codes and opposed Governor William W. Holden. Donnell died in 1867, too soon to tell whether the citizens of eastern North Carolina wanted to continue him in public life. As one might have expected, Arkansas' Allis departed the state during Reconstruction. Sheffey of Virginia held a judgeship, but soon moved to West Virginia to declare his loyalty to the Union. Robert B. Gilliam of North Carolina showed his true colors when he joined the unionist Holden camp, and his neighbors never awarded him postwar elective office. Of the other former speakers suspected of unionist activity, only Arkansas' Lowry held postwar office.[43] Thus, only the most blatantly unionist seem to have suffered politically for their wartime activities.

Other patterns of postwar citizen behavior toward the former speakers reinforces what the Confederacy had lost when the best leaders left office. A few of the truly talented wartime leaders who had left state government for military or national political service again ably served their states and section. Most famous of those were Governor Kemper of Virginia, Chief Justice of the Mississippi Supreme Court Campbell, and federal congressman and United States Senator Whitthorne of Tennessee. Three former speakers died shortly after the war, and twelve of them forsook public service to recoup financial losses.[44] Just as in the war, their loss to the New South was irrecoverable.

Most of the speakers who had served two or more years during the war found that the local citizenry again required their talents. John M. Harrell became Arkansas' Secretary of State. Mississippi's dignified lawmaker Lock E. Houston served as a state judge, as did Alabama's Crenshaw. South Carolina's Aldrich gained election to the state Constitutional Convention of 1865, became the principal architect of the Black Codes, lost office through disfranchisement, and later ably served as a state judge. The Texans, Taylor and Darnell, returned to the state legislatures, where Taylor held the speakership during the 1870's. Georgia's Hardeman also served as postwar speaker.[45] It seems that these representatives continued to gain favor with their local constituents.

The state and county offices with which the postwar voters rewarded those former speakers suggest one important explanation of why they failed as Confederate leaders. Their people had returned them to the limited tasks for which those leaders had prepared, and they rewarded them for services rendered the home community during the war. To be sure, hindrances to successful leadership such as turnover in office, absence of partisan support in the legislature, and tensions with other government authorities made those men appear as followers. Those issues of power point to a major obstacle to their success. They had learned the ways of political authority in local arenas. No doubt a few rose above their training. Always some do. But the larger number of those local leaders, then, surely suffered from the disadvantages of lack of preparation to use Confederate power.

Perhaps even a more important reason for their failure as speakers was the system of political values they had learned during their localist training. Political values are hardly tangible facts. Yet, when one looks at those speakers' behavior patterns in office, those values appeared to determine their uses of power, the language they used to describe their duties, and their appearance as followers. Their values even explain the accusations against them of divided loyalties, if not downright treason, to the national cause. Their localist vision of authority, their desire to concentrate mainly on local issues, and their protection of community interests also are reflected in how they understood the cause. They would not persuade the people to sacrifice further and they did not believe in excessive political power. Thus, Donald's "died of democracy" theme, if transferred from the people to the speakers, should then be changed to say that those men died, or failed politically, because of prior loyalties to their localist world view.

Although these reasons for speaker failure follow from what is known of their career patterns, any final conclusion awaits more information about the formative background, the political values, and the wartime activities of those enormously important mid-level facilitators of local interests. One final incident from the war illustrates this information problem. On May 17, 1864, North Carolina's speaker Donnell presented a memorial before the house to former speaker Nathan Neely Fleming, who had died at the age of 36 in the Battle of the Wilderness. Donnell proclaimed Fleming to have been a "useful and heroic citizen, whose name will ever be cherished in grateful remembrance by his people." But that simply has not been the case for Fleming or for most of the other speakers, and the evaluation of Confederate state leadership remains the poorer for it.

Endnotes

1 Edward Younger (ed.), *Inside the Confederate Government: The Diary of Robert Garlick Hill Kean* (New York, 1957), pp. 214-215; Allan Nevins, *The Statesmanship of the Civil War* (New York, 1954), Chap. 3; David Donald (ed.), *Why the North Won the Civil War* (New York, 1962), pp. 79-90. For another view of the leaders see John M. Murrin, "The American Revolution Versus the Civil War," (unpublished paper given at the Washington Seminar, May 1989.)

2 For example, see William J. Cooper, "A Reassessment of Jefferson Davis as War Leader," *Journal of Southern History* XXXVI (1970); Thomas E. Schott, *Alexander H. Stephens of Georgia* (Baton Rouge, 1988); Rembert W. Patrick, *Jefferson Davis and His Cabinet* (Baton Rouge, 1944); W. Buck Yearns (ed.), *The Confederate Governors* (Athens, 1985); William Morris Robinson, *Justice in Gray* (Cambridge, 1941.)

3 Fletcher Green, *Constitutional Developments in the South Atlantic States* (Chapel Hill, 1930), pp. 84-88; Robert Stanley Rankin, *The Government and Administration of North Carolina* (Chapel Hill, 1955), p. 51; Ralph Wooster, *Politicians, Planters and Plain Folk* (Knoxville, 1975), p. 44.

4 J. Mills Thornton, *Politics and Power in a Slave Society* (Baton Rouge, 1978), p. 116.

5 Yearns (ed.), *The Confederate Governors*, pp. 7, 13; Charles E. Cauthen, *South Carolina Goes to War* (Chapel Hill, 1950), p. 161; John Edwin Johns, *Florida During the Civil War* (Gainesville, 1963) pp. 81, 86; Charles R. Lee, *Confederate Constitutions* (Chapel Hill, 1963).

6 May Spence Ringgold, *Role of State Legislatures in the Confederacy* (Athens, 1966), pp. 56-57; Charles W. Ramsdell, *Behind the Lines in the Southern Confederacy* (Baton Rouge, 1944).

7 Ringgold, *Role of State Legislatures in the Confederacy*, p. 4.

8 For example, see Thornton, *Politics and Power in a Slave Society*.

9 Thornton, *Politics and Power in a Slave Society*; Ralph Wooster, *The People in Power* (Knoxville, 1969), pp. 3-47, 81-106; Lacy K. Ford, Jr., *Origins of Southern Radicalism* (New York, 1988), Chap. 8.

10 Ringgold, *Role of State Legislatures in the Confederacy*, pp. 6, 100.

11 Reuben Davis, *Recollections of Mississippi and Mississippians* (New York, 1889); Frontis W. Johnston (ed.), *The Papers of Zebulon Baird Vance* I Raleigh, 1963), p. 347; Ramsdell, *Behind the Lines in the Southern Confederacy*, Chap. 3; Yearns (ed.), *The Confederate Governors*, pp. 5, 13, 224.

12 Correspondence between the author and William J. Cooper of Louisiana State University.

13 All biographical material and data computed on these speakers, except where otherwise noted, is taken from Charles Ritter and Jon L. Wakelyn, *Speakers of the State Legislatures, 1850-1910* (Wesport, Conn., 1989).

14 Ritter and Wakelyn, *Speakers of the State Legislatures*; James Daniel Lynch, *The Bench and Bar of Mississippi* (New York, 1881).

[15] Nevins, *The Statesmanship of the Civil War.*

[16] Ritter and Wakelyn, *Speakers of the State Legislatures*; John Lewis Poyton, *History of Augusta County,* Virginia (Bridgewater, 1953); Susan Bradford Eppes, *Through Some Eventful Years* (Gainesville, 1968), pp. xv-xvi.

[17] Ritter and Wakelyn, *Speakers of the State Legislatures*; Lynch, *Bench and Bar of Mississippi,* pp. 450-452.

[18] Jerome Dowd, *Sketches of Prominent Living North Carolinians* (Raleigh, 1888).

[19] Helen Lefkowitz Horowitz, *Campus Life* (Chicago, 1987), p. 25; William T. Grant, *Alumni History of the University of North Carolina* (Chapel Hill, 1901).

[20] Ritter and Wakelyn, *Speakers of the State Legislatures.*

[21] Michael W. Fitzgerals, "Radical Republicans and the White Yeomanry During Alabama Reconstruction" *Journal of Southern History* LIV (Nov., 1988), pp. 565-568; Paul D. Escott, *After Secession* (Chapel Hill, 1978); Carl Degler, *The Other South* (New York, 1973).

[22] Emory Thomas, *The Confederacy as a Revolutionary Experience* (Englewood Cliffs, 1971), p. 111.

[23] Ritter and Wakelyn, *Speakers of the State Legislatures.*

[24] James Roger Mansfield, *A History of Early Spotsylvania* (Charlottesville, 1900), pp. 97-99; 1860 Census *Carroll County, Mississippi,* Manuscript Returns, p. 54.

[25] Thomas McAdory Owen, *History of Alabama and Dictionary of Alabama Biography* (4 Vols., Chicago, 1921) III, 422-424; Cauthen, *South Carolina Goes to War,* pp. 19, 21, 23.

[26] Jon L. Wakelyn, *Biographical Dictionary of the Confederacy* (Westport, 1977), p. 270.

[27] Ritter and Wakelyn, *Speakers of the State Legislatures*; Bell I. Wiley (ed.), *Letters of Warren Aiken, Confederate Congressman* (Westport, 1975), pp. 31-32.

[28] William S. Speer (ed.), *Sketches of Prominent Tennesseeans* (Nashville, 1888), pp. 47-50; Robert M. McBride (ed.), *Biographical Dictionary of the Tennessee General Assembly* (2 Vols., Nashville, 1968) II, 484; Peter Maslowski, *Treason Must Be Made Odious* (Millwood, N.Y., 1978), p. 14.

[29] *Journal of the House of Representatives of the State of South Carolina: Being the Sessions of 1861* (Columbia, 1861), pp. 294-295; Kenneth S. Greenberg, *Masters and Statesmen* (Baltimore, 1985), *passim.*

[30] *Journal of the House of Commons of the General Assembly of the State of North Carolina at the Session of 1864-1865* (Raleigh, 1866), pp. 24-30.

[31] *House Journal 1861-62 of the First Session of the Thirty-Fourth General Assembly of the State of Tennessee* (Nashville, 1957), pp. 11, 7.

[32] *Ibid,* pp. 245, 259.

33 *A Journal of the Proceedings of the House of Representatives of the General Assembly of the State of Florida...November 21, 1864* (Tallahassee, 1864), pp. 18, 92, 97, 100; *Journal of the House of Representatives of the State of South Carolina: Being the Session of 1861*, pp. 7-8; *Journal of the House of Representatives of the State of Georgia, at an Extra Session Convened Under the Proclamation of the Governor, March 10, 1864* (Milledgeville, 1864), pp. 118-119, 9; *Alabama House of Representatives, Dec. 24, 1864 Joint Resolution on Impressment* (n.p., n.d.).

34 *Journal of the House of Representatives of the State of Mississippi, At A Regular Session...*(Jackson, 1862), pp. 5-6; Donald (ed.), *Why the North Won the Civil War*, p. 90.

35 *Journal of the House of Representatives of the State of Georgia, at the Extra Session...Convened Under the Proclamation of the Governor, March 10, 1864*, pp. 110-111; *Journal of the House of Representatives of the State of Georgia,...November 6th 1862* (Milledgeville, 1862), pp. 4, 17; *Journal of the House of Representatives of the State of Georgia...November 6th, 1861* (Milledgeville, 1891), pp. 61, 68, 412-417.

36 *Journal of the House of Representatives of the State of Texas, Extra Session of the Eight Legislature* (Austin, 1861), pp. 4, 5; *Ordinances and Constitution of the State of Alabama* (Montgomery, 1861), p. 74; *Journal of the House of Representatives of the State of South Carolina: Being the Session of 1861*, pp. 201, 199, 204.

37 *A Journal of the Proceedings of the House of Representatives of the General Assembly of Florida,...November 17, 1862* (Tallahassee, 1863), pp. 5-6; *Journal of the House of Representatives of the State of South Carolina: Session of 1862* (Columbia, 1862), pp. 5-6; *Journal of the House of Representatives of the State of Texas, Extra Session of the Eighth Legislature*, pp. 263-264; *Resolution of the Legislature, State of Mississippi, Apr. 5, 1864*, (broadside).

38 Georgia Lee Tatum, *Disloyalty in the Confederacy* (Chapel Hill, 1934), p. viii.

39 Ritter and Wakelyn, *Speakers of the State Legislatures; Journal of the House of Commons of the General Assembly of the State of North Carolina, at the Session of 1864-65*, pp. 84, 108.

40 *Journal of the House of Representatives of the State of Georgia, at an Extra Session...Convened Under the Proclamation of the Governor, March 10th, 1864*, p. 93; *Ordinances and Constitution of the State of Alabama*, p. 46; Ritter and Wakelyn, *Speakers of the State Legislatures*.

41 William J. Cooper, *The South and the Politics of Slavery, 1828-1856* (Baton Rouge, 1978); Thomas P. Alexander, "Persistant Whiggery in the Confederate South;" *Journal of Southern History* XXVII (1961), 305-329; also see Marc W. Kruman, *Parties and Politics in North Carolina, 1836-1865* (Baton Rouge, 1983), Chaps. 9-10.

42 Ritter and Wakelyn, *Speakers of the State Legislatures*.

43 Ritter and Wakelyn, *Speakers of the State Legislatures*; Dallas Herndon (ed.), *Annals of Arkansas* (Chicago, 1890), p. 175.

44 Ritter and Wakelyn, *Speakers of the State Legislatures*; Speer (ed.), *Sketches of Prominent Tennesseans*, pp. 47-50.

45 Davis, *Recollections of Mississippi and Mississippians*, p. 41.

Civil War Leaders

Richard M. McMurry

The theme of the Third Annual Deep Delta Civil War Symposium has been broadcast to the world as "Leadership During the Civil War." We have, not surprisingly, focused—or tomorrow we shall focus—on a number of individual "leaders." Robert E. Lee, Nathan Bedford Forrest, Stephen D. Lee, and John C. Breckinridge were all military "leaders" in the traditional usage of that term. One naturally cringes a bit at the thought of including Braxton Bragg, George B. McClellan, and Mansfield Lovell in such a valhalla. If, however, our criterion for a "leader" is someone at the top of a military field force—a general with followers—then they can be squeezed at least into the vestibule of the pantheon wherein Civil War military "leaders" are enshrined. (Although, I might add, the papers given earlier by Art and Larry may force me to do some rethinking about Lovell and Bragg.).

Abraham Lincoln and Jefferson Davis were Civil War "leaders" in the sense that each stood atop the pinnacle of political power in his respective national government. Jedediah Hotchkiss, I submit, was a staff officer, not a "leader." "Leadership" in a political body such as a state legislature seems to me to be almost an oxymoron. Politicians tend to follow far more often than they "lead." Those politicians who dominate legislative bodies, I would suggest, would better be described as "bosses," "operators," "facilitators," or "co-ordinators"—depending upon their individual ways of getting things done—rather than as "leaders."

Permit me, then, for the sake of argument, to suggest that the eight military "leaders" who have been or will be the subjects of our sessions were not "leaders" at all but "commanders" or, in one case, a staff officer acting for a commander—or, at least, they should have been considering the positions they held and the responsibilities they were supposed to exercise. Davis and Lincoln, of course, were commanders-in-chief and were, therefore, even further removed from positions of true "leadership." I have already indicated what I think of politicians. They are rarely "leaders" at all, and most of them belong in the same disgusting subspecies of Homo sapiens with traitors to the country, child molesters, people who poison dogs, academic administrators, and similar useless, parasitic slimeoids.

This distinction between "command" and "leadership" is, of course, to some extent a play on words—on the difference between a "commander" and a "leader"—and it may not apply at all outside the military sphere. Yet, within that sphere, the difference is very real. For decades the United States Army has made a formal distinction between the two, designating "squad leaders" and "platoon leaders" on the one hand and "company commanders" and "battalion commanders" on the other.

"Leaders" are found in the lower echelons of the military hierarchy; "commanders" are more elevated on the chain of authority. For a simplified, but workable, definition we can say that a commander tells his men to "go on, and I will stay back here and supervise your attack"; a leader says "come on, and let's go get 'em!" This, at any rate, is the distinction I wish to draw because I want to talk about a group of men who were literally Civil War "leaders" and to suggest some ways in which their presence or absence may have influenced the course of the war as well as to discuss some avenues of possible research concerning their role in the conflict.

*   *   *   *   *

One of the most frequently found stereotypes in Civil War literature is the newly-minted company or regimental officer arriving at his unit, cocooned in his spiffy new uniform; his buttons, belt buckle, and breastplate as shiny as mirrors; his boots, belt, and cap visor polished to resemble obsidian; his sword flashing brightly in the sunlight; and his mind utterly devoid of any knowledge of military matters.

In truth, such characters were not uncommon sights during the war of the 1860s, especially in the struggle's early months. Neither North nor South had any program or system to provide formal training for officers newly-commissioned from civilian life.[1] Many of the men who were suddenly thrust into positions of military authority owed their selection more to their personality or status in the community or to their family's political connections or prestige than to any demonstrated fitness for the position or to knowledge of military subjects.

The simple fact is that in the spring of 1861 there were not very many men in the United States who were qualified to occupy positions as small unit officers or non-commissioned officers. Most of those elected (for that was the way many such leaders were chosen) or appointed (and appointees often owed their selection to political factors) to such positions in the early days of the war had left their farms, shops, offices, or classrooms and had been suddenly elevated to posts of responsibility in a large military organization. Nothing in their previous experiences had prepared them for the situation in which they found themselves. In their new posts their knowledge—or lack of knowledge—of military matters could quite literally mean life or death to themselves and to those who came under their authority.

Most of these men were intelligent enough eventually to learn most of what they needed to know to function effectively, and most of them were to prove brave enough to win the respect—and sometimes even the admiration—of the men they led. At the beginning of their military service, however, they simply lacked the technical knowledge (to use a not really satisfactory term) to function effectively as small unit leaders.

Such effectiveness, it seems to me, involved thorough knowledge of two areas. One *sine qua non* was a basic familiarity with the confusing and sometimes infuriating military way of doing things—with the routine of life in a military organization; with small unit administration; with the simple daily round of guard mount, guard duty, roll call, and drill; with military customs and paperwork; with inspections, reviews, and cross-country marches. One had to adjust to the military spelling of enclosure and endorsement with "i" rather than "e" and to an alphabet in which the tenth letter was "K" rather than "J" when it came to the designation of companies. One had to know how to use and care for both his own weapons and accouterments and those of his men. One had to know the forty-nine different bugle calls and the thirty-five different drumbeats so well that he could understand them even if, in the confusion of battle, he caught only a few notes.[2] One had to know such things well enough to teach them to his men. More important, if one was to lead effectively, he had to know such matters well enough that his men would believe that he did, indeed, know what he was doing and that he could be entrusted with their lives. Perhaps most difficult and important of all, a leader had to know such things well enough to convince himself that he did, indeed, know what he was doing. Without the self-confidence that comes from an inner conviction that he is able to perform his duties no leader can succeed. Without this self-confidence his men would sense his unsureness and lose confidence in him. In such circumstances his ability to lead would be severely limited.

The second—and for our immediate purposes far more important—area of which a Civil War leader had to have thorough knowledge embraced the manual of arms (both shoulder arms and saber), the drill, and the tactics employed by mid-nineteenth century armies. In those decades troops were supposed to move about the battlefield in compact, ordered formations, much as they would march in a parade. Armies had followed this practice for centuries because it was only in such formations that the officers could maintain control of the troops and direct the unit toward the accomplishment of whatever mission had been assigned to it.

Such closely-knit formations required, among other things, a skillful handling of weapons. Civil War soldiers averaged five feet, eight and one quarter inches in height. The standard Civil War shoulder weapon, the .577 calibre musket or rifled musket, with bayonet affixed was longer than the average soldier. In a closely-packed formation the man who had not thoroughly mastered the manual of arms was apt to make life very comfortable for those unfortunate enough to be standing near him.[3]

Nineteenth-century infantry tactics were, therefore, based on close order drill. That drill, in turn, was conducted by officers who relied on vocal commands, musical signals with drum or bugle, and flags to direct and control the movements of their men. Successful execution of the drill demanded frequent practice under the watchful eyes of officers and non-commissioned officers who themselves had to be well-versed in the drill both at their own level and at all of the levels down to that of the individual soldier. Nor was it enough that only the officer giving the orders know what he was doing. If he became a casualty, the man who took his place had to be equally competent and prepared to step immediately into the vacancy left by his superior. If he was not, the unit's ability to function would suffer and in all probability numbers of its men would die to no purpose.

It is now well understood that nineteenth-century technological changes—notably the percussion cap, the minie ball, and the rifled shoulder arm—had rendered Civil War battlefield tactics obsolescent by increasing the range and accuracy of individual weapons. The degree to which these tactics had been outdated, however, was not as great at the beginning of the war when many units were still armed with smoothbore weapons as it was to become later on when virtually all units carried rifled arms.

Technology, however, had not provided any new means of battlefield communication and control to replace the vocal, musical, and visual signals that had been in use for centuries. Even had new methods of command and control been available in, say, 1862, the armies could hardly have been expected to develop and learn a new system of tactics in the midst of a war. In effect, the Union and Confederate armies had to choose between obsolescent tactics and no tactics, and the obsolescent tactics that were necessary for battlefield control placed a great premium on close order drill.

Battlefields in wartime, so we are told by those who have been on them—and, I hasten to add, I have not—are places of great noise and incredible confusion. This chaotic atmosphere was even more characteristic of Civil War battlefields than it is of modern ones because Civil War armies crowded large numbers of men into relatively small fighting areas and also because the black powder used by nineteenth-century armies produced great clouds of smoke that oftentimes limited visibility. In such an environment it was even more difficult for an officer to maintain control over his men. Nineteenth-century drill was, in fact, intended to overcome these difficulties.[4]

In the Civil War battlefield environment an instinctive knowledge of drill was a great asset to a small unit leader. An officer—and his replacement if he became a casualty—could not afford to forget a command or to get mixed up as to what command was appropriate or as to the direction in which his unit was to move and the commands necessary to get it moving in the proper direction in the correct formation. If he did, his unit was likely to be thrown into confusion and thereby become even more vulnerable to enemy fire. At the beginning of the Civil War there were not many Americans capable of taking charge of a company or a regiment and maneuvering it on either a parade ground or a battlefield.

The absence of a pool of well qualified junior officers and non-commissioned officers was not, of course, unique to the Civil War era. Some three decades before the nation's bloodiest conflict a force of Illinois state militia was called out for duty against some Indians. One company of these militiamen elected as its captain a lanky young man named Abraham Lincoln. Like most antebellum militia units, Lincoln's company was not trained for a real military campaign— nor was its captain.

On one well-known occasion Lincoln had his company formed in line—the men arranged shoulder to shoulder—and marching forward through a field. To his consternation Lincoln discovered that there was a fence stretching across the field and realized that his company's line was too long for the unit to pass through the narrow gate in the fence. In his panic Lincoln forgot the command necessary to get his company from line into column (men marching one behind the other)—or, as Lincoln later put it, "to turn the company endwise"—so that it could pass through the gate. Thinking quickly, Captain Lincoln shouted for the company to halt and then dismissed the men with instructions to form again on the other side of the fence in a few minutes.

Lincoln's lapse of memory during the Black Hawk War was amusing and of no military significance, and his quick thinking solved the problem. Such improvisation in the chaos of a Civil War battlefield, however, could well have meant disaster if the unit was under fire. If the company had been in close proximity to an enemy force, such confusion could have invited a quick counterattack that would inflict heavy casualties, disrupt Lincoln's unit, and perhaps wreck the larger force of which it was a part. Lincoln may well have been, as T. Harry Williams (the patron saint of this symposium) once called him, a masterful "director of war," but as a small unit battlefield leader he— like many inexperienced Civil War officers—proved deficient because of a lack of simple rote knowledge of drill commands.[5]

So long as both opposing armies lacked trained small unit leaders their mutual disadvantages offset each other and there was no impact on the battle or the course of the war other than to increase the length of the casualty list. If, however, one army had such leaders it would enjoy a great advantage over an enemy force that did not. It is my contention that one Civil War army did have a nucleus of trained men to serve as leaders for many of its batteries, companies, battalions, and regiments and that those leaders, while not numerous enough to make that army into a Prussian drill team, were partly responsible for giving it a soundness of command that helps to explain the considerable success that it enjoyed during the war. That success, in turn, prolonged the war for three years with incalculable results on the American nation.

*   *   *   *   *

There were a few men in Civil War America who, in the spring of 1861, were capable of stepping immediately into positions as "line" (leaders of troops) officers or non-commissioned officers and functioning effectively. These were men whose previous military experience had prepared them for such roles. Some of these had served prior to 1861 in the United States Army, Navy, or Marine Corps or in the armed forces of another nation. Others had seen meaningful service in the antebellum militia. The third group consisted of men who had been educated and trained at a military school but who had not seen any active service. (It was possible, of course, for an individual to have been in two of these groups.)

Men who had spent time in active antebellum military service would be knowledgeable to some degree about drill and weapons, although the extent of their knowledge would vary with the length, level, type, nationality, and duration of their service.[6] Militia experience, too, varied. In theory each state was supposed to maintain a "well regulated militia." In practice a few states had a fairly well established military force while in many others the militia had for all practical purposes been discontinued because most men did not want to perform military duty and the political "leaders" caved in to popular pressure. Virginia, for example, had in 1861 a much larger and better equipped militia than did any other Southern state.

It is, however, on the third source of small unit leaders that I wish to concentrate. White Southerners from George Washington to Jefferson Davis to Daniel Harvey Hill placed great emphasis on the value of a military education. By this term they meant a normal education conducted in a military environment. The students—called "cadets"—and faculty members would wear military uniforms. Students would march to class, to meals, and to church. They would spend an hour or so each day engaged in some type of military drill. They would walk guard posts and learn to use and care for various types of weapons and other military equipment. At most such schools they would spend six to eight weeks each summer "in the field" in a camp of instruction undergoing what

Future Civil War Leaders—Members of the VMI Class of 1861. The cadet in the center of the front row is Henry King Burgwyn, who became colonel of the 26th North Carolina and was killed at Gettysburg. The others (although it is not certain which is which) are Lieutenant W. H. Bray, 53rd Virginia, killed at Gettysburg; Lieutenant R. L. Williams, 55th Virginia; Lieutenant Colonel E. M. Morrison, 15th Virginia; and, W. A. Smith, a staff officer in Virginia and in the Trans-Mississippi. *Courtesy of the Virginia Military Institute Archives.*

amounted to basic or advanced training. Old cadets filled positions as officers, sergeants, and corporals in cadet companies and learned to conduct guard mount, drill, inspections, parades, and tactical marches. In the case of one antebellum military school the cadets were sometimes ordered to the state capital to participate in inaugural parades for a new governor or welcoming ceremonies for a visiting dignitary. Such expeditions gave them the experience of troop movements by foot, boat, and rail from Virginia's Shenandoah Valley to Richmond and back—a movement that many of them would make several times in the years from 1861 to 1865. Perhaps most important of all, the cadets were forced to learn to juggle their time to meet the myriad responsibilities that their military duties and their academic work imposed upon them.[7]

In such an environment the cadets received an education that often stressed science, mathematics, engineering, and modern foreign languages. They also received training in military matters, although both the level of the training and its quality varied with the school. Such schools usually began their terms in July, and it was traditional for the cadets to spend the first two months of the school year in field training. For this reason, even a cadet who remained in such a school for only a few weeks underwent a training period that taught him the fundamentals of soldiering. One who stayed in school longer than one year not only went through such basic training himself but he also helped to train others.

Once they had completed their education, the military school graduates returned to civil life. (Very few graduates of Southern state or private antebellum military schools went into the United States military forces.) Some went on to further schooling to study law, medicine, or theology. Others became businessmen, engineers, or teachers. Many of them were able to put their military training to use as members of local militia units. When the Civil War began in 1861 most of the living military school graduates in the Southern states volunteered to join their state's military forces and through that process became part of the Confederate army.

The education and military training that these men received did not make them into budding Napoleons or Hannibals nor did it necessarily make them courageous combat leaders. It did, however, mean that almost all of the men who had experienced it were well-prepared in 1861 to begin service as noncommissioned officers or junior officers. They were able to step unhesitatingly into such positions with a confidence born of the realization that they knew what they were doing and that for them the army camp, the drill field, and the marching column were not new and strange environments.

Since they did not have to train themselves, they could begin immediately to carry out their most important duty—the training of their men. Indeed, many of them began to train Confederate soldiers even before they themselves were in the army. The Corps of Cadets of the Virginia Military Institute, for example, was rushed to Richmond a few days after the Old Dominion's secession to serve as drill instructors ("drillmasters" in the jargon of the day) for the thousands of troops pouring into the capital from all over the South. The Corps of Cadets from the North Carolina Military Institute (at Charlotte) was sent to Raleigh for the same purpose. After two or three months of this work most of these cadets then went directly into state or Confederate military service.

Some of the cadets who were too young to be commissioned remained with and trained active duty units until they were old enough to become officers. (Twenty-one was supposed to be the minimum age for a commission.) Joseph W. Latimer, a member of the Class of 1863 at VMI, served as an artillery drillmaster from April to July 1861. Somehow he then managed to get a commission even though he was under age. Of Latimer, one superior wrote, "as an instructor in the Artillery Drill *his equal is rarely seen, his superior never.*" A subordinate commented, "we have worse Generals by far than he would make." When Latimer died on 1 August 1863 from wounds received a month earlier at Gettysburg, he was a major and a division chief of artillery. He was also a month shy of his twentieth birthday.[8]

From the start the cadets' and former cadets' knowledge of small unit administration, drill, tactics, weapons, and other nitty-gritty facets of military life enabled them to give their companies, batteries (how many antebellum Americans knew how to unlimber, limber, fire, and care for an artillery piece?), battalions, and regiments better administration, more thorough training, tighter discipline, and greater confidence than would otherwise have been possible. An army able to draw upon military school alumni as the nucleus of its junior officer corps would have a ready made cadre of small unit leaders and hence a greater than average strength of command. One—and only one—Civil War army found itself so endowed.

*　　*　　*　　*　　*

By 1861 there were military schools scattered across the South from Lexington, Virginia, to Tallahassee, Florida, to Bastrop, Texas, to Tulip, Arkansas, and there were military departments (analogous to the modern ROTC program although not federally funded) at a number of other schools. At the time the war began, however, most of these schools and programs were small and of recent origin. It is likely that many of them were also of questionable quality as to the education and the military training that they offered. Only the Virginia Military Institute in Lexington (established in 1839) and the South Carolina Military Academy (the Citadel) in Charleston (1843) had been in operation long enough to train significant numbers of men.[9]

At present we do not know how many men attended Southern military schools prior to the Civil War. At VMI 978 men enrolled up through the Class of 1862 (which was sent off to war in 1861), and 455 were graduated (46.5 percent). An 1861 report on the Citadel listed 200 graduates of that school through the Class of 1861. If the dropout rate at the South Carolina school was the same as that in Virginia, the total number of men trained at the Citadel would have been 430. A wild guess would put the total from the other Southern military schools at about 2,000, making a grand total of, say, 3,400 Southerners who had been educated and trained at a Southern military school.

From this total we must subtract the number of those who died prior to their state's secession—96 in the case of VMI; 12 among Citadel graduates; an estimated 100 from the other schools (including those men who attended the Citadel but did not graduate). We must also remove from the total those who did not serve in the Rebel army because of ill health, family or business obligations, service as a chaplain or surgeon, residence abroad, loyalty to the Union, or some other reason. These calculations leave us with perhaps 3,000 men who were fitted in 1861 by education at a Southern military school to fill positions as junior officers or non-commissioned officers.

These men were too few to have had much impact on so large a group as the Confederate army. (If the Rebel army numbered one million men, the three thousand would have been three tenths of one percent of the total.) I believe, however, that these men were not distributed uniformly throughout the Southern forces but that the great majority of them were to be found in the Eastern theater in the Army of Northern Virginia where their presence helps to explain why that army enjoyed such battlefield success during the war, especially in the early years of the conflict.[10]

Almost all Civil War units—North as well as South—were organized by state governments and then turned over to the national war department to help meet the state's troop quota. This method of raising a military force meant that virtually all men who entered Rebel service at the beginning of the war joined state—not Confederate—units.

In addition to the graduates of its own military schools, a state could also draw upon the services of many of its sons who had been educated at the United States Military Academy. Thus an officer who resigned from the United States Army upon the secession of his state usually went to his state capital and joined the state's newly-organized force. Only weeks, or sometimes months, later when his unit was transferred to national control did he become a Confederate officer. Stephen Dodson Ramseur, for example, was graduated from the United States Military Academy in 1860. In April 1861 he resigned from the United States Army. He entered the military service of his native North Carolina as commander of an artillery battery. In July 1861 he and his unit went into Confederate service. When he was killed in late 1864, he was a major general commanding an infantry division.[11]

This state-based method of raising troops meant that a state that had sent large numbers of men into the United States Army in the *antebellum* decades, or had a well-regulated militia or a large number of men who had been educated and trained at a military school was better able to provide its newly-formed armed forces with competent small unit leaders at the beginning of the war than was state that lacked such human resources.

In the Confederacy such qualified men were far more likely to be found in the older states along the Atlantic seaboard than in the newer states to the west. Some statistics illustrate if they do not demonstrate the concentration of trained junior officers and non-commissioned officers in the Eastern Rebel states. In 1861 Virginia had 104 living graduates of the United States Military Academy; the other ten Confederate states had a total of only 184. Early in 1861 a man in Nashville made a count of the officers then on active duty in the United States Army. He found that 304 of them were from the states that were to join the Confederacy. Of these 304 officers, 137 were from Virginia, 40 from South Carolina, and 36 from North Carolina. Seven out of ten of the Southern officers were from those three states. Only 35 of VMI's 978 pre-war cadets were from outside Virginia—and six of them were from North Carolina while five others hailed from the District of Columbia.[12]

When the Southerners began to raise troops for the Civil War, the three Eastern Rebel states were able to place trained and often experienced men in many positions of small unit leadership. In virtually every Virginia regiment, battery, and battalion there was a nucleus of VMI alumni to officer the unit and train the men. Many of the Old Dominion's regiments had more than a dozen such men on their rolls. In the 11th Virginia Infantry, for example, the original regimental commander and five of the ten original company commanders were VMI alumni, and there were seven other VMI men who served with the regiment.

The Rebel government assigned virtually all units raised in Virginia and the Carolinas to the Army of Northern Virginia. Since the great majority of the South's trained officers were from the Eastern states of Rebeldom, they went into, trained, commanded, and led the units formed in 1861 by those states. Almost none of those units served outside the Eastern theater.

In addition to its virtual monopoly of the Eastern Confederacy's supply of trained men, Virginia also drew to her defense a large proportion of the trained officers who were from the Western Confederacy. As a general rule, a state's trained men were among the first to volunteer for its defense. The Confederate government organized its army in Virginia before it organized major forces elsewhere. For this reason, many of the Western units that were formed at the very beginning of the war were rushed to Virginia, taking with them a large number of the Westerners trained as military officers as well as a large share of their states' military equipment. John Bell Hood, Cadmus M. Wilcox, John Pelham, Evander M. Law, Robert E. Rodes, and many others were among the men from Western states with military training and experience who served in Virginia in positions as small unit leaders/commanders.

Bruce Allardice has pointed out that the numerical designation of a regiment is often a good indication of the sequence in which it was organized—that is, the lower-numbered regiments were usually formed before those with higher numbers. It is interesting to compare the numerical designations of Western infantry regiments in the Army of Northern Virginia with those of regiments from the same state in the Army of Tennessee, the Confederacy's main force in the West. In 1864 twenty Alabama regiments were in service in Virginia; the average number was 23.9. Thirty-four Alabama regiments then served with the Army of Tennessee; their average number was 33.4. The average of Louisiana's ten regiments serving in Virginia was 7.7; of the state's nine regiments in the Army of Tennessee, 15.6. Mississippi had eleven regiments fighting in Virginia; the average designation was 19.9. The average number of her thirty-one regiments in the Army of Tennessee was 25.6. Georgia, the only other state with significant numbers of troops in both armies, had thirty-three regiments in Virginia with an average designation of 28. Her twenty-two regiments in the Army of Tennessee carried an average number of 41.1. If Allardice is correct in his belief that a state's trained and experienced manpower tended to be disproportionly concentrated in the state's first-organized and hence lower-numbered regiments, these data are certainly more indications that the Confederacy's best qualified small unit military leaders were to be found in the Army of Northern Virginia.[13]

*   *   *   *   *

In this paper I have suggested that one major factor in the relative success enjoyed by the Army of Northern Virginia was a better level of small unit leadership—especially in the war's early months when the tone for many later military operations and attitudes was set. Such an hypothesis can be neither proved nor disproved. It can, however, be subjected to further testing, and I would like to close with some suggestions for future research along these same lines.

First, we need to know a great deal more about the military personnel available to the states in 1861. Almost a half century ago Douglas Southall Freeman wrote an essay on the Virginians who, as of early 1861, had had military training of some type. We need similar studies of the other Confederate states. Fortunately, Bruce Allardice and James L. Conrad are now at work on such undertakings.[14]

Second, we need to know a great deal more about the Southern military schools and the military programs at other colleges and universities. Some work along these lines has been done. Mabel Altstetter and Gladys Watson authored (in 1936) an article on the Western Military Institute, and John Hope Franklin presented an overview in *The Militant South*. It is unlikely that any other school will have records as complete as those for VMI, but Jim Moody's work on the Citadel and the more general studies by Allardice and Conrad should tell us much more than we now know. I might add that, although I have focused on the Southern military schools, we also stand in need of similar works on such schools in the North and the role of their alumni in the war.[15]

Third, we need studies of individual regiments that will devote space to a collective portrait and evaluation of the unit's officers and non-commissioned officers. Such analyses should answer many questions about the quality of small unit leadership in all theaters of the Civil War and allow some real comparisons of such leadership in different areas, different armies, and at different times during the war. Again, this suggestion applies as much to Northern regiments as to Southern units.

Finally, we need to know more about the Civil War small unit leaders—on both sides—as individuals. Perhaps it is the lingering influence of my mentor Bell Wiley, but it seems to me that historians should make a real effort to publish letters and diaries written by the men who led companies or who served as subordinate line officers and non-commissioned officers. In this connection, I suggest that the compiled service records in the National Archives will be a major source. My work with those records for the VMI alumni who served in the war indicates that such research can teach us a great deal about both those men themselves and also the larger groups of which they were a part and about the nature of the war they fought.

*   *   *   *   *

When we begin to get such information about large numbers of these men, I believe that we will be in a much better position to reach some definitive answers to questions about those men who really exercised "leadership during the Civil War."

Endnotes

1 On occasion some individual units established "schools" to teach their officers the fundamentals of their new jobs. These "schools," however, were often cases of the blind leading the blind because the senior officers who were supposed to instruct their juniors were equally ill-prepared in military drill. "The effect of the volunteer system," wrote T. Harry Williams, "was to ensure that practically all the officers of a regiment would know nothing about war or their jobs." Williams, *Hayes of the Twenty-third: The Civil War Volunteer Officer* (New York, 1965), pp. 28-29.

2 *Casey's Tactics*, one of the basic Civil War drill books, prescribed twenty-six general bugle calls (directed at all members of a regiment) plus an additional twenty-three used to transmit orders to the regiment's skirmishers. There were thirty-five different drum signals (fifteen general; twenty for skirmishers). *Ibid.*, p. 37.

3 A convenient description of "SMALL ARMS OF THE CIVIL WAR" is in Mark Mayo Boatner III, *The Civil War Dictionary* (New 1959), pp. 766-768. On soldiers' height, see Ralph Newman and E. B. Long, *The Civil War*, volume II, *The Picture Chronicle* (New York, 1956), p. 219. For an example of soldiers and their weapons see the photograph of some members of the 33d New Jersey in David Evans, "The Atlanta Campaign," *Civil War Times Illustrated*, XXVIII, no. 4 (Summer 1989), p. 37. See also the comments in Bell Irvin Wiley, *The Life of Billy Yank: The Common Soldier of the Union* (New York, 1951), pp. 26-27.

4 For discussions and descriptions of Civil War small unit tactics as they were supposed to be executed and of the impact of technology (or its lack of impact) on Civil War battles, see Williams, *Hayes*, pp. 31-38; Grady McWhiney and Perry D. Jamieson, *Attack and Die: Civil War Military Tactics and the Southern Heritage* (University, Al., 1982), *passim*; and Paddy, Griffith, *Battle Tactics of the Civil War* (New Haven and London, 1989), *passim*. For a provocative discussion of many facets of warfare that at least touch on the subjects covered in this paper, see John Keegan, *The Face of Battle: A Study of Agincourt, Waterloo & The Somme* (New York, 1977). In practice, of course, such factors as the terrain and enemy fire would work to disrupt a unit. As the regiments split up during a battle, small unit leadership became even more important.

5 Lincoln's adventures in the Black Hawk War are described in Benjamin P. Thomas, *Abraham Lincoln* (New York, 1952), pp. 30-34. William's comment is in *Lincoln and His Generals* (New York, 1952), p. 331.

6 In this connection it should be noted that the Federal government's decision during the Civil War to keep intact the pre-war "regular" United States Army units deprived the Northerners of what otherwise would have been a large number of trained, experienced instructors and small unit leaders. The Federal policy of organizing new units rather than replenishing existing ones with new recruits had the same effect.

7 For an example of Southern opinion on military education see Hill's speech printed in the Raleigh (N.C.) *Standard*, 27 Mar. 1861, and John Hope Franklin, *The Militant South* (Cambridge, 1956).

8 On Latimer see his service record in the Compiled Service Records of Confederate Generals and Staff Officers and Non-Regimental Enlisted Men (microfilm in the National Archives and in many other depositories) and Robert K. Krick, *Lee's Colonels: A Biographical Register of the Field Officers of the Army of Northern Virginia* (2d edition, Dayton, Oh., 1984), pp. 197-198.

9 For comments on antebellum Southern military schools see Franklin, *Militant South*, *passim*, and Richard M. McMurry, *Two Great Rebel Armies: An Essay in Confederate Military History* (Chapel Hill, 1989), pp. 98-105.

10 For helpful information on many of the military schools and their alumni I am indebted to Bruce Allardice of Des Plaines, Il. (Letters and telephone conversations, 1989). It should be noted that some of the schools continued to train men during the war. In VMI's case the 952 members of the greatly expanded wartime classes (1863 through 1868) almost equalled the total of the twenty-one earlier classes. In addition, VMI trained a special class of eighty-five members who were sent to the school in 1861 for military training only and who are known as the Class of 1864-MS (Military Science). See *Register of Former Cadets* [of the Virginia Military Institute] (Lexington, 1957), pp. 33-66. On the Citadel see Charleston *Daily Courier*, 9 May 1861.

11 On Ramseur see Gary W. Gallagher, *Stephen Dodson Ramseur: Lee's Gallant General* (Chapel Hill, 1985).

12 See the sources cited in McMurry, *Two Great Rebel Armies*, pp. 92-94 and 176.

13 Letters from and telephone conversations with Allardice, 1989.

14 For Freeman's essay see his *Lee's Lieutenants: A Study in Command* (3 vols., New York, 1942-1944), I, 701-725.

15 Altstetter and Watson, "Western Military Institute, 1847-1861," *The Filson Club History Quarterly*, X (1936), pp. 100-115.

Appendix

Edwin C. Bearss—Chief Historian, National Park Service and the author of numerous books, including *The Vicksburg Campaign, Hardluck Ironclad, Forrest at Brice's Cross Roads*, and *A Southern Record: The Story of the 3rd Louisiana Infantry, C.S.A.*

Arthur W. Bergeron, Jr.—Historian, Louisiana Office of State Parks and the author or editor of several books, including *Reminiscences of Uncle Silas* and *Guide to Louisiana Military Units, 1861-1865*.

Richard N. Current—University Distinguished Professor Emeritus at the University of North Carolina at Greensboro and the author of numerous volumes, fifteen of which are currently in print and include *Lincoln and the First Shot, The Lincoln Nobody Knows, Old Thad Stevens*, and *Those Terrible Carpetbaggers*.

William C. Davis—President, Museum Editions, Ltd., a division of Historical Times, Inc., and the author or editor of over twenty books dealing with the Civil War, including *The Image of War, Battle of Bull Run, Duel Between the First Ironclads*, and *Breckinridge: Statesman, Soldier, Symbol*.

Herman Hattaway—Professor of History at the University of Missouri at Kansas City, and the author of *General Stephen D. Lee* and the co-author of *How the North Won* and *Why the South Lost*.

Lawrence L. Hewitt—Associate Professor of History at Southeastern Louisiana University and the author or editor of several books, including *Port Hudson, Confederate Bastion on the Mississippi, The Battle of Fort Bisland*, and *The Confederate High Command*.

Archie P. McDonald—Professor of History at Stephen F. Austin State University and the author of nearly two dozen books, including *Make Me a Map of the Valley: The Journal of Jedediah Hotchkiss, 1862-1863*.

Richard M. McMurray—Adjunct Professor of History at North Carolina State University and the author or editor of numerous books, including *John Bell Hood and the War for Southern Independence, The Road Past Kennesaw, Rank and File*, and *Two Great Rebel Armies*.

Grady McWhiney—Lyndon Baines Johnson Professor of American History at Texas Christian University and the author of many books and articles,

186

including *Braxton Bragg and Confederate Defeat, Attack and Die: Civil War Military Tactics & the Southern Heritage,* and *Cracker Culture: Celtic Ways in the Old South.*

Emory M. Thomas—Regents Professor of History at the University of Georgia and the author of many books, including *The Confederacy as a Revolutionary Experience, The Confederate Nation,* and *Bold Dragoon: The Life of J.E.B. Stuart.*

Jon L. Wakelyn—Chair of the Department of History at the Catholic University of American, and the author or editor of several books, including *Biographical Dictionary of the Confederacy.* He is also the co-editor of The American Biographical History Series published by Harlan Davidson, Inc.

INDEX